jon hird

edward de chazal
adrian tennant
nick witherick

move

advanced

teacher's book

MACMILLAN

Macmillan Education
Between Towns Road, Oxford OX4 3PP
A division of Macmillan Publishers Limited
Companies and representatives throughout the world

ISBN 978-1-4050-2299-6

Text © Macmillan Publishers Limited 2007
Text by Jon Hird
Resource materials by Edward de Chazal, Jon Hird, Adrian Tennant
and Nick Witherick
Design and illustration © Macmillan Publishers Limited 2007

First published 2007

Designed by eMC Design
Illustrated by Stephen Elford, Dylan Gibson, Tim Kahane, Robin Lawrie
and Peters & Zabransky.
Cover design by Macmillan Publishers Limited

Authors' acknowledgements:
The author would like to thank the editor Meredith Levy for all her ideas
and hard work.

The authors and publishers would like to thank the following for permission to
reproduce their material:
Extract from 'French Stick to plan to ban English' by Colin Randall, copyright ©
Telegraph Group Limited 2006, first published in The Daily Telegraph 24.7.06,
reprinted by permission of the publisher; Extracts from New Japanese from
Japan-zone online kindly reprinted by permission of www.japan-zone.com.

Although we have tried to trace and contact copyright holders before publication, in
some cases this has not been possible. If contacted, we will be pleased to rectify any
errors or omissions at the earliest opportunity.

Printed and bound in Spain by Edelvives

2011 2010 2009 2008 2007
10 9 8 7 6 5 4 3 2 1

Contents

Teaching notes

Coursebook contents

Module 1 Individuals

Module 2 Pairs

Module 3 Groups

CD-ROM contents

Location	Activities for each unit	Features
• Modules 1–3	• Language activity • Vocabulary activity • Common European Framework linked activity • Language game	• Markbook – helps you to record and update your marks. • Bookmark – helps you to save your favourite activities. • Wordlist – helps you to create your own wordlists. • You can back up, restore and print out your Markbook, Bookmarks and Wordlists. You can also send saved files as emails. • For more information use the Help feature.

Introduction

Welcome to *Move*

Adult learners have a wide variety of reasons for choosing to learn English. Some, for instance, do so as part of a foundation course for university or other course of study; others do so for career reasons in order to gain promotion or perhaps to seek a new job. Yet others are planning to travel and wish to improve their English, or they are studying English as part of their holiday. Some students choose short, intensive courses of study, while others are studying perhaps two or three hours a week over a longer period.

Move recognises that to meet this wide variety of learning needs and teaching contexts, the key feature of a course for adults must be that it builds in a great deal of flexibility, allowing teachers to select from both core and optional material.

Each level of *Move* contains a core course of three modules, and with that there is an extensive range of optional materials, in the Coursebook and Class CD, and also on the CD-ROM and in this Teacher's Book. There are five levels of *Move*, and it is suitable for use with adult students from an elementary level through to an advanced level of English.

The aim of this introduction is to explain both the methodological approach taken by *Move* as a language course, and the features that make up both the core course, and the optional materials.

Methodology

Move recognises that the best way that most students learn is through a discovery approach. Throughout *Move* language is presented in context and students are encouraged to notice its use, meaning and form before plenty of practice is given.

Move attaches great importance to the accessibility of topics through engaging reading and listening texts. Throughout *Move* students are given the opportunity to present personalised and meaningful responses and to discuss their own ideas and opinions as a means of encouraging learning.

Move recognises that students are primarily looking to use their language in communicative situations. Therefore, central to *Move* are exercises and activities that encourage students to communicate their ideas in particular through speaking and listening.

Move recognises that learning a language means a lot more than studying tenses or other isolated grammatical features and individual lexical items. Just as important is the ability to recognise, for example, language chunks such as collocations and fixed phrases and to develop an awareness of the importance of naturalness and register. *Move* covers aspects of these language features throughout.

Each unit of *Move* has a Language study section, which focuses on a key area of grammar or other language. The section starts with examples of the language in context taken from a preceding text or listening activity and then guides the students, encouraging them to notice its use and then work out meaning and form. Plenty of practice is then given through activities which allow the students to engage with the language on a personal level. Grammar reference pages support the Language study sections.

Each unit of *Move* has at least one Vocabulary section and many units have more than one. The students are encouraged to notice how the vocabulary is used in a preceding text or listening activity and it is then extended and practiced, again allowing the students to engage with the language on a personal level.

Throughout *Move*, language is recycled and revised during the course of each module. Additionally, the Review units at the end of each module bring language together from each of the preceding units and provide more overt revision. For further recycling and revision, *Move* has stimulating Extra practice material for each of the main units at the end of each module and the Teacher's Book includes photocopiable resource activities as well as end of unit and end of module tests. There are also CD-ROM activities for each unit (see below).

Move recognises the importance and value of self-study. The Extra practice activities are designed for use as homework or in class. The Grammar reference and Wordlist pages help students to review and keep a record of the language they have studied as they go through the course. The CD-ROM, which can be used on PC or Macintosh platforms, can be used either in school computer rooms or privately at home.

Coursebook organisation

Each level of *Move* contains three stand-alone teaching modules, each of which focuses on one overall topic, such as 'Individuals' or 'Pairs'. The language is recycled and tested within the module. The main advantage of this is that students joining the course at a later stage are not disadvantaged if, for instance, they start their studies from the second module.

Each module contains four main teaching units and a review unit. The four main teaching units each take one aspect of the module's overall topic. So, for instance, the 'Groups' module has topics that include living together, talk talk, net value and team spirit, which examine travel, communication and world events.

The key features of the main teaching units are:

A **Lead-in activity** at the start of every unit. The purpose of the Lead-in is to activate the topic by drawing on students' knowledge and curiosity.

Stimulating **reading texts**. These occur at least once in each unit and include a mixture of global, gist and detailed information tasks. Recognising the importance of authenticity, the texts are based on authentic sources such as magazine and Internet articles and book extracts, and are chosen to be appropriate for use with Advanced students. Students are encouraged to engage with and react to the texts on a personal level. The main reading texts in each unit are recorded to give you the flexibility to use an alternative means of presentation, or for the students to simultaneously listen and read. This can consolidate pronunciation features such as word and sentence stress and intonation, as well as helping students to adjust to the normal speed at which English is spoken.

Stimulating **listening activities**. These occur at least once in each unit and include carefully graded main listening tasks as well as student-to-student listening and speaking interaction. Skills covered include prediction, global and gist listening as well as listening for detail. The listening scripts are reproduced at the end of each module. There are also dedicated pronunciation tasks for all modules.

A **Language study section**. This draws from the reading and listening texts and follows a guided discovery approach. As well as work on traditional grammar such as tenses and word order, the Language study sections also cover broader language considerations such as politeness and register, how to express particular ideas or how to modify language. The sequence of tasks moves from more controlled to freer practice.

Vocabulary input and practice sections. These occur at least once in each unit and draw from the reading and listening texts. They include topic-based lexical sets and other useful language items such as phrasal verbs, phrases, expressions and collocations.

Speaking activities. These occur in a number of sections within every unit and include pairwork and small and larger group discussion opportunities. The speaking activities give the students the chance to respond personally to texts and issues. There are also more substantial speaking activities such as role-plays and presentations.

Writing activities. There are four major tasks in every module. The writing tasks are integrated with other skills work in order to help students to plan and prepare for the written task. There is variety of writing genres, which are chosen as practical examples of writing tasks students are likely to come across in everyday life. These include formal letters, emails, postcards and reviews.

CD-ROM practice at the end of each main teaching unit. This includes four corresponding activities for each unit. (For more details see below.)

The sequence of activity types within units varies to reflect the nature of the material.

The **Review units** focus on the main language presented in the preceding four main teaching units and recycle it through reading and listening texts, speaking activities and games. Review units also feature a song related to the module theme, with a short factfile about the singer / writer. There is also an extended production task, such as a role-play or discussion, using language from the module.

Extra practice pages, which are at the end of each module, offer a chance for further practice and consolidation of the grammar and vocabulary in each unit.

Grammar reference sections, which support each Language study section, are at the end of each module.

A **Wordlist**, with phonetic spellings, for each unit is at the end of each module.

Flexibility

One of the key benefits of *Move* is that as teachers you can combine the core and additional course material to suit your teaching situation and the needs and interests of your students. Each module contains 15 hours of core teaching material (three hours per unit). Therefore using just the core material for each level provides a course of around 45 hours' study. But in addition, you can supplement this with the following additional materials and resources and potentially expand the course to over 90 hours:

Extra practice pages. These can be completed for homework or in class, during or at the end of each unit.

CD-ROM (see page 8).

Teacher's Book optional activities. Throughout this Teacher's Book there are suggestions for additional optional activities to consolidate and extend the language being taught.

Teacher's Book resources. For each of the main teaching units there are two photocopiable worksheets offering different kinds of practice (see page 8).

Tests. There are photocopiable progress tests for the end of each unit, and more substantial tests for the end of each module. There is also a placement test (see page 8).

Common European Framework (CEF) links

There is a dedicated section in this Teacher's Book which explains how *Move* links to the CEF (see pages 9–20). Essentially, this section explains what the CEF is, introduces a photocopiable, detailed mapping document and photocopiable student checklists for each unit that students can use as part of their dossiers. These checklists also draw on the 'Can do' learning aims which appear at the start of each unit of the Coursebook.

The CD-ROM contains one activity per unit which expressly links to the student checklists. Additionally the Markbook feature allows marks for each of the activities to be recorded and printed so that students can add these to their dossiers, and you can also check progress. The bookmark feature also allows students to save their own wordlists or to access particular activities directly. Again, this can be used to contribute towards the student's dossier, and it encourages learner independence.

Other components

Class CD set

There are two CDs in the set. CD1 contains the listening material for the first and second module, while CD2 contains material for the third module. All recorded listening material for the core course, which includes listening and pronunciation activities, is shown with the 🔊 symbol, with the corresponding track number set out alongside the activity in the Coursebook. Optional listening activities, i.e. the main reading tasks, are shown by the 🔊 symbol. The listening scripts are set out in the reference material at the end of each module in the Coursebook, and for convenience, in the teaching notes in this Teacher's Book.

CD-ROM

There are four activities for each of the main units. These provide further practice of language presented in the unit:

Language study activity – focusing on language presented in the Language study.

Vocabulary – recycling language presented in the Vocabulary sections.

'Can do' activity – focusing on one of the main 'Can do' statements in the Common European Framework student checklists. These include reading, listening and writing activities.

Language game – drawing on language from the unit, these are highly interactive fun activities in which students have to perform tasks such as beating the clock, chasing a villain or saving someone from meeting a terrible fate.

The CD-ROM contains a useful Help section which shows students how to use it. Additionally the Markbook feature allows students to record and update their results, as well as to print them out. The Bookmark feature is a space for students to create their own wordlists, revision notes, or shortcuts to their favourite activities. The Help section shows students how to create bookmarks and build their own learning resource.

Teacher's Book

This Teacher's Book contains a range of useful sections:

Teaching tips. This invaluable four-page section provides useful teaching ideas. These include suggestions for five-minute lesson warmers before opening the Coursebook, lesson closing activities, and five-minute revision activities. Tips include ideas for varying speaking activities such as different ways of organising pairwork, how to lead whole class discussions and lots more.

The Common European Framework section sets out how *Move* links with the CEF (see page 9).

The teaching notes provide straightforward and clear procedural notes, with answer keys and listening scripts inserted in the body of the notes for easy reference. You'll also find useful optional activities to add extra practice, alternative ways of presenting new language, cultural background notes and help with pronunciation of difficult words and phrases. The summary at the start of each unit sets out the main learning aims and content of each unit, as well as a preparation checklist for some of the optional activities. The reference section at the end of each unit shows where to find additional study material in the Coursebook and this Teacher's Book.

The Teacher's resource section comprises two parts: a resource pack section, and a test section.

The Resource pack contains 24 photocopiable worksheets, two for each of the main teaching units. These comprise a stand-alone discussion lesson based on the topic of the unit, and a language-oriented activity, which consolidates and extends the language presented in the unit.

There are three kinds of tests. The pre-course placement test is flexible and contains a half-hour multi-choice grammar and vocabulary test, which is easily marked. It includes a suggested additional spoken interview and written task for a more comprehensive assessment of a student's level. The complete test can be administered in under one and a half hours, and is the same test for all levels of *Move*. The end of unit tests are flexible, quick tests which contain grammar, vocabulary and reading skill elements drawn from the unit. The three end of module tests are more substantial tests which assess students' progress against the main learning points in each of the preceding four units. These can be used instead of the end of unit tests or in addition to them. The end of module test also contains a listening element. All of the tests are easily marked.

We very much hope you and your students enjoy using *Move*. The range of material and resources it offers make it a unique course with enough space within each unit for students to get an impressive range of practice, and plenty of variety in their learning experience.

Jon Hird

The Common European Framework and *Move*

Introduction

The Common European Framework (CEF) is a document which has been drawn up by the Council of Europe. Its main purpose is to provide an 'open, neutral framework of reference' to help students, teachers, institutions and employers describe the stages of learning that students typically go through when they are learning a foreign language, and to establish benchmark levels of language proficiency. A range of international language qualifications can also be mapped against these benchmark levels of proficiency.

The Framework sets out six levels of language proficiency. These are A1, A2, B1, B2, C1, and C2. A1 learners are just starting to learn a language. The B1 level represents the threshold level of English and C2 learners are at a very advanced level of proficiency. Each of these levels incorporates a series of statements that describe a wide range of language skills and sub-skills. The main advantage of this is that it enables the individual student to assess their own progress in order to build up a profile of their own learning, and to set learning objectives for the future.

The series of level statements can be made more specific to the course of learning by generating a series of language descriptors that correlate to the level statements. The CEF sets out clear guidelines about how these descriptors should be formulated in Chapter 9, Assessment (pp177–196) of the *Common European Framework of Reference*, and in Appendix A: developing proficiency descriptors (pp 205–216). This document can be downloaded in all European languages from: www.coe.int.

The three criteria of assessment that the guidelines set out are:
1 Validity: what is actually assessed is what should be assessed;
2 Reliability: the accuracy of decisions; and
3 Feasibility: the assessment has to be practical.

Additionally, the guidelines advise that descriptors should be set out as follows:
- Positiveness: although it is easier, particularly at low levels, to describe what a learner can't do, rather than what they can do; if levels of proficiency are to serve as objectives rather than just an instrument for screening candidates, then it is desirable to use positive descriptors.
- Definiteness: descriptors should describe concrete tasks and/or degrees of skill in performing tasks.
- Clarity: descriptors should be transparent, not jargon laden.
- Brevity: no individual student is typical. A range of shorter descriptors helps both students and teachers to identify what is being assessed. Descriptors that are longer than a two clause sentence cannot realistically be used accurately. Teachers also consistently prefer short descriptors.
- Independence: descriptors that are likely to describe a behaviour about which one can say 'Yes, this person can do this' can be used as independent criteria statements in checklists, self-assessment or teacher continuous assessment. Independent descriptors offer greater integrity to those forms of assessment.

The CEF also introduces the concept of a student portfolio. A student portfolio can consist of three strands. Firstly, a language 'Passport' will incorporate the formal qualifications that a student has successfully completed, along with details of courses completed. Secondly, the portfolio contains a personal 'Biography' which can contain notes about what the student found easy or difficult and a record of his or her learning experience. The third element is a 'Dossier', which can contain individual pieces of student's writing in a foreign language as well as recordings of the student speaking it.

The approach used in *Move*

The key point to make is that no coursebook can accurately claim that by completing the activities contained within it a student will have attained a given level of the CEF. *Move* is a short course which has been comprehensively mapped against appropriate levels of the Framework. In completing the course, students are offered a range of activities that are consistent with the aims of the Framework, and which contribute significantly towards the learning progress that a student will make.

CEF mapping document

In the case of *Move Advanced*, the course has been mapped against statements at the C1 and C2 (proficiency) level of attainment. The photocopiable mapping document which follows this introduction uses statements taken from the CEF and provides instances from the course where each skill and sub-skill is presented and practised. The main purpose of this is to provide teachers with a detailed overview of how *Move* relates to the various skills and sub-skills identified in the CEF.

CEF student portfolio checklists

The second set of documents is a series of photocopiable student portfolio checklists, one for each of the main teaching units of the course. As described above, we have followed the guidelines contained within the CEF to generate the descriptors within each of these checklists, and these are linked in turn to the level statements. The purpose of these checklists is to enable students to reflect at the end of each unit in the coursebook, and related CD-ROM activities, on the level of proficiency that they have reached for each of the skills and sub-skills that are set out. The main purpose of the checklists is to provide for the students a record of their ongoing self-assessment, as part of their portfolio Biography.

In completing the student portfolio checklists students can assess how successful they have been, what they need more practice in, and what specific help they could ask their teacher for.

Levels of learning:
1 = a very low level of understanding. The student may recognise the item but not be able to use it at all.
2 = understands and can use a little.
3 = understands and can manipulate the item fairly well.
4 = understands, can self-correct and manipulate the item appropriately most of the time.
5 = the learner has passive understanding, appropriate selection and accurate active use of the item.

How to use the checklists:
1 Once you have completed a unit, give your students a photocopy of the relevant checklist. Avoid giving the impression that you are testing them.
2 Ask students to take the list home and think it over.
3 In the following lesson discuss any points that the students raise.
4 After each review unit ask students to look at the four checklists for that module again and update their assessments.
5 Ask students to keep their checklists and file them with their self-assessment documentation as part of their portfolio.

Coursebook links to the CEF

As well as the photocopiable material contained within this section of the Teacher's Book, there are a number of other 'tools' that *Move* incorporates as part of an integrated approach towards the European Framework. Each module of the course begins with a Contents map which sets out the content of each of the syllabus strands of the course. *Move* has a multi-stranded syllabus which is consistent with the range of skills and sub-skills set out in the CEF.

Additionally, the main learning aims of each of the teaching units are expressed as 'Can do' descriptors. These are replicated in the student portfolio checklists, thus ensuring that what is presented is also what is being assessed.

Revision and testing

The importance of revision work in recycling new language cannot be underestimated. Each module of *Move* contains a review unit, and we recommend that as part of the review process students revisit their student portfolio checklists and re-evaluate their self-assessment after completing each review unit.

This Teacher's Book also contains a comprehensive, photocopiable test section. The placement test provides a benchmark pre-course record of attainment, and there are end of unit and end of module progress tests which either can contribute towards an overall end of course grade, as part of the student portfolio Passport, or alternatively can be integrated into the student's Dossier.

CD-ROM links to the CEF

The CD-ROM contains at least one activity for each unit which has been specifically written to provide further support for one of the descriptors set out in the student portfolio checklists. Other activities for each unit are also consistent with the learning aims recorded on the checklists.

The markbook feature of the CD-ROM allows students to print out their end scores for the activities, and provides a further record of how the student is performing against the descriptors set out in the student portfolio checklist as well as an invaluable document for the student's Dossier.

Concluding remarks

The comprehensive approach in *Move* to the Common European Framework reflects the overall aim of the Framework to provide an ongoing practical and accurate assessment of the level of language proficiency that a student has attained. The 'tools' provided for both teachers and students to record progress allow for a flexible approach which can be tailored to reflect the level of detail needed by individual students and educational institutions.

CEF mapping

Descriptor	Page of CEF	Page of *Move Advanced* containing practice for this descriptor
Can understand a wide range of demanding, longer texts, and recognise implicit meaning.	24	3, 7, 15, 35, 39, 47, 67, 71, 79
Can express him/herself fluently and spontaneously without much obvious searching for expressions.	24	5, 9, 17, 20, 42, 49, 51, 67, 73, 76, 78
Can use language flexibly and effectively for social, academic and professional purposes.	24	4, 7, 8, 13, 16, 19, 37, 44, 68, 73, 76
Can produce clear, well-structured, detailed text on complex subjects, showing controlled use of organisational patterns, connectors and cohesive devices.	24	13, 17, 37, 39, 45, 47, 69, 77, 81
Range (vocabulary)		
Has a good command of a broad range of language, allowing him/her to select a formulation to express him/herself clearly in an appropriate style on a wide range of general, academic, professional or leisure topics without having to restrict what he/she wants to say.	28	2, 7, 8, 13, 16, 34, 43, 44, 47, 72
Has a good command of a broad lexical repertoire allowing gaps to be readily overcome with circumlocutions; little obvious searching for expressions or avoidance strategies.	112	2, 7, 13, 34, 69, 72, 78, 85
Good command of idiomatic expressions and colloquialisms.	112	9, 14, 16, 35, 41, 42, 43
Occasional minor slips, but no significant vocabulary errors.	112	7, 22, 23, 24, 25, 54, 55, 56, 57, 85, 86, 87, 88, 89
Accuracy (grammar)		
Consistently maintains a high degree of grammatical accuracy: errors are rare, difficult to spot and generally corrected when they do occur.	28, 114	8, 20, 22, 23, 24, 25, 36, 48, 54, 55, 56, 57, 68, 80 86, 87, 88, 89
Can qualify opinions and statements precisely in relation to degrees of, for example, certainty/uncertainty, belief/doubt, likelihood, etc.	129	4, 11, 19, 20, 40, 44, 48, 73
Fluency		
Can express him/herself fluently and spontaneously. Only a conceptually difficult subject can hinder a natural, smooth flow of language.	28, 129	5, 9, 17, 20, 42, 49, 53, 76, 82
Can give elaborate descriptions and narratives, integrating sub-themes, developing particular points and rounding off with an appropriate conclusion.	125	13, 37, 45, 51, 69, 81
Interaction		
Can select a suitable phrase from a readily available range of discourse functions to preface his/her remarks in order to get or keep the floor, to gain time and keep the floor whilst thinking, and to relate his/her own contributions skilfully to those of other speakers.	28, 124	5, 11, 44, 73
Coherence		
Can produce clear, smoothly flowing, well-structured speech, showing controlled use of organisational patterns, connectors and cohesive devices.	28, 125	2, 4, 11, 20, 35, 44, 45, 51
Pronunciation		
Can vary intonation and place sentence stress correctly in order to express finer shades of meaning.	117	5, 9, 11, 41, 73
Sociolinguistic appropriateness (function)		
Can recognise a wide range of idiomatic expressions and colloquialisms, appreciating register shifts; may, however, need to confirm occasional details, especially if the accent is unfamiliar.	122	9, 41, 42, 43, 49, 75, 76, 81
Can follow films employing a considerable degree of slang and idiomatic usage.	122	43

Descriptor	Page of CEF	Page of *Move Advanced* containing practice for this descriptor
Can use language flexibly and effectively for social purposes, including emotional, allusive and joking usage.	122	9, 11, 73
Can adjust what he/she says and the means of expressing it to the situation and the recipient and adopt a level of formality appropriate to the circumstances.	124	9, 11, 68, 73
Strategies		
Can plan what is to be said and the means to say it, considering the effect on the recipient/s.	64	2, 37, 45
Can use circumlocution and paraphrase to cover gaps in vocabulary and structure.	64	7, 8, 13, 34, 68, 72
Can backtrack when he/she encounters a difficulty and reformulate what he/she wants to say without fully interrupting the flow of speech.	65	13
Skilled at using contextual, grammatical and lexical cues to infer attitude, mood and intentions and anticipate what will come next.	72	5, 9, 11, 36, 73, 81
Can select a suitable phrase from a readily available range of discourse functions to preface my remarks appropriately in order to get the floor, or to gain time and keep the floor whilst thinking.	86	5, 11, 44, 73
Can relate own contribution skilfully to those of other speakers.	86	5, 9, 11, 44
Can ask follow-up questions to check that he/she has understood what a speaker intended to say, and get clarification of ambiguous points.	87	75
Listening		
Can understand extended speech even when it is not clearly structured and when relationships are only implied and not signalled explicitly.	27, 66	5, 9, 10, 17, 18, 37, 41, 42, 49, 50, 69, 73, 75, 81, 83
Can understand television programmes and films without too much effort.	27	18, 37, 42, 69, 83
Can understand enough to follow extended speech on abstract and complex topics beyond his/her own field, though may need to confirm occasional details, especially if the accent is unfamiliar.	66	10, 17, 18, 37, 41, 42, 69, 73
Can recognise a wide range of idiomatic expressions and colloquialisms, appreciating register shifts.	66	9, 14, 16, 42, 75, 76, 81
Can easily follow complex interactions between third parties in group discussion and debate, even on abstract, complex unfamiliar topics.	66	9
Can follow most lectures, discussions and debates with relative ease.	67	12, 13, 49
Can understand a wide range of recorded and broadcast audio material, including some non-standard usage, and identify finer points of detail including implicit attitudes and relationships between speakers.	68	21, 37, 42, 50, 73
Can follow films employing a considerable degree of slang and idiomatic usage.	71	42
Reading		
Can understand long and complex factual and literary texts, appreciating distinctions of style.	27	14, 34, 39, 79
Can understand specialised articles and longer technical instructions, even when they do not relate to my field.	27	2, 12, 39, 47, 66, 70
Can understand in detail lengthy, complex texts, whether or not they relate to his/her own area of speciality, provided he/she can reread difficult sections.	69	14, 34, 39, 66
Can understand any correspondence given the occasional use of a dictionary.	69	12
Can scan quickly through long and complex texts, locating relevant details.	70	2, 38
Can quickly identify the content and relevance of news items, articles and reports on a wide range of professional topics, deciding whether closer study is worthwhile.	70	77

Descriptor	Page of CEF	Page of *Move Advanced* containing practice for this descriptor
Can understand in detail a wide range of lengthy, complex texts likely to be encountered in social, professional or academic life, identifying finer points of detail including attitudes and implied as well as stated opinions.	70	6, 34, 39
Can understand in detail lengthy, complex instructions on a new machine or procedure, whether or not the instructions relate to his/her own area of speciality, provided he/she can reread difficult sections.	71	47
Spoken interaction		
Can express him/herself fluently and spontaneously without much obvious searching for expressions.	27	2, 5, 13, 15, 37, 41, 67, 82
Can use language flexibly and effectively for social and professional purposes.	27	2, 4, 5, 11, 42, 67, 73, 81
Can formulate ideas and opinions with precision and relate his/her contribution skilfully to those of other speakers.	27	2, 5, 9, 13, 37, 44, 73, 74, 78
Can express him/herself fluently and spontaneously, almost effortlessly.	74	5, 15, 37, 41, 53, 82
Has a good command of a broad lexical repertoire allowing gaps to be readily overcome with circumlocutions.	74	2, 8, 13, 69, 72
There is little obvious searching for expressions or avoidance strategies; only a conceptually difficult subject can hinder a natural, smooth flow of language.	74	7, 8, 13, 45, 72
Can use language flexibly and effectively for social purposes, including emotional, allusive and joking usage.	76	9, 11, 35, 73, 76
Can easily follow and contribute to complex interactions between third parties in group discussion even on abstract, complex unfamiliar topics.	77	5, 13
Can easily keep up with the debate, even on abstract, complex unfamiliar topics.	78	5, 13, 45, 51, 74
Can argue a formal position convincingly, responding to questions and comments and answering complex lines of counter argument fluently, spontaneously and appropriately.	78	13, 45, 51
Can help along the progress of the work by inviting others to join in, say what they think, etc.	79	6, 13, 45, 69
Can outline an issue or a problem clearly, speculating about causes or consequences, and weighing advantages and disadvantages of different approaches.	79	13, 67
Can cope linguistically to negotiate a solution to a dispute like an undeserved traffic ticket, financial responsibility for damage in a flat, for blame regarding an accident.	80	49, 73
Can outline a case for compensation, using persuasive language to demand satisfaction and state clearly the limits to any concession he/she is prepared to make.	80	49, 73
Can understand and exchange complex information and advice on the full range of matters related to my occupational role.	81	6, 9, 47
Can participate fully in an interview, as either interviewer or interviewee, expanding and developing the point being discussed fluently without any support, and handling interjections well.	82	77
Spoken production		
Can give clear, detailed descriptions of complex subjects.	27, 59	7, 8, 10, 20, 45, 69
Can give elaborate descriptions and narratives, integrating sub-themes, developing particular points and rounding off with an appropriate conclusion.	27, 59	8, 10, 11, 20, 35, 45
Can deliver announcements fluently, almost effortlessly, using stress and intonation to convey finer shades of meaning precisely.	60	20
Can give a clear, well-structured presentation of a complex subject, expanding and supporting points of view at some length with subsidiary points, reasons and relevant examples.	60	20, 45, 49, 51
Can handle interjections well, responding spontaneously and almost effortlessly.	60	20

Descriptor	Page of CEF	Page of *Move Advanced* containing practice for this descriptor
Writing		
Can express him/herself in clear, well-structured text, expressing points of view at some length.	27	13, 39, 47, 69, 77
Can write about complex subjects in a letter, an essay or a report, underlining what he/she considers to be the salient issues.	27	11, 13, 40
Can select style appropriate to the reader in mind.	27	17, 37, 39, 47, 69
Can write clear, well-structured texts of complex subjects, underlining the relevant salient issues, expanding and supporting points of view at some length with subsidiary points, reasons and relevant examples, and rounding off with an appropriate conclusion.	61	37, 39
Can write clear, detailed, well-structured and developed descriptions and imaginative texts in an assured, personal, natural style appropriate to the reader in mind.	62	17, 37, 69, 81
Can write clear, well-structured expositions of complex subjects, underlining the relevant salient issues.	62	13, 17, 39, 40
Can expand and support points of view at some length with subsidiary points, reasons and relevant examples.	62	39
Can express him/herself with clarity and precision, relating to the addressee flexibly and effectively.	83	17, 37, 69
Can express him/herself with clarity and precision in personal correspondence, using language flexibly and effectively, including emotional, allusive and joking usage.	83	
Can take detailed notes during a lecture on topics in his/her field of interest, recording the information so accurately and so close to the original that the notes could also be useful to other people.	96	49
Can summarise long, demanding texts.	96	2, 17
Layout, paragraphing and punctuation are consistent and helpful.	118	37, 39
Spelling is accurate, apart from occasional slips of the pen.	118	37, 39

Move Advanced Teacher's Book © Macmillan Publishers Limited 2007 **Photocopiable**

CEF student checklists

Module 1 Unit 1 Behave!

Complete the checklist. Add an extra activity you have done in class or at home.
1 = I can do this with a lot of help from my teacher 2 = I can do this with a little help
3 = I can do this fairly well 4 = I can do this really well 5 = I can do this almost perfectly.

Competences	Page	Exercise	Your score
Language quality I can use discourse markers to contrast information. I can use a rich vocabulary to describe people's personality.	4 2	Language study 1–6 Vocabulary and speaking 1–7	1 2 3 4 5 1 2 3 4 5
Listening I can explain the meaning of sentences from a conversation I have heard.	5	Listening and speaking 1–3	1 2 3 4 5
Reading I can understand detailed abstract information in an article. I can recognise the emphatic use of auxiliary verbs.	2 4	Reading 1–2 Language study 3	1 2 3 4 5 1 2 3 4 5
Spoken interaction I can discuss types of behaviour. I can take turns in a discussion. I can give detailed character descriptions of people.	2 2 5 5 5 2	Lead-in 1–3 Reading 5 Listening and speaking 3 Vocabulary and pronunciation 1–2 Speaking 1–3 Vocabulary and speaking 3–6	1 2 3 4 5 1 2 3 4 5 1 2 3 4 5 1 2 3 4 5 1 2 3 4 5 1 2 3 4 5
Spoken production I can apply given expressions to tell anecdotes of my own.	4	Language study 6	1 2 3 4 5
Writing I can summarise a difficult text.	2	Reading 3–4	1 2 3 4 5
Strategies I can organise ideas systematically to present them well.	2	Reading 5	1 2 3 4 5

Module 1 Unit 2 Form and function

Complete the checklist. Add an extra activity you have done in class or at home.
1 = I can do this with a lot of help from my teacher 2 = I can do this with a little help
3 = I can do this fairly well 4 = I can do this really well 5 = I can do this almost perfectly

Competences	Page	Exercise	Your score
Language quality I can combine words into compound adjectives correctly. I can qualify nouns correctly with a range of modifiers and subordinate clauses.	7 8	Vocabulary 1–5 Language study 1–5	1 2 3 4 5 1 2 3 4 5
Listening I can understand a colloquial conversation between native speakers. I can identify speakers' attitudes.	9 9	Listening and vocabulary 1–6 Listening and vocabulary 3–6	1 2 3 4 5 1 2 3 4 5
Reading I can understand a writer's attitude, even if it is only implied.	6	Reading and speaking 2	1 2 3 4 5
Spoken interaction I can reach an agreed solution with a group of people, establishing criteria, arguing my case and including others. I can sympathise with problems.	6 9	Lead-in 1–3 Listening and vocabulary 5–7	1 2 3 4 5 1 2 3 4 5
Spoken production I can describe buildings, places and objects. I can talk about workspaces.	6 6 9	Reading and speaking 1 Reading and speaking 1 Reading and speaking 1	1 2 3 4 5 1 2 3 4 5 1 2 3 4 5
Strategies I can identify patterns in the language I know and use them to notice similar language and extend my repertoire.	7	Vocabulary 1–5	1 2 3 4 5

Module 1 Unit 3 It's up to you!

Complete the checklist. Add an extra activity you have done in class or at home.
1 = I can do this with a lot of help from my teacher 2 = I can do this with a little help
3 = I can do this fairly well 4 = I can do this really well 5 = I can do this almost perfectly

Competences	Page	Exercise	Your score
Language quality I can communicate what is emotionally significant and emphasise what is important. I can use conventional collocations.	11 13	Language study 1–6 Vocabulary and speaking 1	1 2 3 4 5 1 2 3 4 5
Listening I can follow extended speech on an unfamiliar topic.	10	Listening 1–3	1 2 3 4 5
Reading In can understand correspondence and Internet discussions.	12	Reading and vocabulary 1–3	1 2 3 4 5
Spoken interaction I can discuss social issues and direct action. I can make a case, convince and persuade.	10 12–13 13	Lead-in 1 Reading and vocabulary 4–5 Vocabulary and speaking 4	1 2 3 4 5 1 2 3 4 5
Spoken production I can use emphasis when talking about important events. I can convey vivid impressions skilfully.	11 10	Language study 1–6 Speaking 1–2	1 2 3 4 5 1 2 3 4 5
Writing I can contribute to message boards.	13	Writing 1–5	1 2 3 4 5
Strategies I can notice new synonyms and use my vocabulary range to rephrase when I don't know a word	13	Vocabulary and speaking 3	1 2 3 4 5

Module 1 Unit 4 No pain, no gain

Complete the checklist. Add an extra activity you have done in class or at home.
1 = I can do this with a lot of help from my teacher 2 = I can do this with a little help
3 = I can do this fairly well 4 = I can do this really well 5 = I can do this almost perfectly

Competences	Page	Exercise	Your score
Language quality I can use three-part phrasal verbs correctly.	16	Language study 1–7	1 2 3 4 5
Listening I can understand the details of extended colloquial speech.	17	Listening 1–2	1 2 3 4 5
Reading I can note the details of the way an article is expressed.	14	Reading and speaking 1–4	1 2 3 4 5
Spoken interaction I can discuss motivation and achievement. I can understand and use colloquialisms and proverbs.	14 17 14 14–15	Reading and speaking 1, 4 Vocabulary 2 Lead in 1–2 Vocabulary and speaking 1–5	1 2 3 4 5 1 2 3 4 5 1 2 3 4 5 1 2 3 4 5
Spoken production I can talk about success. I can explain causes and results. I can use idioms in telling an anecdote.	16 17 17 15	Language study 3–7 Vocabulary 1–2 Speaking and writing 1–2 Vocabulary and speaking 3	1 2 3 4 5 1 2 3 4 5 1 2 3 4 5 1 2 3 4 5
Writing I can write a summary of an inspiring life.	17	Speaking and writing 1–3	1 2 3 4 5
Strategies I can stuse dictionaries, scripts and reference books to check my understanding and extend my vocabulary	17 17	Vocabulary 1 Speaking and writing 1	1 2 3 4 5 1 2 3 4 5

Move Advanced Teacher's Book © Macmillan Publishers Limited 2007 **Photocopiable**

Module 2 Unit 1 Telling tales

Complete the checklist. Add an extra activity you have done in class or at home.
1 = I can do this with a lot of help from my teacher 2 = I can do this with a little help
3 = I can do this fairly well 4 = I can do this really well 5 = I can do this almost perfectly

Competences	Page	Exercise	Your score
Language quality I can connect events using the perfect. I can use the correct nouns, adjectives and exclamations to express emotions.	36 34–35	Language study 1–4 Vocabulary 1–3	1 2 3 4 5 1 2 3 4 5
Reading I can understand a piece of contemporary literary prose. I can appreciate the connotations of choice of verb tense.	34 36	Reading and speaking 1–5 Language study 1–4	1 2 3 4 5 1 2 3 4 5
Listening I can understand a literary narrative.	37	Listening 1–2	1 2 3 4 5
Spoken interaction I can discuss a literary text. I can discuss my reading habits and different kinds of texts.	34 37 37	Reading and speaking 1–5 Listening 3–4 Speaking and vocabulary 1–2	1 2 3 4 5 1 2 3 4 5 1 2 3 4 5
Spoken production I can relate an anecdote and bring out its emotional significance.	35	Vocabulary 4	1 2 3 4 5
Writing I can write a fictional narrative using dramatic and descriptive effects.	37	Writing 1–3	1 2 3 4 5
Strategies I can work on texts with other people, give feedback and profit from theirs.	37	Writing 3	1 2 3 4 5

Module 2 Unit 2 A perfect world

Complete the checklist. Add an extra activity you have done in class or at home.
1 = I can do this with a lot of help from my teacher 2 = I can do this with a little help
3 = I can do this fairly well 4 = I can do this really well 5 = I can do this almost perfectly

Competences	Page	Exercise	Your score
Language quality I can use a range of structures to focus attention on important points.	40	Language focus 1–6	1 2 3 4 5
Listening I can understand people's attitudes from the way they express themselves.	41	Listening and speaking 1–3	1 2 3 4 5
Reading I can predict the content of a text. I can find specific information in a difficult text. I can analyse the structure of a text.	38 38 38	Lead-in 1 Reading and vocabulary 1–2 Reading and vocabulary 5	1 2 3 4 5 1 2 3 4 5 1 2 3 4 5
Spoken interaction I can comment on current affairs. I can express surprise or indifference. I can discuss people's characters	38 41 41	Reading and vocabulary 3–4, 7 Vocabulary and pronunciation 1–4 Listening and speaking 4	1 2 3 4 5 1 2 3 4 5 1 2 3 4 5
Writing I can plan and write a well–structured article. I can focus attention on important information.	39 40	Writing 1–3 Language focus 1–6	1 2 3 4 5 1 2 3 4 5
Strategies I can use my knowledge of structures which focus attention to predict what people are going to say.	40	Language focus 4–6	1 2 3 4 5

Module 2 Unit 3 Modern-day icons

Complete the checklist. Add an extra activity you have done in class or at home.
1 = I can do this with a lot of help from my teacher 2 = I can do this with a little help
3 = I can do this fairly well 4 = I can do this really well 5 = I can do this almost perfectly

Competences	Page	Exercise	Your score
Language quality I can contrast British and American English pronunciation. I can use idioms involving parts of the body.	43 42–43	Pronunciation 1–2 Vocabulary 1–4	1 2 3 4 5 1 2 3 4 5
Listening I can understand attitudes in an interview, even when the accent is unfamiliar.	42	Listening and speaking 1–4	1 2 3 4 5
Reading I can understand subtle linguistic and conceptual distinctions that are implicit in things I read.	45	Reading and speaking 1–3	1 2 3 4 5
Spoken interaction I can talk about popular icons and nostalgia. I can discuss the significance of a proverb.	42 42	Listening and speaking 5–8 Lead-in 1	1 2 3 4 5 1 2 3 4 5
Spoken production I can use spoken phrases with say and speak. I can integrate specific expressions smoothly into what I am saying. I can co–operate with a group to brainstorm ideas, plan and deliver a presentation.	44 44 45	Language study 1–6 Language study 5 Speaking and writing 1–3	1 2 3 4 5 1 2 3 4 5 1 2 3 4 5
Strategies I can plan what is to be said and the means to say it, considering the effect on the audience.	45	Speaking and writing 1–3	1 2 3 4 5

Module 2 Unit 4 Safe and sound?

Complete the checklist. Add an extra activity you have done in class or at home.
1 = I can do this with a lot of help from my teacher 2 = I can do this with a little help
3 = I can do this fairly well 4 = I can do this really well 5 = I can do this almost perfectly

Competences	Page	Exercise	Your score
Language quality I can talk about real and unreal past situations. I can use the language of banking and finance.	48 46	Language study 1–5 Reading and vocabulary 4–7	1 2 3 4 5 1 2 3 4 5
Listening I can follow a debate and take notes about the opinions of each contributor and the evidence they quote.	49	Listening and vocabulary 1–3	1 2 3 4 5
Reading I can understand a technical text in detail. I can determine precise shades of meaning from specific verb usages in their broader context.	46 47	Reading and vocabulary 1–5 Language study 4	1 2 3 4 5 1 2 3 4 5
Spoken interaction I can discuss security, crime prevention and civil liberties. I can discuss privacy and public information. I can negotiate a solution to a complex problem.	46 47 49 46 49	Reading and vocabulary 7 Speaking and writing 1–2 Listening and vocabulary 4 Lead-in 1 Speaking 1	1 2 3 4 5 1 2 3 4 5 1 2 3 4 5 1 2 3 4 5 1 2 3 4 5
Spoken production I can express my opinions about a broad topic.	49	Listening and vocabulary 4	1 2 3 4 5
Writing I can give advice and warnings.	47	Speaking and writing 1–4	1 2 3 4 5
Strategies I can take notes effectively and use them to reinforce my knowledge of a vocabulary area.	49	Listening and vocabulary 1–5	1 2 3 4 5

Move Advanced Teacher's Book © Macmillan Publishers Limited 2007 **Photocopiable**

Module 3 Unit 1 Living together

Complete the checklist. Add an extra activity you have done in class or at home.
1 = I can do this with a lot of help from my teacher 2 = I can do this with a little help
3 = I can do this fairly well 4 = I can do this really well 5 = I can do this almost perfectly

Competences	Page	Exercise	Your score
Language quality I can generally discern the best word to use for precision in a particular context.	69	Vocabulary and writing 1	1 2 3 4 5
Listening I can understand extensive discourse and appreciate finer shades of meaning.	69	Listening and speaking 1–2	1 2 3 4 5
Reading I can understand a newspaper article in detail, including colloquial expressions. I can read a text critically, comparing its attitudes with my own.	66 68	Reading and vocabulary 1–5 Language study 5–6	1 2 3 4 5 1 2 3 4 5
Spoken interaction I can discuss family relationships and cultural values. I can discuss the conditions of a non-traditional community and people's responses to it.	66 66 67 69 69	Lead-in 1 Reading and vocabulary 6 Speaking 1 Listening and speaking 3 Vocabulary and writing 2	1 2 3 4 5 1 2 3 4 5 1 2 3 4 5 1 2 3 4 5 1 2 3 4 5
Spoken production I can set out the advantages and disadvantages of a course of action.	67	Speaking 1	1 2 3 4 5
Writing I can describe abstract ideas in detail, and express them in such a way as to make them seem attractive.	69	Vocabulary and writing 2–4	1 2 3 4 5
Strategies I can use ellipsis and substitution.	68	Language study 1–6	1 2 3 4 5

Module 3 Unit 2 Talk talk

Complete the checklist. Add an extra activity you have done in class or at home.
1 = I can do this with a lot of help from my teacher 2 = I can do this with a little help
3 = I can do this fairly well 4 = I can do this really well 5 = I can do this almost perfectly

Competences	Page	Exercise	Your score
Language quality I can form adjectives from verbs and nouns using suffixes. I can use sensitive language and softeners to avoid offence.	72 70 73	Language study 1–7 Vocabulary 1–3 Speaking and pronunciation 1–3	1 2 3 4 5 1 2 3 4 5 1 2 3 4 5
Listening I can appreciate subtleties of tone and attitude, even in extended speech with an unfamiliar accent.	73	Listening 1–3	1 2 3 4 5
Reading I can read an op-ed article and fully understand the viewpoint expressed and its implications.	70	Reading and speaking 1–4	1 2 3 4 5
Spoken interaction I can evaluate the cultural and practical value of minority languages. I can address emotionally difficult topics and achieve a desired outcome without causing unnecessary upset.	70 73	Reading and speaking 4 Speaking and pronunciation 3	1 2 3 4 5 1 2 3 4 5
Spoken production I can use sentence stress to make my point without offending the person I'm addressing.	73	Speaking and pronunciation 1–2	1 2 3 4 5
Strategies I can work with another person to find examples to illustrate particular words.	72	Language study 5–7	1 2 3 4 5

Module 3 Unit 3 Net value

Complete the checklist. Add an extra activity you have done in class or at home.
1 = I can do this with a lot of help from my teacher 2 = I can do this with a little help
3 = I can do this fairly well 4 = I can do this really well 5 = I can do this almost perfectly

Competences	Page	Exercise	Your score
Language quality I can adjust the register of my language to make it appropriate to the situation.	76	Language study 1–6	1 2 3 4 5
Listening I can take notes as I listen and then work with others to reconstruct what was said. I can appreciate subtleties of register and tone in an informal discussion.	74 75	Listening and speaking 1–5 Listening and vocabulary 1–5	1 2 3 4 5 1 2 3 4 5
Reading I can predict statistical information in a text from the language used to set it in context.	77	Reading and vocabulary 1–5	1 2 3 4 5
Spoken interaction I can use vague language in informal communication. I can evaluate the importance and dangers of electronic media. **Spoken production** I can develop an argument and put a case in a debate.	76 74 75 77 74	Language study 1–6 Lead-in 1 Speaking and pronunciation 4 Reading and vocabulary 6 Listening and speaking 5	1 2 3 4 5 1 2 3 4 5 1 2 3 4 5 1 2 3 4 5 1 2 3 4 5
Writing I can collate collected data and write an interesting and convincing survey report.	77	Speaking and writing 1–5	1 2 3 4 5
Strategies I can clarify information and check understanding.	75	Speaking and pronunciation 1–3	1 2 3 4 5

Module 3 Unit 4 Team spirit

Complete the checklist. Add an extra activity you have done in class or at home.
1 = I can do this with a lot of help from my teacher 2 = I can do this with a little help
3 = I can do this fairly well 4 = I can do this really well 5 = I can do this almost perfectly

Competences	Page	Exercise	Your score
Language quality I can use dependent prepositions with verbs, nouns and adjectives.	80	Language study 1–5	1 2 3 4 5
Listening I can understand and empathise with the implicit emotional background of what is being said.	81	Listening 1–5	1 2 3 4 5
Reading I can use a text to provide evidence in support of a viewpoint.	78	Reading 1–2	1 2 3 4 5
Spoken interaction I can discuss work practices and leadership styles. **Spoken production** I can describe college- or work-related problems and give advice to others.	78, 81 81	Lead-in 1–2 Vocabulary and speaking 3–4 Speaking 1–3 Speaking 1–3	1 2 3 4 5 1 2 3 4 5 1 2 3 4 5 1 2 3 4 5
Writing I can write an entertaining dialogue to illustrate a typical situation.	81	Writing 1–2	1 2 3 4 5
Strategies I can work out meaning and usage from context sufficiently well to try using the vocabulary in new situations.	78	Vocabulary and speaking 1–2	1 2 3 4 5

Teaching tips

Starting lessons

Start the lesson with an interesting opener related to the topic of your lesson, before students open their books. The Teacher's notes give ideas for lesson warmers, usually using an opening discussion question. You could also use one of these ideas:

- Show students realia (everyday objects) related to the topic but not too obvious. Ask students to guess the topic of the lesson. For example, for Module 1, Unit 2, Form and function, you could bring in some photos of famous or unusual buildings.
- Ask students to describe and speculate about a magazine picture that is related to the subject of the lesson in some way.
- Write the unit title or the subject of the lesson on the board and ask students to brainstorm words connected to it. You can do this with the class for more control, or with teams of students as a competition for more fun.
- Write a word related to the unit topic on the board (for example, for Module 2, Unit 2, A perfect world, you could write *controversy / controversial, debate, precedent*) and ask students what they associate with that word. This is a good way to discuss how things are seen in different cultures and the differing importance attached to them.
- Write one or two controversial statements relating to the topic on the board. For example, for Module 2, Unit 2: *Cloning human beings should never be legal*. Ask students to discuss the statement(s).
- Write a jumbled list of topic-related verb–noun collocations (for example, for Module 2, Unit 4 *open – a bank account, withdraw – money*), or adjective–noun collocations (for example, for Module 1, Unit 1 *vivid – imagination, optimistic – outlook*) on the board and ask students to match them.

Whole class work

Whole class work needs to address the needs of each student as far as possible. Here are some tips for large or mixed ability classes:

- Make sure that you know the names of everybody in the class! Ask students to make a desk name card.
- The best classroom layout of desks is usually a horseshoe shape so that all students can see and be seen.
- Ensure that every student has the chance to speak. Most students are quite happy to contribute when asked directly but some students will not offer information voluntarily.
- Make sure that everyone has understood the instructions. For more complex tasks, demonstrate the steps with a stronger student. Allow students thinking time before answering or performing a task.
- Ask weaker students easier questions so that they feel encouraged to participate in discussions.
- Do not allow stronger or more outgoing students to dominate. Encourage students to listen and show respect for each other.

- Ensure whatever you write on the board is clear and clearly visible to everybody in the class.
- Try to provide a variety of tasks that will appeal to all learning styles: visual tasks (for example, picture description and speculation, TV and video extracts, newspaper cartoons); physical response tasks (mime, drawing, acting out); audio tasks (songs, sound recognition, dictations, pronunciation tasks, rhymes); mechanical tasks (comprehension questions, gap-fills, rewriting sentences); problem-solving tasks (ranking activities, group discussion tasks requiring agreement, logic puzzles); tasks requiring creativity and imagination (role-plays, writing brochures, making posters, interpreting poems).
- If you have a wide range of abilities, make sure that you have prepared extension tasks for students who work more quickly (extra questions, extra tasks, checking tasks etc) and provide extra support for weaker students while they are doing tasks (checking, offering help etc).

Pairwork and groupwork

Pairwork and groupwork allow students to speak more and exchange ideas and information with other students. Use these tips to ensure that students work effectively in pairs and groups:

- It is usually easier to let students work with their neighbour or neighbours. However, you can swap pairs and groups round for variety now and then by getting them to work with someone else in the class.
- To randomly pair two students: make cards with pairs of words and distribute them at random. Students have to find their partner by asking questions or showing their card. You can use for example, two words that make a compound word (*foot, ball*); pairs of names (*Jekyll, Hyde / David, Beckham*), synonyms (*rich, wealthy*) or opposites (*rich, poor*). For group work: give every student a letter from a set of, say, four letters (*A, B, C,* D) and than ask all *A*s to work together, all *B*s etc.
- Always make sure students know what they have to do. Present the task clearly, using an example. You can demonstrate the tasks using open pairs: ask two students to perform the task or part of the task to the class. Check students have understood the task and allow time for questions.
- Set a time limit for the task. Make sure students know they have to stop when the time limit has been reached, even if they have not quite finished. About a minute before time runs out, warn students to try and complete their task.
- Monitor discussions. Sort out any problems, praise students and make a note of recurring errors for later discussion and correction.

Always ensure whole class feedback so that students feel their activity had a point or an end result. Ask students to report back to the class, discuss their results or ask individual pairs or groups to perform their role-play etc to the class.

Correcting and praising

Students need to feel that they are making progress and achieving something. Encourage students as much as possible by praising them both for effort and for achievement:

- Smile and make positive comments.
- Always begin by focusing on what students have done well before correcting mistakes.

The level of language correction necessary will depend on the type of activity you are using. Explicit and frequent correction will be necessary in accuracy tasks such as controlled grammar, pronunciation and vocabulary activities. In fluency activities and warmers, it is unnecessary to correct every mistake if students are able to convey their message. In these cases, you can correct indirectly as follows:

- Correct students by adding a comment which repeats the correct formulation or pronunciation, rather than drawing attention to the mistake directly.
- Make a note of frequent mistakes and correct them on the board with the whole class after the activity has finished.
- Ignore minor mistakes completely!

Dealing with cultural differences

The huge advantage of having multilingual or multicultural classes is that students bring a wealth of different experiences and opinions to the language class. Exploit this by:

- asking students to compare the material in their student's book with their own country and customs as much as possible (ask, for example: Do you have this tradition/type of house etc in your country? Are there any famous eccentrics in your country?). Discussing idioms and popular sayings is often a good way to discuss the importance of things in different cultures.
- asking students to reflect on their own experiences and compare them with those of students from different countries (ask in Module 2, Unit 2, for example: *Is GM food controversial in your country? Is there much debate about 'designer babies'?*).

However, be aware that not all students will possess the same degree of awareness about popular culture, such as famous people, famous buildings and places, music, sports, technology etc. You can get students to share knowledge by:

- mixing students from different countries and backgrounds when doing pairwork and groupwork
- asking the class to define potentially problematic terms or explain proper names that come up in the Coursebook material. Scan texts for these in advance.
- doing specific cultural recognition activities (for example, in Module 1, Unit 1, by doing a quiz on famous people and their achievements or in Module 1, Unit 2, by asking students to guess the names of famous cities or landmarks).

Using reading materials

- Before reading a text, students can use the photos, the title and the general look of the text to predict the content of the text and the text type. If students already have some ideas about the text before they read it, they will be able to deal with it more confidently. Predicting also motivates students to read the text to find out if their ideas are correct. Ask questions such as: *Look at the title: what does it tell you about the subject of the text? Look at the photos: who is the text about? Where does this text come from – a teenage magazine, a newspaper?*
- Pre-teaching vocabulary can give students extra support when reading a text. You can pre-teach particular items from the text by deciding in advance which items might cause difficulty and writing them on the board. Or you can choose a vocabulary set which covers several items in the text (for example, in Module 2, Unit 2 there is a text on 'designer babies' which includes the words *genetic disease*, *donor* and *blood transfusion*: you could pre-teach / elicit a 'medical' set which includes things like *transplant*, *organ donor*, *key-hole surgery*, *benign / malignant*). You can also do word building exercises (focusing on verbs, nouns, adjectives) which include words from the text (for example, in Module 2, Unit 2: *donor – donation*, *embryo – embryonic*, where *donor* and *embryo* are the words in the text).
- All *Move* reading texts are recorded on the CD which means that students can listen to the text while they read it. This helps learners who prefer learning orally rather than visually and is a good pronunciation help for all students. It also means that learners have to read at a certain speed; it is therefore sometimes a good idea to let students listen and read the first time they read a text and have to perform a gist-reading task. Simply listening to a reading text can also be useful, particularly for 'spoken' texts such as interviews.
- Jigsaw reading tasks are a good way of exploiting reading texts in pairs and groups. Divide a text into sections; ask students to read one section, find out information and then share this information orally with their partner or group members.
- Reading texts often contain a lot of unknown vocabulary. Emphasise again and again that students don't have to understand every word! Students need to understand enough to complete the main task. Advise students to always try and work out the meaning of the word from the context – by looking at the type of word (adjective, noun, verb etc) and 'clues' about the meaning of the word in the lines before and after.
- If students need to look up the meanings of unknown words, encourage them to use a good monolingual learner dictionary. This type of dictionary gives a simple definition in English as well as an example, making the meaning clearer than a translation – which may well have several meanings. You can build dictionary work into your class (finding definitions, discussing different forms of a word, explaining dictionary abbreviations etc) so that students can get the maximum help out of their dictionaries and become more independent learners.

Speaking

- Encourage students to speak as much as possible and stress that they should not worry about making mistakes.
- Make sure students speak with correct pronunciation and intonation. Ask students to repeat new words in class, in chorus and individually; ask students to repeat sentences from listening and reading texts or their own sentences, with correct rhythm and sentence stress.
- Speaking about concrete, personal topics is easier than discussing abstract situations. Personalise tasks as much as possible, so that all students have the chance to say something.
- Train students to use strategies to help them make the best use of the language they have. For example, you can train students to describe things when they don't know an English word using phrases such as *It looks like a …, It's made of …, It's used for …* (Practice task: *You are in a chemist's and want to buy plasters and mouthwash, but you don't know the English words. Explain to the chemist what you need.*) Teach the use of fillers such as *Well, Actually, Anyway, What I mean to say is …* which allow students to keep a conversation going while looking for the language to express something.
- Use pairwork for checking and comparing answers to tasks, so that students have more opportunities to speak.

Using listening materials

- Before listening, as before reading, exploit the pictures in the book and any other clues to the content of the listening text.
- Tell students not to panic if they can't understand some of what they hear. Make sure they understand that they are listening to perform a task and if they can complete the task, they have been successful.
- Encourage students to use clues in people's voices which show their feelings, age, attitudes etc to reinforce understanding of the content.
- Allow students to listen to the material more than once, if they wish.
- You can direct students to use the listening scripts in the Coursebook to support their understanding and check answers.
- Encourage students to watch English TV, listen to radio and interact in English as much as possible outside their classes in order to 'tune their ear' to the English language.

Writing

- Brainstorm ideas on the board before students write to make sure all students have something to write about.
- Tell students to use any similar texts in the Coursebook as models.
- Tell students to think carefully about what they write and revise their work when they have finished: Is it interesting? Are there any repetitions or unclear parts? Is it grammatically correct?
- Make sure somebody reads or listens to written work: check writing tasks individually yourself; ask students to read a partner's work and check it; ask students to read out an answer or task to the whole class and the class to comment.
- The optional activities in the teacher's notes contain several extra writing tasks which can be used both for language consolidation and for practising writing skills.

Reviewing and revising

Build in regular revision of structures and vocabulary. The teacher's notes contain suggestions for unit-related revision activities at the end of each unit. Students can use the Grammar reference to revise or check structures at any time. They can revise vocabulary by studying the Wordlist and playing these word games:

- **Explain it:** Students work in teams of four. They write out all the nouns/adjectives/verbs in the Wordlist on small pieces of paper. They then work with another team. Teams take turns explaining words. Each member of a team must pick up a word and explain it to their team while the other team times them (1 minute). If the team gets the word in time, they get a point.
- **Categories:** Write umbrella nouns from the Wordlist on the board (for example: *social issues, behavioural traits*). Students work individually or in teams and make a list of as many words as possible which fit these categories.
- **Countdown:** Write a (long) word from the Wordlist in jumbled form on the board. Teams of students try to make a word using all the letters. Follow up with students making a new word with the same letters (the team with the longest word wins).
- **Collocations:** Write a noun from the Wordlist on the board. Teams of students make lists of verbs that go with the noun (set a time limit for this). Check the collocations on the board. The team with the most correct ones wins. (For example, *chess: play, watch, understand, practise, compete at, win at, lose at, like, dislike, hate, enjoy …*). You can also practise other collocations, such as noun–noun (*chess board, chess champion, chess match, chess set …*).
- **Pictionary:** Students choose a word from the Wordlist and draw a picture on the board. The class or their team guesses the word.
- **Comparisons:** Write two nouns from the Wordlist on the board. Students work individually or in teams. They have to compare the two things. (For example, in Module 2, Unit 3: *equality, world peace. Equality is more achievable than world peace.*)

- **Crosswords:** Students work in pairs. They make a completed crossword grid using ten words from the Wordlist. Then they make an empty, numbered grid and write clues for the words. Pairs exchange their crosswords with another pair and complete them.
- **Headlines:** Students make headlines using only the words in the list and prepositions. For example, *Mischievous eccentric becomes avid collector of garden gnomes* (Module 1, Unit 1). They then write a short story for the headline.

Ending or filling in lessons

Sometimes you will need a short activity or game to change the pace of the lesson, end a lesson on a positive note or just provide a bit of fun. Here are a few ideas that can be used with different topic and language areas:

- **Charades:** Students mime a film, book, item of vocabulary or phrase for the class or their team to guess.
- **Bingo:** Write twenty large numbers (over 100) on the board. Students choose five and write them down. Call out the numbers on the board at random. The first student to tick off their numbers is the winner. You can also play this with categories of words or a list of unit-related words.
- **Find someone who …:** Write a list of questions on the board (Find someone who was born in the same month as you, someone who likes cats, someone who knows what [a word from the Wordlist] means, etc). Students move around the class asking questions, and find at least one name for each question.
- **Picture dictation and drawing:** Describe a scene or a person. Students draw a picture. Students then compare pictures with a partner and discuss any differences. Students can also dictate pictures to each other.
- **Coursebook picture dictation:** Students choose a picture in one of the units already covered in their book and describe it to the class or to a partner without showing them the picture. The class or their partner listens and then has to find the correct picture in their book.
- **Five things:** Ask students to think of five things …
  – they do well / badly.
  – they hate to eat / love to do.
  – that are small / disgusting / beautiful / blue … etc.
  – that make people embarrassed / angry / happy … etc.
  Students discuss their ideas with a partner.
- **Memory game:** Bring ten objects from home or collect ten things from students in class. Hold the objects up to the class to memorise first and then put them in a dark bag or put them on the teacher's desk and cover them with a blanket. Students have to say what is in the bag or under the blanket, giving a description of each object.
- **Chinese whispers:** Whisper a fairly complex sentence to a student at the front of the class. Students take it in turns to whisper the sentence to another student. The last student writes it on the board. Whisper different sentences at intervals, so about five sentences are circulating in a clear progression. Compare the sentences on the board to the original sentences.

- **Stand in line:** Write the words of a long sentence on individual cards. Give out the cards at random to students. Students with cards go to the front of the class in turn. They show the class their word and take their place in the sentence, moving around until students form the correct sentence.
- **General knowledge quiz:** Students work in teams. They write ten general knowledge questions on the topic of the unit. Teams take turns to ask their questions.

Emergency lessons

The *Move Advanced* Teacher's Book contains 24 photocopiable resource sheets (see pages 88-117). Twelve of these are one-page games and communicative activities and twelve are 45-minute discussion lessons requiring little or no preparation. Both types are linked to the topic of the units in the Coursebook and can be used as emergency lessons or activities.

Below is an idea for an emergency lesson, built around a single activity. It requires no preparation and can be used at any point in the book, with any topic.

Storytime

- Explain that students are going to write a story using ten words from their Coursebook.
- Students work in small groups. Each group chooses ten words from the previous two units: three nouns, three verbs, three adjectives and one adverb. They can do this using the Wordlists for the correct module. Check the groups' word lists to ensure that they have complied with the instructions.
- The groups discuss and write down their story.
- Each group checks its story carefully. Encourage students to revise their work.
- The groups present their story to the class. The group can nominate one person to read out the story or they can take it in turns to read a section. They can draw pictures, use realia or make sound effects to add interest.

Behave!

Topic	Language study	Vocabulary	Main skills
• Eccentrics • Are you a nonconformist?	• Contrast (discourse markers)	• Behavioural traits (adjectives and their collocations) • Taking turns in a discussion	• **Reading:** predicting and checking; summarising information • **Speaking:** discussing types of behaviour; discussing pressure to conform in different countries; taking turns and interrupting • **Listening:** identifying main information • **Pronunciation:** stress and intonation in discussions

Learning aims

- Can use discourse markers to contrast information
- Can discuss types of behaviour
- Can take turns in a discussion

Warmer

- Ask students to look quickly at the photos. Explain that all these people are regarded as *eccentric*, and write the word on the board. Ask: *What does 'eccentric' mean?* Elicit a definition from the class and then compare it with a dictionary definition.

Eccentrics

Lead-in

Background information

German-born Albert Einstein (1877–1955) is considered by many to be the most important scientist of the 20th century. He was noted for his eccentric hairstyle and character and later in life he needed to spend a lot of time alone.

Salvador Dalí (1904–1989) was a Spanish artist best known for his surrealist work, identified by its dreamlike images. His eccentric manner and appearance often drew more public attention than his artwork.

Frida Kahlo (1907–1954) was a Mexican painter whose work combined realism, symbolism and surrealism. She was noted for her extroverted behaviour and her flamboyant clothes.

Björk (born in 1965) is an Icelandic singer famed for her unusual appearance and quirky music. She was voted the world's most eccentric star in 2006.

Ozzy Osbourne (born in 1948) is a British singer in the heavy metal band *Black Sabbath*. He is known for his unconventional behaviour in *The Osbournes*, a reality TV series about his daily life with his family.

Vincent van Gogh (1853–1890) was a Dutch painter who lived in France. In later years he suffered from mental illness and he spent some time in a psychiatric clinic after cutting off part of his left ear. He committed suicide in 1890.

1

- Students work in groups. They identify the people in the photos and discuss the questions.
- Check the answers with the class.

Answers
a Albert Einstein   b Salvador Dalí   c Frida Kahlo

2

- Discuss the question with the class.

3

- Read out the quote and check any problematic vocabulary.
- Discuss the questions with the class. Elicit some examples of people who might fit each description.

Reading

1

- Students work in pairs and discuss the questions.
- Draw attention to the difference in stress between *eccentric* and *eccentricity*.

2

- 🔊 **01** Students read the interview and check their answers to Ex 1. They can listen to the text on CD.

Answers
1 True. They have a sunny outlook on life and are curious.
2 True. They regard the person making fun of them as the one with the problem.
3 False. Eccentricity is a conscious choice not to conform.

Optional activity

More questions
You could ask further questions about the interview to check comprehension and / or to practise scan reading. For example, *What prompted David Weeks to make a scientific study of eccentricity? Why has psychiatry overlooked eccentricity? Do men or women tend to be obsessive collectors? What example of this does David Weeks give? Are eccentrics generally more or less healthy than the average person? How often do eccentrics go to the doctor, on average? What makes a person eccentric? Are men or women more likely to be eccentric? Does David Weeks consider himself to be eccentric?*

3
- Ask the question and elicit the answer from the class (he is positive). Ask students to find key sentences / phrases in the interview that support this conclusion.
- Students summarise David Weeks' ideas. Remind them that only the main points should be included.

4
- Students work in pairs. They compare their summaries and discuss possible improvements.
- As a class, students decide which are the key points that need to be included. Build up a model summary on the board.

Possible answer
David Weeks is positive about eccentricity. His results show that eccentrics are healthier and require less medical help than other people. This is due to their optimistic outlook and a low level of stress because they don't feel the need to conform. David Weeks thinks we can learn from their curiosity and their ability to hold on to their dreams.

5
- Students give themselves a score (1–5) and then discuss the questions in pairs.
- Students report back to the class.

Vocabulary and speaking

1
- Students read the words and identify the main stress.

2
- 🔘 **02** Students listen and check their answers in Ex 1. Check that they can pronounce all the words correctly.

Answers
con<u>ven</u>tional   <u>cur</u>ious   <u>gloom</u>y   in<u>tel</u>ligent
<u>mis</u>chievous   o<u>pin</u>ionated   re<u>bell</u>ious   un<u>or</u>thodox

3
- Students work in pairs. Encourage them to look back at the interview to see the words in context, and to use dictionaries to check their meaning.
- Explain that some of the words may be either positive or negative depending on the context and the speaker's interpretation.

Answers
conventional: usually negative when describing people; similar: ordinary, orthodox; opposite: unconventional, non-conformist
curious: usually positive; similar: inquisitive, questioning; opposite: indifferent
gloomy: negative; similar: miserable; opposite: cheerful
intelligent: positive; similar: clever, bright; opposite: dim, stupid
mischievous: usually positive (it is normally used affectionately); similar: playful; opposite: solemn, serious
opinionated: usually negative; similar: dogmatic, pig-headed; opposite: broad-minded

rebellious: either positive or negative; similar: defiant, disobedient; opposite: obedient
unorthodox: either positive or negative, but usually negative; similar: unconventional; opposite: conventional

4
- Look at the example with the class. You could give a further example by choosing a different adjective and describing yourself.
- Students work in pairs and describe themselves.
- Students report back to the class.

Optional activity

Famous characters
- Students think of famous people, alive or dead, who can be described by each of the adjectives in Ex 1. They can work individually or in pairs.
- Read out each adjective in turn. Students say the names that they have thought of. You can ask them to justify their choices and invite others to agree or disagree.

5
- Look at the sentences and check that students understand all the adjectives.
- Students complete the sentences and then check by looking for the collocations in the text.

Answers
1 imagination   2 collector   3 side   4 traits
5 outlook

6
- To model the activity, give an example of your own, for example: *My nephew has a very vivid imagination. He's always pretending to be someone from Lord of the Rings …*
- Students work in pairs and describe people they know.
- Ask some students to report back on a person described by their partner.

7
- Students complete the task individually or in pairs.
- Check answers with the class.

Answers
1 avid / keen collector
2 fertile / overactive imagination
3 gloomy / positive / serious outlook
4 dark / feminine / sympathetic side
5 unconventional traits

Language study

Contrast

Note
The aim of this language study is to review some of the more frequent contrastive discourse markers, focusing on their position in relation to the two ideas they are contrasting.

1

- Explain to students that they need to look for words / phrases that indicate a contrast between two different ideas.
- Students underline the discourse markers.
- Check the answers with the class.

Answers
a on the other hand   b but   c while   d however

2

- Students complete the table, working either individually or in pairs.
- Check the answers with the class.
- Tell students to look back at the sentence with *on the other hand* in Ex 1. Ask: *Where else can we put this phrase?* (after *And*, after *tends* or at the end of the sentence). Do the same for *while* (after *In Great Britain*) and *however* (at the beginning or at the end of the sentence).

Answers

Must always go between the ideas they are contrasting	Can also go before the first idea they are contrasting	Can also go in various positions in the second sentence
yet but	while	however on the other hand

3

- Elicit the answer to the question.
- Refer students to the Grammar reference on page 26 if necessary.

Answer
To emphasise the contrast.

4

- Look at the example. Ask: *What other word can we use instead of 'yet'?* (but), *How can we use 'even though' in a different position?* (Van Gogh sold only one painting in his lifetime, even though …).
- Point out to students that there are several ways of joining the sentences, but they are only required to use two for each item. Encourage them to use a range of discourse markers.
- Check the answers with the class.
- Ask: *What else do you know about any of the people in Exercise 4?* Discuss this with the class.

Possible answers
There are various possibilities. The following are the most likely.
1 … in popular music, **yet** he has been …
   … in popular music, **even though** he has been …
2 … eight years old, **yet** he went on …
   … eight years old. **However, / Nevertheless**, he went on …
   … eight years old. He went on, **however**, to become …

3 **Whereas /While** most people …, *Nirvana* front man Kurt Cobain …
   Even though most people …, *Nirvana* front man Kurt Cobain …
   … fame and fortune, **but / yet** *Nirvana* front man Kurt Cobain …
   … fame and fortune. **However**, *Nirvana* front man Kurt Cobain …
   … fame and fortune. *Nirvana* front man Kurt Cobain, **however**, …
4 … most subjects. **However**, he did, excel …
   … most subjects. He did, **however**, excel …
   … most subjects. He did excel, **however**, in geometry …
   … most subjects. He did excel in geometry, **however**, …
   … most subjects, **but** he did excel …
5 **Even though** Dalí based his appearance …, his paintings were …
   … a century earlier, **but / yet** his paintings were …
   … a century earlier. His paintings, **however**, were …
   … anything but retrospective, **however**.

5

- Students complete the task individually or in pairs.
- Draw attention to the stress on both the auxiliary and the main verb in the first clause and on the information that contrasts in the second clause (underlined in the answer key below).

Answers
1 I <u>did</u> <u>want</u> to go, but it was just im<u>poss</u>ible.
2 I <u>do</u> <u>like</u> them, but I've just listened to them <u>too</u> <u>much</u>.
3 I <u>did</u> en<u>joy</u> it, but I was <u>glad</u> to get <u>home</u>.
4 I <u>do</u> a<u>gree</u> I should do it more, but <u>sometimes</u> I just <u>can't</u> be <u>bothered</u>.
5 We <u>did</u> <u>like</u> each other, but it just <u>wasn't</u> to <u>be</u>.
6 I <u>did</u> <u>feel</u> for them, but there was <u>nothing</u> I could do to <u>help</u>.

6

- Look at the example. Make it clear to the students that they can adapt information in the sentences to fit with their own situations.
- Students work in pairs and tell each other about their own situations.
- Ask some students to report back on one of the situations described by their partner.

Are you a nonconformist?

Listening and speaking

1

- Students work in pairs and discuss the definition. Compare their ideas with the Macmillan English Dictionary definition:

nonconformist /nɒnkənˈfɔːmɪst/ noun [count]
    someone who does not think or behave in the usual way

2

- 🔘 **03** Look at the photos with the class. Ask: *Where do you think these people are from? What do you think they're like? Who do you think is the most conventional? Who is the most nonconformist?*
- Students listen and complete the task.
- Check the answers with the class.

> **Answers**
> 1 People live in many different ways, with different values, tastes and habits.
> 2 If you don't like spending time with other people, life will be very difficult. People don't like it if you don't follow the crowd.
> 3 People don't like you being different. They attack you and try to make you conform if you behave in an unusual or unconventional way.

Listening script 03

(T = Teacher; A = Alex; M = Mette; N = Natsuko)

T: Right, we're going to talk a bit about nonconformism. Er ... Alex, what about you? Are you a nonconformist? Do you follow society's rules for behaviour, dress and things like that, or don't you care what other people think of you?

A: Er, well, I suppose I'm quite conventional really. I don't think I deliberately try to be different for the sake of it. In some ways I don't actually want to stand out. Probably because I'm too lazy. I think you have to have time to think about projecting an alternative image. You have to, er, work at being different. I'm not bothered about standing out from the crowd.

T: Is it difficult to be a nonconformist in Germany?

A: Well, it depends where you live. Germany's such a big country. If you live in a small village in the south, I don't think people perhaps are as tolerant about people being different. But I come from Berlin, so for me ...

M: Berlin? Great city!

A: Er, yeah ... Anyway, in a big city like Berlin there are lots of people from different countries, and lots of different lifestyles. There's no one norm that everyone follows, so it's harder to say what conformism and nonconformism is. On the whole, German people are quite individual and ...

M: That reminds me of a trip I took to, er, Berlin last year. I was just amazed, you know, how individual people were there. Everybody looked so different. In my town people all dress the same way.

T: So is there a lot of pressure to conform in Denmark, then, Mette?

M: Definitely. It's a small country and it's like, everybody thinks the same. People tend to do everything in groups. In kindergarten, you have to have the whole class to your birthday and then in school you have to do endless cooperative projects. If you don't like spending time with other people, you've had it, you don't fit in and er ...

N: Sorry to interrupt, but Denmark sounds a lot like Japan with the group ... er ... mentality, you know. We have a saying in Japanese – in English it's something like 'The nail that sticks out gets hammered down'. People don't like you being different. You're made to conform in school and at work.

A: I've never ... er ... been to Japan but I've seen some Japanese TV shows on TV in Germany. They're wild, there's just no limits to what people do on those shows. That doesn't fit with conformism.

M: And you look quite unconventional, don't you? You know, your clothes and ...

N: Wait a minute! Just because I like wearing unusual clothes doesn't mean I'm a non-conformist. In fact in Tokyo I don't look unconventional! All my friends dress like this. I think ...

A: And don't people in Japan ...

N: Just let me finish, please. I think nonconformism has more to do with personality and how you view other people.

M: Yeah, you have to be very tolerant towards other people and also be quite thick-skinned yourself ... To get back to what I was saying before, I like doing things by myself. I've always liked doing my own thing. I suppose other people would say I'm a loner. Some people say I'm stuck up. A lot of people don't like it if you don't follow the crowd. They feel threatened somehow.

A: Talking of threatening situations ...

3

- Students work in groups and discuss the questions.
- Ask the groups to report back to the class.

Vocabulary and pronunciation

Taking turns in a discussion

1

- Students listen to the discussion again and complete the six phrases.
- Play the CD again, pausing to check the answers.

> **Answers**
> 1 Anyway, ...   2 reminds me of ...
> 3 to interrupt, but ...   4 a minute!
> 5 let me finish please.   6 back to what I was saying, ...

2

- Students put the phrases from Ex 1 into the table and then add the phrases in the box.
- Check the answers with the class.

> **Answers**
> Interrupting: That reminds me of ...
> Sorry to interrupt, but ...   Can I add something?
>
> Preventing interruption: Wait a minute.
> Just let me finish, please.
> Before you comment, can I just ...
> Can I finish what I was saying?   Hang on!
>
> Returning to a topic: To get back to what I was saying, ...
> Where was I?
>
> Changing the topic: By the way, ...   Incidentally, ...

Speaking

1
- Look at the diagram. Explain that after adding two topics of their own, each group will discuss the five topics.
- Divide the class into groups of three or four. Ask them to agree on two topics of their choice to add to the diagram. Explain that the topics need to be in the form of statements which people could agree or disagree with.

2
- Students prepare for the discussion by thinking of reasons for and against the topics.

3
- In their groups, students discuss the topics for ten minutes. Encourage them to use some of the phrases from Vocabulary and pronunciation Ex 2 in the course of the discussion and when moving on to a new topic.
- Students report any interesting points from their discussions back to the class.

Optional activity

Opinions essay
- Students write an essay of about 200 words giving their opinion on one of the topics in the Speaking section. You could outline the following plan:
  – Introduce the argument (2 or 3 sentences).
  – Present and contrast the arguments for (4 or 5 sentences) and against (4 or 5 sentences).
  – Give your opinion (4 or 5 sentences).
  – Summarise and conclude the argument (2 or 3 sentences).
- Encourage the students to use the language of contrast (eg *on the other hand, whereas, yet, nevertheless*), opinion (eg *as far as I'm concerned, in my opinion, I believe*) and conclusion (eg *in summary, to sum up, in conclusion*).

Revision activity

Eccentrics quiz
- Read out the following incomplete sentences. Working individually or in teams, students decide what the missing information is and write it down.
- Check the answers with the class. Give one point for each correct answer. The student / team with the most correct answers is the winner.

1 Playwright Oscar Wilde was a familiar sight walking his favourite pet through the streets of London in the late 1800s. This favourite pet, however, was a _____ .

2 The eccentric film producer Howard Hughes kept several _____ in his house on large salaries, yet he rarely saw them and usually refused to follow their advice.

3 Even though she has her own house, Argentinian Roxana Pons, spent the whole of 2005 living in a _____ she had built in a tree in her garden.

4 In 2006, Turkish student Sefa Boyar studied hard for his university entrance exam. He did so, however, not to help him pass the exam, but because he wanted to _____ as a protest against the university selection process.

5 Even though American oil tycoon HL Hunt had a $700 million fortune, he regularly used to steal his secretary's _____ .

6 American businessman Brian Hughes would regularly scatter jewels outside his favourite restaurant and watch passers-by pick them up. The jewels, however, were _____ .

7 Whereas most people feel lucky if they find a five pound note in the street, a passer-by in Wales in 2006 grabbed £700 when a man shouting 'Who wants free money?' threw _____ into the air.

8 Albert Einstein was offered the presidency of _____ in 1952, but he turned it down.

Answers
1 lobster   2 doctors   3 nest
4 answer all the questions incorrectly   5 lunch
6 fake   7 £20,000   8 Israel

Extra practice
Students complete the Extra practice material on page 22, either in class or for homework.

Extra practice answers
1 1 rebellious   2 conventional   3 gloomy
4 opinionated   5 curious   6 unorthodox
7 obsessive   8 mischievous   9 intelligent
10 nonconformist

Advice in shaded column: Be yourself

2 1 outlook   2 collector   3 traits   4 side
5 imagination

3 1 yet   2 whereas / while   3 whereas / while
4 However   5 while / whereas   6 Whereas / While
7 even though   8 nevertheless

References
Grammar reference: Coursebook page 26
Wordlist: Coursebook page 28
Photocopiable resources: Teacher's Book pages 88–89
Test: Teacher's Book pages 121–122

CD-ROM
Unit 1 Behave!
Listening activity: He's not as normal as some
Vocabulary activity: TV preview – At home with the Hampsons
CEF-linked activity: I can take turns in a discussion
Game: Witch's pot (adjectives to describe behavioural traits)

Form and function

Topic	Language study	Vocabulary	Main skills
• Modern wonders (buildings and design) • Your workspace and you	• Describing buildings, places and objects (structures used to describe nouns)	• Compound adjectives • Expressing sympathy and annoyance	• **Reading:** understanding gist • **Speaking:** discussing architecture and design preferences; sympathising and expressing annoyance; talking about workspaces • **Writing:** a description of your favourite place • **Listening:** understanding gist and identifying key topics; understanding vocabulary in context

Learning aims

- Can describe buildings, places and objects
- Can talk about workspaces
- Can sympathise with problems

Ideas for preparation

- Pictures of the Seven Wonders of the Ancient World (see Warmer activity below)
- Information from the website of the New7Wonders Foundation (www.new7wonders.com) on the winners of the competition for the New Seven Wonders of the World (see Lead-in Ex 3 below)

Warmer

- Ask: *What were the original Seven Wonders of the World?* If you have pictures of them, you can use these as prompts.
- Produce a class list of suggestions and then compare them with the actual list.

Modern wonders

Lead-in

Background information

The original Seven Wonders of the World were:
- the Great Pyramid of Giza (Egypt)
- the Hanging Gardens of Babylon (modern-day Iraq)
- the Temple of Artemis at Ephesus (Turkey)
- the Statue of Zeus at Olympia (Greece)
- the Mausoleum of King Mausollos at Halicarnassus (now Bodrum in Turkey)
- the Colossus of Rhodes (Greece)
- the Pharos, or lighthouse, of Alexandria (Egypt)

Of these, only the Great Pyramid remains. The first known list of Seven Wonders comes from Greece and dates from the second century BC.

The worldwide survey to establish the New Seven Wonders of the World was conducted by New7Wonders Foundation, which has the aim of documenting,

maintaining and restoring world heritage sites. Voting took place via their website and the winners were announced on 7/7/2007.

1
- Students work in groups and discuss the questions.
- Students check the answers on page 29.

2
- Discuss the questions with the class. Make a class list of the most important features on the board.

3
- In groups, students discuss the list of buildings and monuments and agree on the seven that they feel are the most impressive. Encourage them to think of reasons for their choices.
- Students could compare ideas with other groups.
- If possible, name the seven winners in the New7Wonders competition. Students compare this 'official' list with their own.

Optional activity

Our Seven Wonders
- Students decide on 'The Seven Wonders of our Country or Town / City'. This can be done in pairs, in groups or as a whole class discussion.
- You could have a class vote for the top building or monument in their country or town.

Reading and speaking

1
- Check the meaning of the words in the box.
- In groups, students brainstorm other adjectives (eg well-built, picturesque, solid, uninhabited, etc).

2
- Students discuss the questions in pairs or small groups, and then as a class.

3
- 04 Students read the article and answer the questions. They can listen to the article on CD.
- Check the answers with the class.

Answer
Yes, he likes its appearance (he calls it ultrachic, ultramodern, sparkling and sensuous) and the fact that it is 'sensible': it is environment-friendly and energy-saving and provides 'desirable' working space.

4
- Students answer the questions and compare their answers with a partner.
- Check the answers with the class.

Answers
1 Its official name is *30 St. Mary Axe*. Its nickname is *the Gherkin* because of its shape.
2 A cigar, a rocket, a bullet, a lipstick, a Zeppelin airship, a lava lamp, a bandaged finger, a pineapple, a pine cone. (Students' own preferences.)
3 Most people love and appreciate it, but some Londoners hate it for desecrating the ancient City.
4 It has a unique shape and an energy-saving design.

Optional activity

More about the Gherkin
- You could ask further questions about the article to check comprehension and/or to practise scan reading, for example: *How high is the Gherkin and how many storeys does it have? Is it the tallest building in London? Who designed it? Who were the original owners? How many triangular windows are there? Are there offices on all levels? In what ways is it environment-friendly? What's in the basement?*

5
- In groups, students discuss the statements.
- Students report back to the class.

Vocabulary

1
- Students complete the task and compare answers with a partner.
- Check the answers with the class. For item 7, note that *environment**ally** friendly* is also commonly used.
- Give special attention to the pronunciation of *frivolous*: /ˈfrɪvələs/.

Answers
1 well-known icon: an icon that most people know
2 much-loved tourist attraction: an attraction which is loved a lot
3 frivolous-looking shape: a shape that looks frivolous
4 Zurich-based insurance company: a company that is based / has its headquarters in Zurich
5 pie-shaped pieces: pieces shaped like parts of a pie
6 window-facing working space: working space that faces a window
7 environment-friendly design: a design that is friendly / not harmful to the environment
8 energy-saving design: a design that saves energy

2
- Look at the examples with the class. Explain that the words in italics are examples only – there are many possibilities. Elicit a few other examples for these two adjectives.
- Students complete the exercise individually or in pairs. Explain that they may have to rely on their intuition to arrive at some of the answers and encourage them to compare the items with expressions in their own language.
- Check the answers with the class.

Answers
The nouns in brackets are examples – other alternatives are possible.
1 well-loved (*toy, pet, book*)
   badly loved X
   much-loved (*building, person*)
2 rainy-looking X
   expensive-looking (*watch, clothes*)
   tasty-looking (*sandwich, cake*)
3 American-based (*company, organisation, artist, actor*)
   London-based (*company, organisation, artist, actor*)
   Britain-based X
4 sky-shaped X
   heart-shaped (*earring, box, leaf*)
   crescent-shaped (*earring, blade, beach*)
5 south-facing (*terrace, window, garden*)
   sea-facing (*room, flat*)
   room-facing X
6 world-friendly X
   child-friendly (*restaurant, furniture*)
   tourist-friendly (*resort, town*)
7 time-saving (*device, appliance*)
   food-saving X
   money-saving (*scheme, idea*)

3
- Refer students back to item 2 in Ex 2. Ask: *What kind of word goes with '-looking' to make a compound adjective?* (an adjective).
- Students work in pairs and list as many adjectives with *-looking* as they can.
- Check the answers with the class. Write the adjectives on the board for students to copy down.
- Ask: *What could be described by each of the compound adjectives?* Brainstorm some ideas with the class.

Possible answers
good-looking, ordinary-looking, funny-looking, strange-looking, unusual-looking, odd-looking, weird-looking, angry-looking, forward-looking, backward-looking, similar-looking, tired-looking, old-looking, expensive-looking, cheap-looking, etc

4
- Students rewrite the sentences, using compound adjectives to replace the words in italics. Ask them to compare answers with a partner.
- Check the answers with the class.

Answers
1 The building is really eye-catching.
2 I rent a third-floor flat.
3 It's a non-smoking flat.
4 I have a two-bedroom flat.
5 The cupboards were badly made and don't open properly.
6 There's a good café nearby where you can get a great all-day breakfast.

5
- Students work in pairs and describe where they live (their home or their city / town / village), using at least three compound adjectives.
- Students report back to the class.

Optional activity

What can you see?
- Students work individually or in pairs. Say: *Think of compound adjectives for things you can see in the classroom or through the window.*
- Give them one or two examples, eg *a well-used dictionary, a brand-new book, a newly built office block.*
- Ask some students to say one of their answers. The others have to look around or outside the room and point to an object that fits the description.

Language study

Describing buildings, places and objects

Note
The aim of the language study is to review the different ways in which nouns can be described. Note that a noun to which an adjective, a relative clause or a phrase is added is known as a *noun phrase*.

1
- Students complete the task individually or in pairs.
- Check the answers with the class.

Answers
1 well-known*, contemporary, much-loved*, sparkling*, calm, gray, high, genuine, fresh (* You may see these described as participles functioning as adjectives.)
2 glass, floor
3 whose original owner was Swiss Re
4 generated at street level
5 from outside

2
- Students answer the question.
- Check the answers. Remind students that adjectives can also go after the noun when preceded by *be*, for example: *The surfaces and walls are **ultrachic** and **ultramodern**.*
- Refer students to the Grammar reference on page 27 if necessary.

Answers
Before the noun: adjectives, nouns used as adjectives
After the noun: relative clauses, clauses beginning with a participle, phrases beginning with a preposition

3
- Look at the example with the students. Refer them back to the photos on page 6, and ask: *Which building is this?* (St Basil's Cathedral in the Kremlin).
- Students complete the task.
- Check the answers with the class. For each answer, ask *Which building / monument is this?*

Answers
It's a ruined city discovered in 1908 perched high in the Andes plateau in Peru. (Machu Picchu)
It's a 4,500-year-old pyramid made of two million blocks of stone rising 150 metres out of the desert in Egypt. (Great Pyramid of Giza)
It's a copper statue of a woman at the entrance to the harbour in New York. (Statue of Liberty)

Optional activity

Where in the world?
- Students write a description of three other places in the photos on page 6 of the Coursebook. Tell them to use the descriptions in Ex 3 as a model.
- Students work in pairs or small groups. They read their descriptions to each other and guess which places are described to them.

4
- Students complete the task. They can compare their answers in pairs or groups.
- Check the answers with the class.

Answers
1 My favourite place to eat is a family-run pizza restaurant called Luigi's just round the corner from my house.
2 My favourite item of clothing is a faded old denim jacket with a hole in the sleeve which / that I've had since I was in my teens.
3 My favourite film is *No Way Out*. It's a fast-paced thriller starring Kevin Costner with a great twist at the end.
4 My favourite place anywhere in the world is Pushkar in India. It's a small chilled-out town surrounding a holy lake with over 400 temples.

5
- Students adapt the sentences and write their own descriptions. You could give them one or two examples of your own to model the activity, for example: *My favourite place anywhere in the world is Lindisfarne. It's a magical little island about a mile off the north-east coast of England that you can drive to when the tide is out.*
- Students work in pairs or small groups and read their sentences to each other. Encourage them to ask questions to find out as much as possible about the things described.

Writing

1

- Look at the competition announcement and check that students understand the task.
- Students write their entry for the competition. They could complete this task for homework.

2

- Students read each other's entries. They can be passed around the class or displayed on the classroom wall.
- Students vote for the competition winner.

Your workspace and you

Listening and vocabulary

1

- Discuss the questions with the class.

2

- 🔘 **05** Tell students that they are going to hear someone talking to a friend about working at home.
- Students read the list of topics, then listen and tick the ones they hear.
- Check the answers with the class.

> **Answers**
> work and free time   his business   work colleagues
> his social life   communication   independence

Listening script 05

(K = Kyle, N = Nicola)

K: Hello, 643 1845.

N: Hi, Kyle. How's it going?

K: Oh hi, Nicola. It's going OK but I'm getting a bit sick of sitting at my desk every day. This isn't what I expected working at home would be like!

N: Come on, it can't be that bad. This is your dream job, remember? No 9 to 5, no boss, no boring meetings … I bet you're still in your pyjamas right now watching the daytime soaps!

K: Yeah, I wish! I've got so much work I don't even have time to have lunch, let alone watch TV. I'm just up to my eyes in paper and more paper. I can't see my desk for work.

N: Oh, poor you! But I suppose that's good news, isn't it? It means your company is doing well.

K: Yes, it is. I've been inundated with great projects, which is pretty amazing after such a short time. It usually takes a while to get the quality of work I've been getting, so of course I'm really pleased it's worked out. I just never realised how little time I'd have. Basically I'm just at work all the time – all day and then usually most of the evening as well. But I must admit I miss the drinks after work with the lads and the office gossip. I felt I saw my colleagues a bit too much outside work when I had my office job, but now I'm fed up with being on my own and looking at the same four walls all day.

N: Well, I can imagine it's a bit lonely at times. I certainly want a job where I work with other people. Perhaps not in an office, but definitely with other people … But Kyle, you must talk to people on the phone at least?

K: Sometimes, of course. But most people do business by email. I know it's cheaper than phoning but it's just so anonymous. And people send me mails about every little thing. I get a new email every ten minutes and it's driving me mad. I just can't get anything done.

N: Oh dear, I'm sorry. I thought you'd be happy working for yourself at home. You certainly whinged enough about your office job!

K: Yeah, I suppose on balance, working at home is still better than working in an office. It's great that *I* decide what I do with my time rather than someone else – even if I do end up deciding to work all the time. Anyway, sorry, Nicola, I know I'm being a pain in the neck going on like this. I'll stop moaning now!

N: Well, the good news is I'm coming up to the city tomorrow. So cheer up! You can take me out for a drink – just pretend I'm one of the lads!

3

- Students answer the questions in pairs.
- Check the answers with the class.

> **Answers**
> He's mainly negative about working from home because he has no free time and he feels isolated and lonely. He likes his independence but he misses his social life.

4

- Students complete the tasks.
- Check the answers with the class. For item 1, explain that we can also just say *I'm sick of*. Point out that *sick of*, *miss* and *fed up with* can be followed by either a noun or an *-ing* verb form.

> **Answers**
> 1 <u>I'm getting a bit sick of</u> sitting at my desk every day.
> 2 <u>I don't even have time to</u> have lunch <u>let alone</u> to watch TV.
> 3 <u>I miss</u> the drinks after work with the lads.
> 4 <u>I'm fed up with</u> being on my own.
> 5 I get a new email every ten minutes and <u>it's driving me mad</u>.

5

- Students make two lists. They can work individually or in pairs.
- Check the answers with the class.

> **Answers**
> Sympathising: Come on, it can't be that bad.
> Oh, poor you!   What a shame!   Oh dear, I'm sorry.
> How awful!   Cheer up!
>
> Expressing annoyance: Stop moaning!   Oh, just shut up.
> Oh, change the record!   Put a sock in it!
> You're not the only one with problems, you know.

6

- Students listen again and complete the task.
- Check the answers with the class.
- You could play the CD again, pausing at the phrases that Nicola uses. Ask students to repeat, giving attention to the intonation.

Answers

Come on, it can't be that bad.   Oh, poor you!
Oh dear, I'm sorry.   Cheer up!

Optional activity

Sounding sympathetic

- Students work in pairs. They take it in turns to say a sentence from Ex 4 and to reply with one of the expressions in Ex 5.
- Ask some pairs to say their dialogues for the class.

7

- Students work in pairs. They each turn to their page in the Coursebook, read their role cards carefully and think about what they are going to say.
- Students role-play the discussion with their partner.
- Ask some pairs to perform their role-play for the class.

Reading and speaking

1

- Students complete the questionnaire.
- They turn to page 32 in the Coursebook to calculate their score and read the analysis.
- Students report back to the class.

Revision activity

Who or what am I?

- Read the following descriptions to the students and ask them to guess what / who is being described. The answers are in brackets.
  I'm a huge a palace with 600 rooms located at the end of The Mall in central London. (Buckingham Palace)
  I'm a sixties pop group from Liverpool known as 'the Fab Four'. (The Beatles)
  I'm a sports event that is held every four years, comprising about 30 different sports. (the Olympic Games)
  I'm a marble tomb with jewel-encrusted walls on the banks of the Yamuna river in Agra, India. (the Taj Mahal)
  I'm a 300-metre-high tower made of steel overlooking the river Seine in Paris. (the Eiffel Tower)
- Divide the class into teams and ask them to prepare four or five similar descriptions.
- Teams compete against each other, taking it in turns to read out a sentence for the other team to guess. A correct answer gets one point. The team with the most points at the end is the winner.

Extra practice

Students complete the Extra practice material on page 23, either in class or for homework.

Extra practice answers

1. 1 a second-floor window
   2 are hand-made
   3 an eye-catching black and gold dress
   4 the longest-standing records in sport

2. 2 f   3 b   4 k   5 e   6 i   7 j   8 g   9 a
   10 h   11 l   12 c

3. (individual answers)
   Examples: dull-coloured, blue-coloured; best-known; poorly-paid; unusually shaped; strange-looking, odd-looking; UK-based, office-based; narrow-minded, fair-minded; eco-friendly; well-dressed; money-saving

4. 1 It's a hand-held device that allows you to talk to other people wherever you are.
   2 It's a two-wheeled mode of transport (which was) invented by a Scotsman in the mid-1800s.
   3 It's a statue of a human figure with outstretched arms, overlooking Rio de Janeiro in Brazil.
   4 He's an American actor (who was) born in 1963 of British, German and Cherokee Indian descent.

5. (answers at the bottom of page 23)

6. 1 sick, moaning   2 alone, bad   3 mad, poor
   4 fed up, sock, problems

7. (individual answers)

References

Grammar reference: Coursebook page 26
Wordlist: Coursebook page 28
Photocopiable resources: Teacher's Book pages 90–91
Test: Teacher's Book pages 123–124

CD-ROM

Unit 2 Form and function
Language exercise: Every word helps paint a picture
Vocabulary activity: The Franklin Hotel
CEF-linked activity: I can sympathise with problems
Game: Swamp disaster (compound adjectives)

It's up to you!

Topic	Language study	Vocabulary	Main skills
• Moments in time (the best day of my life) • Changing the world (Supporting causes by wearing wristbands)	• Adding emphasis	• Social issues and direct action	• **Listening:** understanding gist and key information; understanding vocabulary in context • **Speaking:** describing one of the best days of your life; talking about social issues and direct action • **Reading:** understanding main information • **Writing:** a message board thread and comments

Learning aims

- Can use emphasis when talking about important events
- Can discuss social issues and direct action
- Can contribute to message boards

Warmer

- Write *civil rights* on the board and ask: *What are civil rights?*
- Students can discuss this in pairs, then brainstorm ideas and produce a class definition. Compare with the Macmillan English Dictionary definition below.

civil rights /ˈsɪvl raɪts/ noun [plural]
> the basic rights that all people in a society should have, for example the right to be treated fairly by the law, the right to express your ideas, and the right to practise your religion

Moments in time

Lead-in

Background information

Martin Luther King was a pastor and an American civil rights campaigner. He was a brilliant speaker and organised the protest movement, based on a principle of non-violence, which ended segregation on buses. He went on to fight against injustice and inequality and led protests all over the USA. In 1968 he was assassinated.

Nelson Mandela helped to secure the abolition of apartheid in South Africa. He was a prominent member of the African National Congress, which fought against the government's apartheid policies. He was sentenced to life imprisonment in 1964 and was not released until 1990. In 1994 he became South Africa's first democratically elected president.

Aung Sab Suu Kyi is leader of the National League for Democracy in Myanmar (Burma), fighting for democratic rule and human rights against the ruling military junta. She has been repeatedly placed under house arrest for her political activities. In 1991 she won the Nobel Peace prize.

Mother Teresa was an Albanian nun who devoted her life to the sick and those living in poverty. She taught for 17 years in India before moving to the slums to care for the people there. She died in 1997 and was declared a saint in 1993.

Mahatma Gandhi was an Indian lawyer who fought against colonial injustice in India and for independence from British rule. His methods were based on non-violence and included fasts and a 200-mile march. He was arrested and jailed several times. He was assassinated in 1948.

1

- Students work in pairs or small groups and discuss the people in the photos. Encourage them to use the words in the box.
- Check the students' ideas in class discussion.

Listening

Background information

Bob Geldof, born in County Dublin in 1951, was the lead singer of the punk group *The Boomtown Rats* in the 1970s and 1980s. He is now famous for his humanitarian activities aimed at combatting world poverty, especially in Africa. The Live 8 concerts, linked to the British-based Make Poverty History campaign, took place in 2005, following the success of the Live Aid concerts 20 years earlier, which had raised more than £50 million for aid to Africa. At the Live 8 event, over 1,000 musicians performed in 11 concerts around the world. Millions of people put their names to a petition aimed at altering the aid and trading policies of the wealthy G8 nations (Canada, France, Germany, Italy, Japan, Russia, UK, USA). As a result, the G8 leaders pledged to substantially increase aid and to cancel the national debt of 38 of the world's poorest countries.

1

- 🔊 **06** Ask students what they know about Bob Geldof and the Live 8 concerts in 2005.
- Students listen and make notes on the questions.

Listening script 06

It was my sister who got tickets for the Live 8 concert in London – one of the concerts that Bob Geldof organised for 'Make Poverty History'. She thought it might cheer me up because I'd had a terrible year and I was feeling a bit depressed. Yeah, so there we were in Hyde Park, and the sun was blazing down and this vast crowd of people was chilling out, enjoying the music and there was a ... a great feeling, really laid-back. Everyone on stage was talking about the message, the meaning of ... of the concert, that it was a political event, not a party. The crowd was lapping it all up but the speeches rang a bit hollow to me somehow.

But, then ... er ... Bob Geldof came on stage and he ... er ... sang one of my favourite songs, *I don't like Mondays*. It was magical. And with him up there singing on stage, the mood in the crowd seemed to intensify. There was this fantastic buzz, a feeling that this was a very special day, that ... that something momentous was taking place. It was as if anything was possible, that music really could change the world, you know. It's hard to describe now, such a long time after the event, and it's probably even harder to understand what it was like if you weren't there. It was like everyone's hope was embodied in this one man. The whole crowd was on a high. And then I just realised that my own experiences were so ... so trivial, compared to what's happening in other parts of the world. I failed my exams and broke up with my boyfriend – well, so what? People are dying of hunger. It's things like that that are important. You can't just live your life for yourself, everyone has a responsibility to other people. I know it sounds, well, trite now, when I put it like that, but it was an absolute revelation to me then, at that moment in time. That day was a huge turning point in my life.

Possible answers

The event: one of the Live 8 concerts, held in London, organised to combat world poverty

Jodie's feelings at the start: a bit depressed because she'd had a bad year; rather detached from the mood of the crowd; not impressed by the speeches

How it changed her life: Bob Geldof sang one of her favourite songs and she felt at one with the crowd, sharing a special moment. She was inspired by the feeling of hope and belief in the possibility of making a positive change in the world, beyond her own individual concerns.

2

- Ask students to read the sentences from the recording and to try to remember some of the missing words.
- Students listen again and complete the sentences.
- Check the answers with the class.

Answers

1 laid-back   2 lapping it all up, hollow   3 intensify, buzz
4 was embodied   5 revelation   6 turning point

3

- Students work in pairs and discuss the meaning of the words, consulting a dictionary where necessary.
- Discuss the meanings with the class.

Suggested answers

1 relaxed and at ease
2 accepting it without question; empty, without substance
3 become stronger and more powerful; feeling of pleasure and excitement
4 was represented
5 sudden insight and understanding
6 moment of significant change

Speaking

1

- Give students time to reflect on the two situations and to think out what they want to say.
- In pairs, students describe their experiences.
- Invite some students to describe one of their experiences to the class.

2

- Discuss the questions. If some students support a cause or have experience of fund-raising for charity, encourage them to tell the class about these activities.

Optional activity

Our concert

- Say: *Imagine you are organising a charity event. It could be a music concert, a comedy show or a one-off play. What would be your ideal line-up of five bands or other performers, and why?*
- Students work in pairs or small groups. They decide on their line-up and then share ideas with the class.

Language study

Adding emphasis

Note

The aim of the language study is to review and present some ways in which emphasis can be added to language, as a means of making the students' language more dynamic, colourful and interesting.

1

- Students complete the task.
- Ask: *Which words are being emphasised and which words give the emphasis?* Elicit the following points:
  - *even* is commonly used to give emphasis to comparative adjectives.
  - Adverbs such as *very, really, extremely* are used to give emphasis to adjectives not in the comparative or superlative form.
  - *just* may be used to give emphasis to some verbs and verb clauses.
  - *you know* is a very common phrase, often used at the end of a clause or sentence, to give emphasis to what you are saying in general.
- Refer students to the Grammar reference on page 27 if necessary.

Answers

1 a, e   2 d, f   3 c   4 b

2
- Students complete the task.
- Check the answers with the class. Elicit or explain the following:
  - *without doubt* can be used at various positions in the sentence. For example, it could also go at the beginning or the end of sentence 2a.
  - *so* can be used to give emphasis to some adjectives (*It was so peaceful. She's so rude!*). It is also used with adverbs (*Don't speak so quickly. You've done so well!*).
  - *at all* is only used when the sentence has a negative element. It can add emphasis to a noun or a pronoun (*I had no idea at all, It's nothing at all*) or to what you are saying in general (*I don't understand this question at all*).
  - *absolutely* and *totally* are used to give emphasis to absolute (not gradable) adjectives.

Answers
1 using a phrase to add emphasis to what you are saying in general
2 adding emphasis to a verb
3 adding emphasis to a noun
4 adding emphasis to a noun
5 adding emphasis to an adjective
6 adding emphasis to a noun
7 adding emphasis to what you are saying in general
8 adding emphasis to an adjective
9 using a phrase to add emphasis to what you are saying in general
10 adding emphasis to an adjective

3
- Students work individually or in pairs and complete the task. Encourage them to refer to Exs 1 and 2, but also to draw on their intuition and put the words where they 'feel' right.

4
- 07 Students listen and check their answers to Ex 3.
- Play the CD again. Pause after each sentence and ask students to repeat some of the emphatic phrases: *totally speechless, so good*, etc. Point out that the voice often rises and falls sharply when we are expressing strong feelings.
- Ask students to say the whole sentences with appropriate intonation.

Answers and listening script
1 I **just** couldn't believe it. I was **totally** speechless.
2 It was **so** good to see them again after all that time, **you know.**
3 It was a **complete** shock. I had no idea **at all** what they'd been planning.
4 It took us an **absolute** age to get to the top, but it was **well** worth it. The views were **absolutely** stunning.
5 The **whole** day was amazing **from start to finish**. It was **even** better than I'd dared imagine.
6 It was **without doubt** the **single** best moment of my **entire** life.

5
- Give students time to think about which of the sentences could describe moments or days in their life. In pairs, they tell each other about these times.
- Students report back to the class.

6
- Give students plenty of time to prepare. Tell them to use emphatic language as in Exs 1–3.
- Students give a brief description of their day. Their partner asks questions to find out more information.

Optional activity
Strong feelings
- Students make a list of things they love or hate.
- Ask a student to choose something from his/her list and ask someone else *What do you think of …?* The second student replies and then asks the next question, directing it to a different person.
- Students must answer using emphatic words and phrases wherever appropriate.

Changing the world
Reading

Background information
In 2004 the Lance Armstrong Foundation, a charity for cancer sufferers, created the *Livestrong* wristband, the first coloured wristband for people to buy and wear in support of a cause. By early 2005 wristbands had become popular with many other charities.

1
- Use the photo to introduce the word *wristband*. Ask: *How do these wristbands help to support charities?*
- Students identify the issues that are shown on the wristbands in the photo.

Answers
cancer (Livestrong), anti-bullying (Beat Bullying), help for poor countries (Make Poverty History)

2
- Discuss the questions with the class.

3
- 08 Students read the comments and complete the task. They can listen to the comments on CD.
- Check the answers with the class.

Answers
1 True.
2 False. He thinks wristbands can be a great conversation starter when other people don't know about them.
3 False. She also thinks they can raise awareness.
4 True.
5 False. She wants people to protest directly.
6 True.

4
- Students discuss the comments in pairs or groups.
- Ask some students to give their views to the class.

5
- Discuss the questions with the class.

Vocabulary and speaking

1
- Students match the words, then check with the text.
- Note that other collocations are possible: *express commitment, show solidarity, show / spread awareness.*

Answers

do something about something   express solidarity
eradicate poverty   give money to charity   raise money
raise awareness   show commitment   spread the word
support a cause

2
- Students work in groups and discuss the questions.

3
- Students look back to the message board texts to find the alternative words or phrases.

Answers

1 issues   2 stand for   3 conversation starter
4 follow the crowd   5 smug   6 guilty conscience

Optional activity

Attitude idioms
- Refer students to item 4 in Ex 3 and ask: *What does 'swim against the tide' mean?* Then write the following on the board and discuss the meanings.
  sit on the fence (refuse to support either side in an argument)
  put your head in the sand (avoid facing a problem)
  stick your neck out (take a risk)
  toe the line (accept the rules, even if you don't agree with them)
- Students work in pairs or small groups and tell each other about a time when one or more of the idioms could have been used about themselves.

4
- Students work in pairs. They each read their own role card and prepare their arguments. Encourage them to use the language in Exs 1 and 3.
- Students role-play the discussion with their partner.
- Ask some pairs to perform their role-play for the class.

Writing

1
- Students work in groups. Each student chooses a topic and starts a 'thread'. The 'message boards' are passed round so that everyone adds a comment to each thread.

- The message boards return to the person who started the thread. He/She makes a general statement to the group about the direction the discussion has taken.
- Discuss the results of the activity with the class. Ask: *Did people have strong feelings about your topic? Was there any disagreement? Were you surprised by any comments?*

Revision activity

A matter of emphasis
- Write the following phrases on the board:
  absolutely ridiculous   without doubt   even bigger
  a complete waste of time   simply amazing
  just couldn't believe it   nothing at all   so annoyed
  from start to finish   a single thing   a total disaster
- In small groups, students produce a description of an event using as many of the phrases as possible.
- Invite students to read out their stories and award a point for each phrase that is used correctly.

Extra practice

Students complete the Extra practice material on page 24, either in class or for homework.

Extra practice answers

1 1 segregation   2 non-violent protest
   3 Democratic rule, military rulers
   4 Equality, apartheid   5 civil rights movement

2 1 They are **by far** the greatest band **ever**. (They are the greatest band **ever by far**.)
   2 It was a **huge** mistake. It looks **even** worse than before.
   3 There's **absolutely** no chance **at all** of it happening in the near future.
   4 They are **loads** cheaper than when they **first** came out.
   5 I **just** don't understand what they were thinking of. It's **so** ugly.
   6 The **whole** thing was a **total** disaster **from start to finish**.

3 (individual answers)

4 1 vast   2 by far   3 single   4 awesome
   5 simply   6 anywhere   7 highly   8 real
   9 very   10 much   11 just

5 1 express / show   2 eradicate   3 raise
   4 show / express   5 spread

References

Grammar reference: Coursebook page 27
Wordlist: Coursebook page 28
Photocopiable resources: Teacher's Book pages 92–93
Test: Teacher's Book pages 125–126

CD-ROM

Unit 3 It's up to you!
Language exercise: History in the making
Vocabulary activity: Green Action Group
Language exercise: I can contribute to a message board
Game: Crossword (social issues)

No pain, no gain

Topic	Language study	Vocabulary	Main skills
• Getting to the top (Life of a sumo wrestler)	• 3-part phrasal verbs	• Proverbs and idioms: success • Motivation	• **Reading:** identifying key information • **Speaking:** talking about success, motivation and overcoming problems; explaining causes and results; discussing an autobiography • **Listening:** understanding gist and key information • **Writing:** a blurb for a biography

Learning aims

- Can talk about success
- Can discuss motivation and overcoming problems
- Can explain causes and results

Warmer

- Write *proverb* on the board and explain the meaning (a short well-known statement that gives practical advice about life). Elicit one or two proverbs in the students' own language.
- Say: *Think of another proverb and translate it into English.* Students can do this in pairs, using dictionaries if necessary.
- Ask some students to read out their translations, and write them on the board. The others suggest improvements to the translation if necessary.

Getting to the top

Lead-in

1

- Students work in pairs and discuss the meaning of the proverbs.
- Elicit a version of each proverb in the students' language if possible. If there is no equivalent, ask them to explain the message in their own words. The meanings are as follows:
  - a Important things often take a long time to do.
  - b If you want something enough, you'll find a way to achieve it.
  - c You need to take time off work to enjoy life – you shouldn't be serious all the time.
  - d You should think carefully before making an important decision.
  - e You should take an action now, instead of putting it off until later.

2

- Discuss the question with the class.

Reading and speaking

Background information

The Japanese sport of sumo is a competition between two wrestlers who compete in a ring 4.5 metres in diameter. The main aim is to push your opponent out of the ring or to force any part of his body, other than the soles of his feet, to touch the ground inside the ring.

1

- Look at the photo on page 15. Ask: *What's the sport?* (sumo wrestling), *Where does it come from?* (Japan).
- Students work in pairs and discuss the questions.

2

- 09 Ask students to predict the answers to the questions by looking at the photos.
- Students read the article and find the answers to the questions. They can listen to the article on CD.

Answers

The problem was his height: he was 169 cm and needed to be 173 cm to become a sumo wrestler. He raised his height by having a silicone implant embedded under his scalp.

3

- Without looking at the article, students tick the things they remember from their reading.
- Students look through the article to check their answers. They write down the adjectives used to describe each thing they have ticked in the list.

Answers

Mainoumi's speed – dazzling
his build – pint-sized
his weight – puny
his command of conventional techniques – supreme
his tricks and manoeuvres – dizzying
his friend – close
his injuries – terrible

4

- Students discuss the questions in pairs or small groups.
- Students report back to the class.

Vocabulary and speaking

1

- Students find the idioms in the article and decide what they mean. They could compare answers with a partner.
- Check the answers with the class.

Answers

1 to be very successful   2 in whatever way possible

2

Background information

The expression *win hands down* comes from horse racing, referring to a jockey who is so far ahead that he doesn't have to urge his horse on with the reins.
The phrase *with flying colours* comes from the old practice of flying flags from all the masts of a sailing ship as a sign of victory.
Throw in the towel comes from boxing. If a fighter is obviously losing, a trainer may throw a towel or sponge into the ring to concede defeat.

- Students complete the matching task.
- Check the answers with the class. Pick out some of the idioms and ask: *Where do you think this expression came from?*

Answers

1 c   2 h   3 g   4 e   5 f   6 a   7 b   8 d

3

- Ask a student to read out the example. You may want to give a further example of your own.
- Students work in pairs and complete the task.
- Students report back to the class.

Optional activity

Sports idioms
- Write some or all of the following idioms on the board and say: *Decide which sport each idiom comes from and what it means.*
  1 *The ball's in your court.*
  2 *It was below the belt.*
  3 *It's par for the course.*
  4 *I backed the wrong horse.*
  5 *She jumped the gun.*
  6 *They moved the goalposts.*
- Students discuss whether or not they have similar idioms in their language.

Answers
1 Tennis. It's your responsibility to take action.
2 Boxing. It was cruel and unfair.
3 Golf. It's usual or expected in this situation.
4 Horse racing. I supported someone / something that has failed.
5 Running. She acted too soon.
6 Football. They changed the rules without warning.

4

- Ask students to explain what *must-see* means.

Answer

It describes something which is so good that everyone should see it

5

- Elicit the meaning of *must-have*.
- Students work in groups and discuss the questions. Ask them to try to reach a consensus.
- Ask some groups to report their ideas to the class, and invite discussion.

Optional activity

must-
- Write the following *must-* expressions on the board and elicit the meanings.
  must-visit, must-watch (for TV), *must-read, must-win* (for a specific sports match / point, etc)
- Say: *Think of things which can be described by each of the expressions.* Students discuss this as a whole class.

Language study

Three-part phrasal verbs

Note

The aim of the language study is to review the concept and form of three-part phrasal verbs and to present the students with some common and useful examples.

1

- Ask: *What is a three-part phrasal verb? What three-part phrasal verbs do you know?* Write two or three examples (eg *run out of, get through to, keep up with*) on the board and check their meaning.
- Students find the three-part verbs in the sentences and complete the matching task.

Answers

2 come up with, d   3 put up with, a   4 stood up for, c

2

- Students look at the sentences in Ex 1 and answer the question. Emphasise that three-part phrasal verbs are inseparable – that is, the parts cannot be separated by an object. For example, we cannot say ~~come an idea up with~~ or ~~come up an idea with~~.
- Refer students to the Grammar reference on page 27 if necessary.

Answer

The object goes after the second particle.

3

- Students match the two parts of the quotations. Do the first one with the class as an example, and ask students to explain what it means in their own words.

- Students complete the matching task.
- Check the answers with the class.

Answers

1 d   2 e   3 f   4 c   5 a   6 b

4

- Discuss the meaning of the verbs with the class.

Answers

1 run out of: use all of something and not have any left
2 look up to: admire and respect someone
3 get on with: do something without delay
4 put up with: tolerate
5 stand up to: not allow yourself to be treated badly by someone (especially someone in authority)
6 fall back on: use or do something else after other things have failed

5

- Students choose their favourite quotation and compare their ideas with a partner. You could take a class vote on the most popular quotation.

6

- Students read and complete the sentences. Encourage them to use dictionaries to check the phrasal verbs.
- Check the answers and the meanings of the new verbs.

Answers

1 came back from
2 face up to
3 came up with, dropped out of
4 putting up with, stood up to

7

- Read out the instruction. Elicit one or two examples of people who have overcome difficulties to succeed.
- Students think of their own example and describe the person to their partner.
- Ask some students to tell the class about the person described by their partner.

What motivates you?

Listening

1

- 🔘 10 Check that students understand the meaning of *motivate* and *motivation*. Ask: *What are some things that motivate people to succeed in their lives?*
- Read through the list in the box. Students listen and choose the correct reason for each speaker.
- Check the answers with the class. Ask other questions to follow up: *Who gave Max praise when he was young? Which famous person inspired Chloe? How did failure at school help Tom? Who was the family member who motivated Ellen?*

Answers

1 praise   2 a famous person   3 failure
4 an inspirational family member

Listening script 10

Max   What motivates me? Well, I think my motivation is rooted in my childhood. I was an only child and my parents thought everything I did was fantastic. For example, when I built something with building blocks, they'd praise me so much you'd think I'd built the Taj Mahal! And when we played games, they always let me win hands down and told me how clever I was. My confidence today is definitely due to the way I was brought up. And today I'd have to say that it's still praise that motivates me to do things. The downside is, though, that I just can't put up with criticism. I try not to show it but even the slightest hint of negativity makes me feel quite vulnerable.

Chloe   Last year I was feeling quite depressed. The stupid thing was that there was no particular reason for it. I'd passed my exams with flying colours and had started college, training to be a physiotherapist, my dream job. And I just felt so down. Maybe it was the anti-climax after studying so hard for exams and the high of getting through them. But suddenly I just couldn't see a reason to get out of bed in the morning. Then ... well, I hate to admit this because it sounds so corny, but I was encouraged to get on with my life after seeing Kylie Minogue on TV. It was just after she'd had breast cancer, she'd been through chemotherapy and lost her hair. And suddenly there she was in New York looking so full of life. And I thought: 'What's up with you? If she can get on with life, you can.' So I really made an effort and now I feel great. And it's all down to Kylie!

Tom   My motivation? Well, I haven't always been as motivated as I am now. My parents are real high-fliers. They're both architects. They always put pressure on me to do well at school and they were quite disappointed that I was just average. Anyway, when I was 16, I decided to throw in the towel at school. I suppose you could say failure forced me to do something different. I dropped out of school – much to my parents' disappointment – and I concentrated on what I really enjoyed: art. I'm a freelance artist now. To be honest, I don't think I'll ever make it big as an artist, but I love what I'm doing – and that spurs me on to try and be better. And because my parents can see I'm happy, they've accepted what I do and are even quite proud of the fact that I stood up for what I wanted.

Ellen   I know I'm going to be successful simply because I know I can achieve whatever I want to achieve. And I think this is because, er, all my life I've had a very strong role model. My mother got divorced when I was two and was left to look after three small children on her own. She also worked part-time as a doctor. When I was older, my mum told me she knew it was a sink or swim moment in her life. And she didn't want to sink, she wanted to show everybody she could manage her family life and be successful at the same time. She was just determined to do it, you know – by hook or by crook. I've sort of inherited the same ... er, determination and strong belief in myself. I owe everything to my mum.

2

- Students listen again and answer the questions.
- Check the answers with the class. Encourage students to use the three-part phrasal verbs used by the speakers in the recording.

Answers

1 It gave him confidence but also means he can't put up with criticism.
2 There was no particular reason. Maybe it was due to a feeling of anti-climax after her exams.
3 She saw Kylie Minogue who had been through chemotherapy for breast cancer and looked full of life. She thought that if Kylie could get on with her life, then she could too.
4 Because he was just an average student and he dropped out of school at 16.
5 They accepted his decision and were proud that he had stood up for what he wanted.
6 It made her determined to manage her family life and succeed in her career at the same time.

Vocabulary

1
- Students listen again and write the missing words and phrases. Ask them to compare answers with a partner.
- Students check their answers in the listening script. Check the meanings with the class.

Answers
1 is rooted in   2 due to   3 down to   4 spurs me on
5 role model   6 owe

2
- Ask: *What are some things that you are strongly motivated to do?* Encourage students to think of particular activities and elicit a range of answers.
- Students work in small groups and discuss the questions.
- Students report back to the class.

Speaking and writing

1
- Students find the meaning of the words in their dictionaries. They can do this individually or in pairs.

2
- Students read both summaries and discuss the questions with a partner.
- Students tell the class about their conclusions.

3
- Ask: *What's the purpose of a blurb on the back of a book?* (to give people an idea of what the book is about and to convince them to buy it).
- Read out the instructions. Ask: *What examples of inspiring people can you think of?* Elicit a few examples.
- Choose one of the examples and ask: *What information would you include in a blurb for a biography about this person?*
- Students choose a person to write about. The research and writing can be done for homework.
- Encourage students to read each other's blurbs and to give feedback.

Revision activity

Phrasal verb quiz
- Divide the class into two teams.
- Read out list 1–10 below and award one point to the team of the person who first calls out the missing preposition (in brackets). The team gets an extra point if they can give an example sentence using the verb correctly. If they make a mistake, the other team has a chance to make a sentence and get the point. The team with the most points at the end is the winner.
- Alternatively, you could do this as a written quiz. Teams of four or five write their prepositions and sentences on a piece of paper. At the end they pass their answers to another team who award points.

1 run out   (of)   6 stand up   (to/for)
2 look up   (to)   7 fall back   (on)
3 come up   (with/against) 8 get on   (with)
4 make up   (for)   9 drop out   (of)
5 put up   (with)   10 face up   (to)

Extra practice

Students complete the Extra practice material on page 25, either in class or for homework.

Extra practice answers
1 1 d   2 e   3 b   4 c   5 a
2 1 flying start   4 hands down
    2 sail through   5 flying colours
    3 steals the show   6 sink or swim
3 2 came back from   6 face up to
    3 making up for   7 put up with
    4 ran out of   8 looked up to
    5 came up against
4 2 2, 5   3 1, 2   4 3, 6   5 5, 4   6 4, 3
5 1 must-watch   2 must-win   3 must-see
    4 must-have   5 must-have   6 must-visit

References
Grammar reference: Coursebook page 27
Wordlist: Coursebook page 28
Photocopiable resources: Teacher's Book pages 94–95
Test: Teacher's Book pages 127–128

CD-ROM
Unit 4 No pain, no gain
Language exercise: When the going gets tough
Vocabulary activity: The route to total success
CEF-linked activity: I can discuss motivation and overcoming problems
Game: The big squeeze (three-word phrasal verbs)

Before starting this unit, ask students to read the Grammar reference on pages 26–27 and study the Wordlist on page 28 of the Coursebook.

Warmer

- Say: *Think about the life of a full-time university student doing a three-year course. What are the pros and cons?* Discuss the question and list ideas on the board.

Lead-in

1

- Students discuss the questions in pairs or small groups.

Million dollar boy

1

- Invite students to guess the answer to the question.

2

- 🔊 **11** Students listen and check their answers in Ex 1.

Answers

Advertisements created by buying a certain number of pixels on the page. They connect with the buyer's own website.

Listening script 11

(SP = Presenter, P = Paul, A = Alex, C = Chris)

SP: While most of his fellow students were already running out of what little cash they had during fresher's week, Nottingham University student Alex Tew made over £100,000. The 21-year-old undergraduate then went on to net more than a million dollars during his first term at university. So what was the secret of Alex's sudden wealth? Our business correspondent Paul Benn takes up the story.

P: Alex Tew came up with the idea one night in August 2005 while he was contemplating the financial consequences of starting a university course. The fees and accommodation for the first year alone were starting to look daunting and with no finances to fall back on Alex was dreading running up huge debts. As Alex tells us himself …

A: I've always been an ideas sort of person and I like to brainstorm at night before I go to sleep – it's my most productive time. So I wrote down 'How can I become a millionaire before I go to university?' It was a rather ambitious question, but I went with it. Then I wrote down the attributes that this idea would need: it had to be simple to understand and to set up; it had to attract a lot of media interest; and it needed a good name. After I wrote down those three things, the idea just popped into my head. I'd like to say it was more dramatic than that, but it wasn't.

P: Alex's idea was to design a web page consisting of exactly one million pixels, the dots which make up a computer screen, and to sell those pixels as advertising space, costing a dollar per pixel. Clicking on that space would take you to the buyer's website. Alex immediately got on with setting up the website and he bought the domain

name 'milliondollarhomepage.com' that same evening. To get things up and running, he sold his first block of 100 pixels, which is the minimum number the eye can read, to his brothers and some friends. He then used that money to pay for a press release and that's when the site really took off. Advertisers were attracted to it by its novelty and by the curiosity factor, and with people flocking to take a look at the website, that made the advertising good value for money. Chris Magras, Chief Executive of engineseeker.com, an Arizona-based company, bought 6,400 pixels as soon as he heard about the Million Dollar Homepage.

C: It was ingenious. It is easy to make money on the Internet, but it is very difficult to have a unique idea, and this was. The results for us were amazing. We used to get 40,000 visitors a day to our site – that's now up to 60,000.

P: And back in his student digs, when he wasn't catching up with course work or attending lectures, Alex managed to keep track of the money rolling in, which it did at the rate of tens of thousands of pounds per week. And not for one minute did Alex consider dropping out of university. And in a final typically inventive money-spinning twist, Alex sold the last 1000 pixels for 38 times their face value via an ebay auction at the beginning of his second university term. As seems to be the norm with Internet-based business, the Million Dollar Homepage rapidly spawned hundreds of copycat sites, but none were anywhere near as successful as Alex's. Experts agree that the Million Dollar Homepage's success is down to three things: the power of word of mouth, that it's the rags-to-riches story of an ordinary student, and that it was a truly innovative yet simple idea. Expect to hear more from Alex Tew in the near future.

3

- Students listen again to hear what the figures refer to.

Answers

1 Alex made **a million** dollars in his first term at university.
2 He had the idea in August **2005**.
3 He sold his first block of **100** pixels to his brothers and some friends.
4 A company executive from engineseeker.com bought **6,400** pixels as soon as he heard about the Homepage.
5 Alex was **21** when he became a millionaire.
6 engineseeker.com used to get **40,000** visitors a day, but now they get **60,000**.
7 Alex sold the last **1000** pixels for **38** times their face value via an ebay auction.
8 He earned **tens of thousands** of pounds per week.

4

- Students use the verbs to complete the extracts.

Answers

1 running out of   2 came up with   3 fall back on
4 got on with   5 dropping out of   6 was down to

5

- Students write sentences containing the extra words.

Answers

1 He was worried about his **financial** situation and the **huge** debts **that he would be running up.**

2 He came up with the **ingenious** idea of a website **consisting of just one page made up of a million pixels that he would sell to advertisers for a dollar a pixel.**

3 Alex decided the web page would need a **memorable** name **that would capture the imagination.** He thought of and bought the **domain** name 'milliondollarhomepage.com' that **same** evening.

4 Most of the companies **that bought webspace** reported an **immediate** increase in the number of hits **on their websites** as well as **increased** sales.

5 **Numerous other** websites copied Alex's idea, but none achieved anything like the **phenomenal** success **of the Million Dollar Homepage.**

6

- Students discuss the question in pairs or groups.
- Ask the survey question and have a class vote.

Innovation

1

- Students read the extracts and choose the correct alternatives.

Answers

1 yet   2 however   3 While   4 Even though   5 whereas

2

- Discuss the question with the class.

3

- Students answer the questionnaire.

4

- Students calculate their scores and read the analysis.

5

- Students work in pairs and discuss the questions.
- Students report back to the class.

Speaking

1

- Students work in groups and decide on the greatest innovation for each category.

2

- Students read the survey results on page 29. Ask: *Were your results the same or different?*

3

- Give students plenty of time to plan their presentations. They could do some research as a homework task.
- Students each give their presentation to their group. The group then votes for the winning innovation.

4

- Students read the survey result for the overall winner on page 32. Ask: *Do you agree with this result?*

Vocabulary

1

- Read through the instructions with the class.
- Students play the game. At the end, they check the answers on page 32 and calculate their scores.

2

- In groups, students discuss people, places or things that can be described by some of the sentences in the game.

Song

Background information

American singer Patti Smith came to prominence during the punk era with her 1975 debut album *Horses* and the hit single *Because the night.* She is considered one of rock music's most influential female musicians.

1

- Look at the photo of KT Tunstall and ask: *Do you know the singer? What do you know about her?*
- Students read the factfile and answer the questions.

Answers

1 KT learned to play piano, flute and guitar as a teenager. She did a music course in London and then became involved in the local music scene back in St Andrews.

2 She was constantly told that at 25 she was too old to start a successful career as a recording artist.

3 She appeared on a TV show as a last-minute replacement for another act and was a tremendous success.

2

- 🔘 **12** Students listen to the song and read the lyrics.
- Discuss the questions with the class.

3

- Students turn to page 29 to check their ideas.

Answers

1 She suddenly sees that the person she is looking at is how she wants to be.   2 She is singing about Patti Smith.

4

- Students discuss their interpretations of the lyrics.

Possible answers

1 She has lived a lot and had many experiences.

2 I feel inspired, motivated and empowered.

3 Her lyrics make you concentrate on what she is saying and wait for the next thing she says.

4 She makes me feel positive and strong.

5

- Students discuss the question in pairs or small groups.
- Students report back to the class.

References

Module 1 test: Teacher's Book pages 129–131

UNIT 1
Telling tales

Topic	Language study	Vocabulary	Main skills
• A chance encounter (extract from *An equal music*) • The end of a nightmare (extract from *A goat's song*)	• Connecting events using the perfect	• Feelings (nouns and adjectives) • Books and reading	• **Reading:** speculating about and analysing key features of a literary text • **Speaking:** describing emotions; discussing literary texts; talking about books and reading • **Listening:** identifying key information and key features of a literary narrative • **Writing:** a short narrative

Learning aims

- Can discuss literary texts
- Can connect events using the perfect
- Can write a fictional narrative using dramatic and descriptive effects

Warmer
- Ask: *Who are the most famous couples in your country?* Students share their ideas with the class.

A chance encounter

Lead-in

Background information

Mark Antony was one of the three rulers of the Roman empire when he met Cleopatra, queen of Egypt, in 41 BC. Although he made a political marriage with Octavia, the sister of Octavian (later the emperor Augustus), he soon returned to Egypt, divorced Octavia and married Cleopatra. When Octavian conquered their forces in 31 BC, they both committed suicide. The actors playing Antony and Cleopatra in this photo are Richard Burton and Elizabeth Taylor – themselves a famous couple, who married and divorced twice.

Crown Prince Naruhito is the eldest son of Emperor Akihito and is heir apparent to the Japanese throne. He married Masako Owada, the daughter of a diplomat, in 1993.

Brad Pitt and Jennifer Anniston are American actors who married in 2000 and became America's 'golden couple'. They divorced in 2005, however, after Brad Pitt became romantically linked with the actress Angelina Jolie.

Fred and Wilma Flintstone are a married couple in the American cartoon comedy series *The Flintstones*, set in a fantasy version of the Stone Age. The series was originally screened from 1960 to 1966.

1
- Look at the photos and discuss the questions with the class.

2
- Students discuss the question in pairs or groups.
- Students report back to the class.

Reading and speaking

Background information

Vikram Seth was born in Calcutta, India in 1952. His first novel was published in 1986 and his epic of Indian life, *A suitable boy*, published in 1993, won several literary awards. *An equal music* is Seth's third novel, published in 1999. It is set in contemporary Europe and focuses on the lives of classical musicians.

1
- 🎧 **13** Students read the extract and think about the questions. Ask them to note down two or three adjectives which describe their feelings. They can listen to the extract on CD.
- Students share their ideas with a partner and then report back to the class.

2
- Explain to students that the answers to the questions are not stated directly in the text – they will need to draw conclusions from the way actions are described. Ask them to underline parts of the text that support their answers.
- Students work in pairs and complete the task.
- Students report their ideas back to the class.

Suggested answers
1 In London. (The extract mentions Oxford Circus, and a bus with stairs and a bus conductor; the narrator pays for the taxi in pounds.)
2 The man is desperate (he pounds the window and shouts, his fists are clenched) and he is very moved (his eyes are filled with tears). Julia is less agitated, but she is very aware of him (her eyes open wide and they follow his) and she is troubled (her eyes are full of perplexity).
3 They had a relationship ten years ago (the man is now 'a decade older'). It was obviously an important relationship – at least to the man, since he goes to such lengths to try to see her again.
4 He is extremely disappointed and upset.

Optional activity

More questions

- You could ask further questions about the extract to check comprehension and/or practise scan reading, for example: *How does the narrator try to get Julia's attention? How do the passengers on each bus react to this? Who on the other bus first notices his actions? What does this person do? What does the narrator hold against the glass? What is Julia's reaction to this? What number is Julia's bus? When he tries to get off the bus, how do the other passengers react, and how is he hindered? Are the streets busy? Who is just about to take the taxi? What is frustrating about the taxi journey? Does the taxi catch up with the bus? How does he catch up with the bus? How does he feel as he goes up the stairs in the bus?*

3

- Students identify the features in the text and underline examples.
- Discuss the effects created by these features.

Suggested answers

Short sentences: they emphasise each action and the film-like sequence of the actions.
Present simple used for narrative: this makes the story more immediate and urgent. The events seem to be happening as we read.
Repetition: this is used for emphasis and to increase tension.
Descriptive verbs: they give the text colour and drama (*pound, rummage, push, stare, plead, blurt out, gasp*).

4

- Discuss the questions with the class.

5

- Ask some questions to stimulate ideas, for example: *Does the man forget about Julia? Does she still care about him? Do they see each other again? Where do they meet, and what happens?* Brainstorm a few ideas.
- Students write an account of what they think happens.
- Ask some students to read out their paragraphs.

Vocabulary

1

- Students complete the table and then check their answers in the text.
- Check the answers with the class. Ask: *In two pairs of words there's a difference in stress between noun and adjective – which are they?* (despe<u>ra</u>tion – <u>des</u>perate, hesi<u>ta</u>tion – <u>he</u>sitant).

Answers

desperate	hesitation	astonishment	dismay
perplexity	annoyed	hope	

2

- Students complete the task individually or in pairs. Explain that in several cases more than one answer is possible.

- Check the answers with the class.

Suggested answers

1 alarm / dismay   2 annoyance / alarm / dismay
3 hope   4 annoyance   5 hesitation   6 perplexity
7 astonishment / alarm   8 desperation / perplexity

3

- Ask: *What other words have a similar meaning to 'alarmed'?* Elicit a few ideas.
- Students find synonyms for the remaining adjectives.

Possible answers

1 worried, frightened	5 upset, distressed
2 frantic, despairing	6 puzzled, confused
3 unsure, timid	7 irritated, displeased
4 amazed, surprised	8 optimistic, confident

4

- You could model the activity by giving an example of your own. Describe a situation you have experienced and include one or more of the adjectives in Ex 1.
- In pairs, students describe their own situations.
- Ask some students to tell the class about their partner's experience.

Language study

Connecting events using the perfect

Note

The aim of this language study is to consider an 'umbrella' function of the perfect tenses as a means of describing a situation (present, past or future) which is in some way connected with what came before it.

1

- Discuss the question with the students. Encourage them to think of the present perfect as a present tense that primarily describes a present situation. Elicit the following points about each extract:
  1 The narrator is stating that the bus is there now (because it stopped in the past). When and why it stopped is not important.
  2 In *I have lost too much time*, he is stating that he does not have enough time to get to the bus (because he lost time in the past). How, why and when he lost the time is not important. Similarly, in *Her bus has moved away*, he is stating that the bus is now no longer there (because it moved away).
  3 He is stating that the situation of not seeing the woman exists now (and it began years ago). Students should be familiar with this use of the present perfect to convey a situation / action that started in the past and continues to the present.

Answer

Its function is to express a present situation and to connect this with something that happened, or started happening, in the past.

2

- Explain that there are parallels between the present perfect and other perfect tenses. In all cases, they connect an event or situation to something that happened earlier.
- Look at each sentence and discuss the questions with the class.
- Refer students to the Grammar reference on page 58 if necessary.

Answers
1 a past perfect continuous, past perfect simple
   b future perfect simple
   c present perfect continuous, present perfect simple
2 a The function of the past perfect is to connect a past situation with something that happened, or started happening, at an earlier time in the past.
   b The function of the future perfect is to connect a future situation with an event that will happen, or will start happening, at an earlier time in the future.
   c The function of the present perfect is to connect a present situation with something that happened, or started happening, at a time in the past.
3 a continuous   b simple

3

- Students read and complete the text.
- Check the answers with the class. For items 1, 8 and 9, ask about the difference between the simple and continuous forms.

Answers
Where there are two possibilities, the more likely is first.
1 have been delving (emphasises activity, repetition of individual research tasks and duration) / have delved (emphasises completion and the research as a whole)
2 have identified
3 had finally had
4 has found
5 have been looking
6 has always been
7 will / may / might have become
8 have been coming up (emphasises repetition of individual cases) / have come up (emphasises result and the situation as a whole)
9 have been seeing (emphasises activity and repetition of individual cases) / have seen (emphasises result and the situation as a whole)
10 have developed

4

- Students complete the text.

Answers
1 has done   2 have lost   3 has got   4 have reminded
5 will have been   6 had known

5

- Students discuss the first question in pairs and then turn to page 61 to check their ideas.
- Discuss the second question with the class.

Optional activity

What's your excuse?
- Tell the students that you are going to read out some comments. Tell them: *Respond with an explanation, using the present perfect.*
- Give the following example: *You look exhausted.* Elicit a suitable response, for example: *I am. I've been up since 5.30.*
- Read the following comments and elicit responses. *I haven't seen you for ages.   Look at the state of you! What have you been doing?   You seem in a good mood. What's the matter?   What have you been up to lately? I like your hair.   You're late.*

The end of a nightmare

Listening

Background information

Dermot Healy is an Irish novelist, playwright and poet. He has also written screenplays, directed plays and appeared in films. *A goat's song* (1994) is set in the west of Ireland and centres on the life of playwright Jack Ferris and his actress lover Catherine.

1

- 14 Students listen to the first part of the extract and choose the correct answers.
- Check the answers with the class.

Answers
Main character: male   Background: break up
Mood: desperation   Setting: rural
Main character's work: author and fisherman

Listening script 15

He survived the minute only to find that the clock had begun another. And then he knew, with a sense of furious sadness, that this would be followed by another minute, and another, and throughout each one he would be like he was now, only worse. He wrote to Catherine. *Please come back to me. I want you. I am sober.*
He dropped the letter off in Corrloch and went into O'Malley's bar and bought a bottle of vodka. He walked across the fields with the dog and lay down on the old bed.
The skipper met him on the road as he was setting off for Corrloch.
'Jack,' he said. 'Have you finished with the writing?'
'I think so.'
'Good, I need you out on the blue.'
'When?'
'Tomorrow. We could get in a couple of weeks before the storms. The forecast is good.'
He would have refused but could not. De Largey came for him in a car. They drove down the valley in silence. They went to sea for two weeks after the flatfish. It was a sober, spiritual time.

2

- 🔘 **15** Students listen to the second part of the extract and make notes about the events.
- Students work in pairs. They use their notes to tell each other their version of the story, and discuss any differences.
- Explain that the extract they have heard is the very end of the novel. Ask: *Is it a happy ending?*

Note

The extract looks like a standard happy ending. However, it isn't as it seems. The novel actually opens with the same scene: Jack waiting for Catherine to come after receiving her letter. However, what the reader learns from the beginning of the book is that she doesn't turn up because she hears that Jack has started drinking again. Jack then has a nervous breakdown. The rest of the novel tells their story up to the arrival of the letter.

Listening script 15

He was standing one morning by the skipper in the wheelhouse. On the radio, various voices of other fishermen were cajoling, complaining, cursing, talking of the forthcoming storms. Their voices were always in the background, and sometimes the sound of the radio would drown out the sound of the sea. Then suddenly Jack heard Catherine's voice.

'Calling the *Blue Cormorant*.'

The strange feeling of her personality at the end of the radio unnerved him. Each nuance was hers and yet not hers. She was present in the small engine room in a disembodied way, full of tact, irony, and sounding genteel.

'That's for you, I'll warrant,' said the skipper.

'That's Catherine,' said Jack, disbelievingly.

'Jack,' she said. 'Are you there?'

'Jack Ferris here. Over.'

'When will you be coming in?'

'Friday at eight. Over.'

'Oh, that's a pity. Did you get my letters?'

Jack looked around and whispered into the mike: 'No. Over.'

'That's strange. You should have had them by now.'

'They haven't arrived, Catherine. Over.'

'You don't sound like yourself.'

'Neither do you. Over.'

'Have you been drinking?'

'No,' he lied. 'Over.'

'Well, that's wonderful. You sound very business-like. Over.'

'Under the circumstances, so would you. Over.'

'Am I embarrassing you?'

Her voice, filled with static, cut through the quiet, while the boat drifted in a calm east wind on a sea that was suddenly without landmarks, on a day that could have belonged to any of the seasons, in a sea that could have been any sea.

'I've made my mind up what to do. I'm sure you'll be glad to know.'

'You have? Tell me. Over.'

The radio gave a hoarse crackle. A whistle blew. A sound like a strimmer went through the airwaves.

'What did you say? Can you please repeat the message, Catherine. Over.'

'I'll be down next weekend. I'll leave a letter in the house.'

'See you then. Over.'

'Goodbye, Jack. Over.'

'Goodbye, Catherine. Over.'

He threw open the door of the light-keeper's house. He stepped into the hallway and found the letter for which he had prepared himself waiting inside the hall door. Then his heart began its furious beat. He kissed the damp envelope and tore it open. *It was good to hear your voice. I hope your remember your promise to me. We must stay sober. And I have to admit I'm also fighting off wretched imaginings that someone else will be enjoying you in my place – but I'm trusting you, treading thin ice in the hope that someday we'll be skating along without fear.*
I love you.

His world had been magically restored. The nightmare was over. *Jack,* she had written. *I love you and want to be with you. We have a break this weekend and I'll be down to see you. There are other people and we could be with them. But we know we want to be with each other. Let's grow old and sober together.*

He saw himself waiting on the bridge the following afternoon. He saw her alight from the car and begin running towards him. Overcome with happiness he sat there in the December dusk. The bark of a dog flew by.

3

- Students check the meaning of the literary terms. Elicit some examples of alliteration (eg *the sweet smell of success*), metaphors (eg *Their relationship is on the rocks. The news made my blood boil.*) and similes (eg *He eats like a pig. He's as strong as an ox.*).

4

- Students work individually or in pairs and identify the techniques.
- Check the answers and discuss the effects created by these techniques.

Answers

1 descriptive adjective   2 alliteration   3 metaphor
4 simile   5 descriptive verb   6 metaphors

Optional activity

Similes

- Write these words on the board:
  an ox a bat a mouse a parrot a pancake a lion the hills a flash
- Tell the students: *I'm going to read out the beginnings of some common similes. Complete them using the words on the board.*
- Read out the following list. Students call out the endings. (The correct endings are in brackets.)
  as quiet as (a mouse)   *as blind as* (a bat)
  as strong as (an ox)   *as quick as* (a flash)
  as old as (the hills)   *as sick as* (a parrot)
  as flat as (a pancake)   *as brave as* (a lion)
- In pairs, students tell each other about people or things in their own experience that can be described by the similes. For example: *I was as sick as a parrot when I failed my driving test.*

Literature and you
Speaking and vocabulary

1
- Students think about their answers to the questions and tick the appropriate reading genres. They then discuss the questions in pairs.
- Do a quick survey of the most popular genres.

2
- Check the meaning of the expressions in the list. Ask students if they are positive or negative.
- In pairs, students tell each other about something they have read. Encourage them to use words from the box.
- Students report back to the class. Find out if other students have read the same thing and ask: *Do you have the same opinion?*

Writing
1
- Give students time to decide which title they prefer. Brainstorm possible story ideas for each title.

2
- Students make notes for their story.

3
- Students write their story. Refer back to Listening Exs 3–4 on this page and encourage them to use some of these techniques in their stories.
- Students swap stories and give each other feedback.

Revision activities

Perfect situations
- Write the following verbs on the board:
  1 *grow up*   2 *forget*   3 *arrive*   4 *improve*   5 *lose*   6 *change*   7 *be married*   8 *go out*   9 *stop*
- Tell the students: *I'm going to read out some sentences. You need to rephrase them, using the verbs on the board in one of the perfect tenses.* Read out sentences 1–9 below and elicit the answers.
  1 *The kids are a lot bigger than when I last saw them.*
  2 *I couldn't remember her name.*
  3 *At last they're here!*
  4 *The situation was better than before.*
  5 *I can't find my mobile.*
  6 *This place isn't like it was when I was last here.*
  7 *They were no longer there when I arrived.*
  8 *It's our fifth wedding anniversary next month.*
  9 *Is it still raining?*

Answers
1 The kids have grown up (a lot) since I last saw them.
2 I'd forgotten her name.
3 At last they've arrived.
4 The situation had improved.
5 I've lost my mobile.
6 This place has changed since I was last here.
7 They had left when I arrived.
8 We'll have been married for five years next month.
9 Has it stopped raining?

2   Mime game
- Write the adjectives from page 34 Vocabulary Ex 1 on the board.
- Model the activity by miming an everyday activity (eg writing an email, ironing, opening a letter, etc) in the manner of one of the adjectives. Students guess the adjective.
- Invite other students to mime different adjectives for the class to guess.

Extra practice
Students complete the Extra practice material on page 54, either in class or for homework.

Extra practice answers

1 1 dismayed 2 hesitantly 3 astonishment 4 desperation 5 perplexity, sympathetic 6 annoyance, confusion

2 1 has found 5 had slept 2 will have risen 6 had done 3 had lived / been living 7 has evolved 4 had spent

3 1 have shared 4 has been evolving 2 will not have increased 5 has been studying 3 have evolved 6 have been sharing

4 (individual answers)

References
Grammar reference: Coursebook page 58
Wordlist: Coursebook page 60
Photocopiable resources: Teacher's Book pages 96–97
Test: Teacher's Book pages 132–133

CD-ROM
Unit 1 Telling tales
Language exercise: Telling tales
Listening activity: Types of literature
CEF-linked activity: I can discuss literary texts
Game: Witch's pot (adjectives to describe books)

A perfect world

Topic	Language study	Vocabulary	Main skills
• Seeking perfection (designer babies) • Nobody's perfect (perfectionists)	• Focusing attention on important information	• Collocations: discussion issues • Phrasal verbs: debate and discussion • Phrases to express surprise or indifference	• **Reading:** understanding key information and text structure • **Speaking:** discussing genetic engineering and other current affairs topics; talking about perfection and perfectionists; expressing surprise and indifference • **Writing:** a short article • **Listening:** identifying key information • **Pronunciation:** stress and intonation when expressing surprise and indifference

Learning aims

- Can focus attention on important information
- Can comment on current affairs
- Can express surprise or indifference

Ideas for preparation

- Newspaper, magazine or internet articles on current technological / scientific issues, ideally ones with some ethical debate
  (see Optional activity p51)

Warmer

- Ask: *What scientific issues have been the subject of debate in recent years?* Brainstorm ideas. Make a note of the issues, to be used for the Writing activity later in the unit.

Seeking perfection

Lead-in

Background information

Cloning is the process of recreating an identical copy of an original organism. Cloning in animals essentially involves removing the nucleus from a non-reproductive cell of one organism and transplanting this nucleus into a reproductive cell of another organism from which the nucleus has been removed. The 'new' cell is stimulated to divide and develop into an embryo, which is implanted into the womb of a 'mother'.

1

- Ask the question. Students give information or speculate about Dolly the sheep. They then check their ideas with the paragraph on page 61.
- Ask: *What do you know about cloning?* Brainstorm some ideas.

Suggested answer

Dolly was cloned, so she was a 'perfect' copy of another sheep.

Reading and vocabulary

1

- Check that students understand the vocabulary in the box. Note that *controversy* can be pronounced /ˈkɒntrəvɜːsi/ or /kənˈtrɒvəsi/.
- Students replace the underlined phrases. They will need to change the form of some verbs.
- Check the answers with the class.

Answers

1 rekindled debate	4 caused concern
2 make headlines	5 has set a precedent
3 inspired sympathy	6 create controversy

2

- 🔊 16 Students read the text and find the answers to the questions in Ex 1. Ask them to underline the parts of the article which give the answers. They can listen to the article on CD.
- Check the answers with the class.

Answers

1 The birth of the first 'designer baby'.
2 His embryo was genetically selected so that he could save the life of his sick sister.
3 The parents' dilemma: whether to use genetic screening to have a baby who could be a donor for their daughter or to let their daughter die.
4 Some people worry that parents will use genetic screening in the future to select other characteristics such as eye colour, beauty or intelligence. Rich people could use the technique to buy 'perfect' children.
5 It means that other parents will use the case as an example of what is legally possible.
6 He started a website which offered the embryos of models.

3

- Discuss the questions with the class.

4

- Elicit the meaning of *pan out* (to develop or eventuate) by asking the students to look at the verb in context in the article.
- Discuss the questions with the class.

5

- Look at the example for paragraph 1. Tell students: *The aim here is to discover the basic structure of the article.* Encourage them to think about the general purpose of each paragraph.
- Students work in pairs and complete the task.
- Discuss the answers and build up a general structure model on the board. (Students will use this structure model for the Writing activity on page 39.)

Suggested answers

Paragraph 1 introduces and summarises the controversy.
Paragraph 2 defines key terminology.
Paragraph 3 explains the cause of concern.
Paragraph 4 discusses the implications of designer babies.
Paragraph 5 identifies specific groups worried about the problem.
Paragraph 6 predicts what will happen.

6

Background information

GM (genetically modified) food is produced from plants which have had their genetic make-up modified in the lab. Basically, scientists 'cut and paste' a gene from another organism into a plant's DNA to give it a new characteristic. The first step is identifying a gene for a particular characteristic, such as resistance to herbicides or pests, or the production of bigger yields. The gene, which may come from any other organism, is inserted into the DNA of a plant cell, giving it that characteristic.

- Ask: *What is GM food?* and elicit answers.
- Students read the article. In list 1–6 they choose the correct alternative for each of the underlined verbs in the article.
- Check the answers with the class.

Answers

1 happened	2 clearly explains	3 mentions
4 minimised	5 dismissing	6 become less intense

7

- Students discuss the question in pairs, in small groups or as a class. (Note that there is a practice exercise which gives more information about the GM food debate on page 55 of the Coursebook.)

Writing

1

- Students follow the instructions and make notes for their article.

2

- Students write an article of 200–300 words. This could be done in class or for homework. Encourage students to use some of the language in Reading and vocabulary Exs 1 and 6.

3

- Pairs exchange their articles and give each other feedback.
- Students report back to the class. You may wish to develop some of the issues into a class discussion.

Language study

Focusing attention

Note

The purpose of the language study is to review or present some of the ways in which sentences can be 'fronted' as a means of focusing attention and giving emphasis. It focuses on the structures *It is / was … that / who …, What … is / was …* and noun phrase + *is / was …*

1

- Students read the sentences and answer the question.
- Check the answer with the class.

Answer

They help to focus attention on the important information.

2

- Students match the phrases with the patterns.
- Check the answers with the class.
- Refer students to the Grammar reference on page 58 if necessary.

Answer

1 b   2 a   3 c, d

3
- Look at the pair of examples with the class. Point out that the two structures are giving the same information, but in a different order in the sentence and so with a slightly different emphasis.
- Students complete the task individually or in pairs.
- Check the answers with the class.

Answers
1 a It's the clarity of the images that amazes me.
   b What amazes me is the clarity of the images.
2 a It's what they will come up with next that really frightens me.
   b What really frightens me is what they will come up with next.
3 a It's the distances involved that I can't get my head round.
   b What I can't get my head round is the distances involved.
4 a It was watching it live on TV that really brought it home.
   b What really brought it home was watching it live on TV.
5 a It's not knowing what the long-term dangers are that worries me.
   b What worries me is not knowing what the long-term dangers are.
6 a It's how so much can be stored on something so small that I just don't understand.
   b What I just don't understand is how so much can be stored on something so small.

4
- You could elicit some ideas for item 1 as an example. Then give students time to think of some ideas for the other sentences in Ex 3.
- Brainstorm ideas with the class.

Possible answers
1 photos of space / detailed satellite images / electron microscopy
2 cloning / genetic engineering technology / weapons and warfare technology
3 space / the universe / nanotechnology
4 the moon landing / a space shuttle take-off / military activity
5 cloning / genetic engineering / GM foods / pollution / mobile phone microwaves
6 computer technology / microchips / MP3 players / DVDs

5
- Students complete the matching task.
- Check the answers with the class.

Answers
1 b   2 h   3 e   4 d   5 a   6 c   7 f   8 g

6
- Students write their own sentences and then read them to their partner. Encourage them to ask each other questions and discuss ideas.
- Students share some of their ideas with the class.

Nobody's perfect
Listening and speaking

1
- Students consider the question, then discuss it in pairs.

2
- 🔊 17 Look at the photo with the class. Ask: *What's the relationship?* (mother and daughter) *Are they similar? What do you think they've got in common?*
- Students listen, check their ideas and answer the question.
- Check the answer with the class.

Answer
They're both perfectionists.

Listening script 17
(Z = Zoe, E = Ellie)
Z: What's all that noise? Ellie, it's 2 o'clock in the morning. Why on earth are you hoovering the living room now?
E: Oh, sorry, Zoe. I didn't mean to wake you up. It's just, well, you know my mum's coming tomorrow and I want everything to look tidy.
Z: You're kidding me, aren't you? You're hoovering at 2 o'clock in the morning just because your mum's coming. Who cares if there's a bit of dust?
E: You haven't met my mum yet, have you? She's got a thing about cleaning and everything being tidy. As soon as she gets through the door, she'll look how clean everywhere is. She'll be peering in the fridge and the oven and checking out the bathroom …
Z: Yeah, but so what? I mean we're students, she won't expect everything to be perfect.
E: Well, actually that's where you're wrong. My mum's a perfectionist, she likes everything to be in its proper place and she's really fussy about everything she does. She even irons socks!
Z: Are you having me on? How can you iron socks? It certainly sounds like she expects a lot from people! But it doesn't mean you have to worry about it. You've left home now, this is your place, not hers.
E: Yeah, I know, it's stupid. Perhaps I'm more like my mum than I imagined. What a horrible thought!
Z: Mm, now I think about it, you are a bit of a perfectionist yourself. I mean, you're totally organised. All your CDs are in alphabetic order and your shoes together in neat rows.
E: OK, OK, I know I'm strange like that. But at least I'm not as bad as my mum. She can't stand other people not living up to her standards and when people do things wrong – well!
Z: Mm. Your mum sounds lovely. I'm really looking forward to meeting her!
E: Oh, she's OK deep down … Listen, sorry, I woke you. I know you've got to get up early tomorrow.
Z: Oh, it doesn't matter, I'll put the alarm on. See you in the morning.
E: Yeah, 'night … I think I'll just clean the fridge before I go to bed …
Z: Whatever. Just do it quietly!

3

- Read through the list and check any problematic vocabulary.
- Students listen again and tick the items that describe Ellie's mother. <u>Alternatively</u>, they could do the task from memory and then listen again to check.
- Check the answers with the class.

Answers
2, 3, 6, 8

Optional activity

You and perfectionism
- Students grade themselves on a scale of 1–5 (1 = highest) for each of the eight characteristics in Ex 3. They then explain and compare their ideas in pairs.

4

- Students discuss the question in pairs or groups.
- Ask some students to report back their ideas and invite class discussion.

Vocabulary and pronunciation

1

- Refer students back to the listening exercise and ask the questions. Say: *Try to remember how Zoe felt and the actual words she used.*
- Students check the answers in the listening script. Then check the answers with the class.

Answers
1 She's surprised. (*Why on earth are you hoovering the living room now?*)
2 She doesn't care / She's indifferent. (*Whatever.*)

2

- Students complete the task individually or in pairs.
- Check the answers with the class. Explain that most of these expressions are informal.

Answers
1 S 2 I 3 S 4 I 5 I 6 S 7 I 8 S
9 I 10 S

3

- 🔘 18 Students listen and repeat the phrases. Encourage them to mimic the stress and intonation.

4

- Read through the instructions with the class.
- Students work in pairs. Student A chooses a sentence from page 61, to which Student B responds, and the conversation continues from there. Encourage students to be as emphatic as they can in their responses.
- Pairs swap roles. Student B starts another conversation from the list on page 64.
- Ask some pairs to act out one of their dialogues.

Revision activity

The best thing about … is …
- Brainstorm some topics about which the students have strong opinions, for example, *learning English, men, women, music,* etc. Write them on the board.
- Write these sentence beginnings on the board:
  The best thing about … is …
  The worst thing about … is …
  What I don't understand about … is …
  What fascinates me about … is …
- Tell the students: *Choose one of the topics on the board, or think of your own. Complete the sentences about this topic. Three of the sentences must give your true opinion and one must be false.*
- Students work in small groups. In turn, they read out their sentences and the others guess which sentence is not true. If someone guesses correctly, he / she gets a point. For every incorrect guess, the speaker gets a point.
- Students share some of their ideas with the class.

Extra practice

Students complete the Extra practice material on page 55, either in class or for homework.

Extra practice answers

1 1 making 2 rekindles 3 modified 4 set
   5 are causing 6 govern 7 banned 8 to create

2 1 pan out 2 played down 3 touch on
   4 come about 5 die down 6 spelt out, ruled out

3 1 is not knowing the long-term effects of GM food.
   2 the feeling of helplessness that really frustrates me.
   3 I don't understand is why on earth anyone would want to live here.
   4 not knowing who has got access to all your personal details on the Internet that worries me.
   5 it Crick and Watson who discovered the structure of DNA?

4 2 The worst thing about being my age is …
   3 One thing that really annoys me about the media is …
   4 The biggest advantage of being able to speak English is …

5 (individual answers)

References

Grammar reference: Coursebook page 58
Wordlist: Coursebook page 60
Photocopiable resources: Teacher's Book pages 98–99
Test: Teacher's Book pages 134–135

CD-ROM

Unit 2 A perfect world
Language exercise: What amazes me is …
Vocabulary activity: Smoking ban discussion
CEF-linked activity: I can express surprise and indifference
Game: Cats in hats (focusing attention)

Modern-day icons

Topic	Language study	Vocabulary	Main skills
• Keeping a legend alive (a tribute artist, nostalgia) • How star-struck are you?	• Spoken phrases with *say* and *speak*	• Idioms with parts of the body	• **Listening:** understanding gist and key information • **Speaking:** talking about popular icons and celebrity culture; discussing the value of nostalgia; using spoken phrases • **Pronunciation:** American English • **Reading:** understanding key information; completing a quiz and discussing the analysis

Learning aims

- Can use spoken phrases with *say* and *speak*
- Can talk about popular icons and celebrity culture
- Can contrast British and American English pronunciation

Ideas for preparation

- Newspaper or magazine articles on the following topics: business, computers, football and music (you may want to add other topics)
  (See Optional activity p57)

Warmer

- Write *icon* on the board and ask: *What different meanings of the word 'icon' can you think of?* Students can discuss this in pairs, then brainstorm ideas and produce a class definition.
- Compare with the Macmillan English Dictionary definitions below:

  1 a small picture on a computer screen that you choose by pressing a button with your mouse in order to open a particular program
  2 someone who is very famous and who people think represents a particular idea
  3 a picture or model of a holy person that is used in religious worship in the Orthodox Church

- Ask: *Who would you say are modern-day icons?* Brainstorm ideas.

Lead-in

1

- Read out the proverb and check that students understand the meaning of *imitation*, *sincere* and *flattery*.
- Discuss the questions with the class.

Possible answers

The proverb means that it is a compliment if somebody copies your behaviour or appearance – it shows that their admiration is genuine.
Imitation can go too far when somebody tries to model themselves entirely on another person, to the point of obsession.

Keeping a legend alive

Listening and speaking

1

- Check that students understand the meaning of *tribute artist / tribute band.*
- Discuss the questions with the class. Ask: *What tribute bands do you know of? Have you ever seen any?*

2

Background information

Elvis Presley (1935–1977) made his name as a rock 'n' roll singer in the 1950s and became widely known as 'The King' in a musical career of over two decades, setting record after record for concert attendances, TV ratings and record sales. He became one of the best-selling artists in music history and the best-selling solo performer. Elvis has more posthumous sales than any other artist. He also starred in a number of films. A combination of overwork, weight gain, depression, bad diet and abuse of prescription drugs brought about his death at the age of only 42.

- **19** Look at the photo and ask: *Who is this man imitating?* (Elvis Presley). Ask: *What do you know about Elvis?* and brainstorm ideas.
- Students listen to the interview and make notes on the four topics.

3

- Students compare notes with a partner and listen again if necessary.
- Check the answers with the class.

Answers

a He didn't know what to expect as it is a different culture.
b He was nervous, his knees started to buckle.
c There were 36,000 fans, there were kids aged 12, 14, 18, they were singing Elvis's songs, the music blew their minds. It blew Shawn's mind.
d Elvis goes on and on, he had an impact – an effect on the world.

Listening script 23

(I = interviewer, S = Shawn)

I: Oh my gosh, Shawn, you know, it's been about a year since we saw each other last and you were on your way to perform in Switzerland. Yeah, I want you to tell me about that experience. Did you know you would be singing for 36,000 screaming fans before you got there?

S: Had no idea. You know, a lot of us were … we didn't even know what to expect, you know what I mean, going to a different country, as they say, you know, there's different cultures and there's different this and there's different that, I think that the strongest thing that we found out is that music is … is a powerful tool. And it's funny how you can go over there and throw this music at kids who are, you know, 12, 14, 18 years old and it just, you know, blew their minds, and it blew our minds because it just goes to show how strong and universal music really is, and you know it's a tool that is very, very, powerful and …

I: And how universal Elvis is.

S: That's … yeah, that was my next point. For a man to be away and out of the public eye, so to speak, physically, let's say, but how he still goes on and on and on, and it's funny, we brought that show over there and we were backstage and we'd gotten there and, you know, we were nervous to begin with, so we kinda peeked out at the crowd and boy, I looked out at that crowd and my knees liked to buckle, I just went, whoa, wait a minute, it was something to be sought after, something I'll never forget. Hopefully I'll get a chance to go back there. The people in Switzerland are incredible.

I: They love this. You're bringing them closer to the King, it … really… you were there, if you missed it the first time round, you're getting it the second time around. You know, it's wonderful.

S: I really appreciate that. We really try to work hard and I've said it before and I'll say it again, he had impact, impact, impact. And again for a guy like that to have an effect on the world, and I mean that, the world. When you go over to Switzerland and, you know, they're singing stuff like *In the Ghetto* back to you and, it's like, man, you know, we're how many thousands of miles away from the States and … just amazing, amazing. You know, I'm not necessarily saying I'm filling anybody's shoes, because Lord knows I couldn't do that. God puts special individuals on this earth for a certain reason. He put both hands on Elvis, I swear, you know, unbelievable.

I: Well, you're an inspiration to everyone who wants to pay tribute to him, no matter what their capacity.

S: I appreciate that, to everybody out there who feels that way, you know, I'm trying everything to uphold it, you know, an image is a hard thing to keep up.

4
- Discuss the questions with the class.

5
- Students work in pairs and discuss the questions.
- Ask students to report their ideas to the class. Make two lists on the board for questions 2 and 3 and encourage class discussion.

6
- Check that students understand the meaning of *nostalgia*. Read out the instructions and elicit a few examples from some of the topics listed.
- Students work in small groups and discuss their ideas. They prepare a brief informal presentation of their ideas to the class.

7
- Students work in pairs. They each read their own role card and spend some time preparing their arguments.
- Students role-play the discussion with their partner.
- Ask some pairs to perform their role-play for the class.

8
- Discuss the question with the class.

Optional activity

My icons
- Ask: *Who have been your icons from childhood up to now?* Students briefly discuss the question in pairs.
- Students prepare a brief presentation about one of their icons. Encourage them to include relevant information about the person's life and to say why they consider this person to be an icon.

Vocabulary

1
- Students discuss the question with a partner and check by looking at the expressions in context in the script.
- Check the answers with the class. Point out that these expressions are both metaphors using parts of the body.

Answers
it blew their minds = they found it really exciting and amazing
out of the public eye = not constantly in the media

2
- Draw attention to the cartoon. Ask: *Which of the idioms does the cartoon illustrate?* (She loves to be waited on hand and foot), *What does this idiom mean?* (She likes people to do everything for her).
- Students work in pairs or groups and discuss the meaning of the idioms. Encourage them to think about any similar idioms in their own language.
- Check the answers with the class.

Suggested answers
1 She likes people to do everything for her.
2 Her appearance is striking and attracts everyone's attention.
3 He always looks neat and tidy.
4 His outrageous outfits surprise and shock people.
5 He really cares about his performances and puts a tremendous amount of effort into them.
6 She always thanks her fans very sincerely.
7 Success has made him arrogant and self-important.
8 Everybody is talking about her.

3

- Students work in pairs and discuss the questions. Ask them to try to think of at least one performer for each expression.
- Students report back to the class.

Optional activity

More body idioms

- Tell the students: *Guess which word is missing from these sentences. They're all parts of the head and face.*
- Read out sentences 1–7. Students give their suggestions for the missing words. <u>Alternatively</u>, you could ask them to write down the words and check their answers at the end.
- Check that students understand the meaning of the idioms and ask: *Are there any similar idioms in your language?*

1 *She looked incredible! I couldn't believe my _____ .*
2 *I want to go into the shop for a minute. Can you keep an _____ on my bag?*
3 *Oh, I can't think of his name! It's on the tip of my _____ .*
4 *He never listens. Everything just goes in one _____ and out the other.*
5 *It's none of your business. Keep your _____ out!*
6 *Tell me all about it. I'm all _____ .*
7 *Calm down. Keep your _____ on!*

Answers

1 eyes   2 eye   3 tongue   4 ear   5 nose
6 ears   7 hair

4

- Students read the situations and match them with the idiomatic expressions.
- Check the answers with the class. Then ask students to suggest other ways of expressing the meaning of the idioms.

Answers

1 d   2 c   3 e   4 b   5 f   6 a
Possible alternatives:
a Be sensible!   d Stop putting pressure on me!
b Wish me luck!   e Look carefully!
c Let yourself go!   f I'll help you if you help me.

Optional activity

Quick response

- Students work in pairs. Tell them: *Write six two-line dialogues. The reply in each one must be an idiomatic expression from Exercise 4.*
- Give an example. Elicit the reply for the following: *Quick! We've got to go now. Why are you always so slow?* (Keep your hair on!)
- Students write their dialogues.
- Pairs join up to form groups of four. In turn, pairs read out the first line of each of their dialogues. The other pair responds with the appropriate expression.
- Ask some pairs to read their dialogues to the class.

American English

Pronunciation

1

- 🔘 **20** Students listen, concentrating on the underlined sounds in each pair of words. For each word they tick the correct column to indicate a British or American accent.

Answers

2 British, /ɑː/   6 American, /ɜːr/
3 American, /ɑː/   7 British, /eə/
4 British, /ɒ/   8 American, /eər/
5 British, /ɜː/

2

- 🔘 **21** Go through the British English pronunciation of the words with the students.
- Students listen to the British and American pronunciation of each word and make a note of the difference. They then group the words into four patterns.
- Check the answers with the class.

Answers

British	American	
/ɑː/	/eɪ/	(tom<u>a</u>to, v<u>a</u>se)
/ɪ/	/aɪ/	(v<u>i</u>tamin, sem<u>i</u>, pr<u>i</u>vacy)
/juː/	/uː/	(n<u>ew</u>, st<u>u</u>dent)
difference in stress		(garage, ballet, café)

Optional activity

American and British vocabulary

- Ask: *What words do you know that are different in American English and British English?* Give an example: *trousers* (British) and *pants* (American).
- Either brainstorm examples with the class or put students into pairs / groups to produce their own lists. Compile a list of words on the board and ask students to copy them down.

Possible answers (British / American)

car / automobile   taxi / cab   bonnet / hood
boot / trunk   petrol / gas   lorry / truck
motorway / freeway   main road / highway
crossroads / intersection   pavement / sidewalk
lift / elevator   underground / subway   shop / store
city centre / downtown   chemist's / drugstore
flat / apartment   wardrobe / closet   handbag / purse
tap / faucet   curtains / drapes   rubbish / garbage
crisps / chips   sweets / candy   biscuit / cookie
chips / (French) fries   banknote / bill   bill / check
timetable / schedule   holiday / vacation   film / movie
autumn / fall

Language study

Spoken phrases with *say* and *speak*

> **Note**
>
> The purpose of this language study is to present some common spoken phrases that include *say* or *speak*. The phrases in the unit have a range of uses and meanings, but all have the general function of commenting on what has been said or signalling what is about to be said.

1
- Students match the phrases with their uses.
- Check the answers with the class. Ask: *Are there similar phrases in your language? Do they have the same meaning?*
- Refer students to the Grammar reference on page 59 if necessary.

Answers

1 a   2 d   3 b   4 c

2
- Students complete the task.
- Check the answers with the class.

Answers

1 so to speak
2 let's say
3 as they say
4 I've said it before and I'll say it again

3
- Students work in pairs. They discuss the meaning and use of each phrase.
- Check the answers with the class. Ask: *Are there similar phrases in your language? Do they have the same meaning?*

Answers

1 to refer back to something you have previously said
2 to introduce something new relating to a subject that someone has just mentioned
3 to show you are giving your opinion
4 to emphasise a statement, often when it may seem to contradict something
5 to add an opinion that seems to be the opposite of what you have just said, although you think both are true

4
- Look at the example and check that students understand the task. Tell them: *Express your opinions about things you feel strongly about.*
- Students write their answers.
- Working in pairs or groups, students read their sentences to each other. Encourage them to ask questions to find out more about each other's ideas.

5
- Read through the instructions and check that students understand the activity.
- Students have their discussion in groups of three.

- When groups have finished one discussion, they can write down five different phrases from the box, choose a different topic and play again.

> **Optional activity**
>
> **Class discussion**
> - Have a class discussion on one of the topics in Ex 5, or on a different topic. Students score a point each time they use one of the phrases in the box correctly. Change the topic as appropriate.

6
- Look at the examples for *business-speak* and check that students understand them. Make it clear that *-speak* refers to specialist language or jargon. Words like *meeting* or *office* could not be described as *business-speak* because they are in general use.
- Brainstorm ideas with the class. Alternatively, students can make lists in pairs or groups before reporting back to the class.

Example answers

1 USP (= unique selling point), turnover, assets, shareholders, takeover
2 download, upload, spam, blog, browser, server, URL
3 offside, penalty shoot-out, get sent off, header, handball, on the bench
4 gig, riff, groove, jam, solo, chorus

> **Optional activity**
>
> **More *-speak***
> - Put the students into small groups and give each group an article on business, computers, football or music. You may like to add articles in other fields that have specialist language.
> - Tell the students: *Find as many examples of business-speak / music-speak* (etc) *as you can in your article. Underline them and check their meaning.*
> - Students form new groups with people who have read different articles. In turn, they introduce and explain the vocabulary they have found to the other members of the group.

How star-struck are you?

Reading and speaking

1
- Write *adulation* and *emulation* on the board and check that students understand the meaning (*adulation* = great praise or admiration, especially for someone who is famous; *emulation* = trying to be like someone else, usually because you admire them).
- Students work in pairs or small groups and discuss the questions.
- Students report back to the class.

2
- Read through the quiz and check any problematic vocabulary. Give special attention to the idiomatic expressions *chuck their money about* (spend money freely and carelessly), *hang out their dirty laundry* (reveal private problems to the public), *be in seventh heaven* (feel extremely happy), *a bunch of freeloaders* (people who expect to receive things without giving anything in return).
- Students do the quiz. Alternatively, they can work in pairs, reading out the quiz statements and recording their partner's answers.
- Students calculate their score and read the analysis on page 64. If they completed the quiz for a partner, they can read the analysis to them. Ask: *Do you agree with the analysis?*

3
- Elicit or explain the meaning of *obsession*.
- Discuss the questions with the class. Encourage students to pick out statements in the quiz that they feel are obsessive, and to give reasons.

Speaking and writing

1
- Ask: *Do you know any celebrities who have had trouble with obsessive fans? Who else has suffered from being famous?* Elicit a few examples from the class. You may want to introduce the word *stalker* (someone who has an obsession with another person and follows them all the time in a threatening manner).
- Students work in groups and brainstorm ideas. One student should take notes on this discussion.

2
- Groups select their material and plan their presentation. Tell them to ensure that everyone has a part to play in the presentation. You may want to give them time to do some research to find or check information.

3
- Groups give their presentations to the class. Encourage discussion at the end of each presentation.

Revision activities

1 Body idioms
- Make a simple drawing of a person on the board and make sure it clearly includes the following features: hands, feet, fingers, heart, head, hair, eyes, eyebrows, lips.
- Tell the students: *Think of an idiom that includes the feature I point to.* As you point, students give sentences with the idioms they have learnt. For example, if you point to the lips, students could respond: *His / Her name is on everyone's lips.*
- You could add a competitive element, by dividing the class into teams and giving a point for each correct idiom.

2 *Say and speak* chain
- Write these expressions on the board:
  As they say …
  I have to say …
  I've said it before and I'll say it again …
  Personally speaking …
  As [name] was saying, …
  That said, …
- Choose a topic about which the students will have strong views and state your opinion about it, using one of the expressions. One of the students responds to what you have said, also using one of the expressions. The next student responds to this, and so on. Continue until the chain reaches a natural conclusion.
- Students work in groups of three or four. They choose a different topic and make another chain.

Extra practice
Students complete the Extra practice material on page 56, either in class or for homework.

Extra practice answers
1 1 nose   2 hair   3 eyebrows   4 head   5 eye   6 lips

2 1 e   2 d   3 f   4 b   5 a   6 c

3 1 I'll keep / be keeping my fingers crossed.
2 You should let your hair down once in a while.
3 I want to thank you from the bottom of my heart.
4 Get off my back!
5 It blew my mind.

4 1 speaking of
2 That said, as we were saying, I have to say
3 I've said it before and I'll say it again
4 Don't say, as they say, so to speak, let's say, Personally speaking

5 1 d   2 b   3 a   4 c

References
Grammar reference: Coursebook page 59
Wordlist: Coursebook page 60
Photocopiable resources: Teacher's Book pages 100–101
Test: Teacher's Book pages 136–137

CD-ROM
Unit 3 Modern-day icons
Language exercise: But I have to say this
Vocabulary activity: Celebrity gossip column
CEF-linked activity: I can contrast British and American English pronunciation
Game: Neighbourhood (idioms with parts of the body)

Safe and sound?

Topic	Language study	Vocabulary	Main skills
• Identity theft • Caught on camera (video surveillance)	• Using modals to express real and unreal past situations	• Banking • Expressing certainty and drawing conclusions	• **Reading:** understanding and identifying key information; understanding vocabulary in context • **Speaking:** talking about identity theft and other crimes; giving advice and warnings; using the language of banking; discussing video surveillance • **Writing:** website tips • **Listening:** identifying gist; understanding vocabulary in context

Learning aims
- Can talk about real and unreal past situations
- Can discuss crime prevention and civil liberties
- Can give advice and warnings

Ideas for preparation
- Newspaper, magazine or internet articles on the topic of finance / money
  (see Optional activity p60)

Warmer
- Ask: *How many different crimes can you think of?* Brainstorm ideas and make a list on the board.
- Ask: *Which are the most and the least common? Which are the most and the least serious?*

Identity theft

Lead-in

1
- Read through the items in the box and check that students understand what is meant by *credit history*, *criminal record* and *political affiliation*.
- In pairs, students discuss the questions and make two lists: *Private* and *Public*. Invite class discussion.

Reading and vocabulary

1
- Discuss the question with the class. Reach agreement on a definition and write it on the board.

2
- 🎧 **22** Students read the article and check their answer to Ex 1. They can listen to the article on CD.

Possible answer
Identity theft is stealing information about someone in order to use their bank account or credit card, to open new accounts or to take out loans in their name. The motive may also be for terrorism, drug trafficking or illegal immigration.

3
- Students look at the text and complete the task.
- Check the answers with the class.

Answers
1 True.
2 False. Fraudsters can trick you by phoning you, by observing your PIN code, by using attachments to cash machines, by getting your details from your rubbish or by memorising them in shops and restaurants.
3 False. 10% of identity theft is committed by people related to the victims.
4 True.

4
- Students work individually or in pairs. They write the correct names from the article.
- Check the answers with the class.

Answers
1 Scott   2 Rose   3 Scott   4 Rose   5 both
6 Scott

5
- Discuss the meanings with the class.

Answers
1 information on the credit card: name of cardholder, number, bank account, date of issue
2 written statements showing how much money you owe somebody for goods or services you have received
3 a bank account which you can use to withdraw money at any time and which supplies you with a chequebook
4 money that a lender charges for lending you money
5 internet banking services
6 the amount of money you have in your account

6
- Students work individually or in pairs and complete the matching task.
- Check the answers with the class. Point out that *take out* can be used with both *money* (*take out money* = withdraw from your account) and *loan* (*take out a loan* = obtain a loan).

- To consolidate meaning, ask whichever of the following questions are appropriate: *When did you last withdraw / transfer / deposit some money? Have you ever taken out a loan? When will you pay it off? Have you ever / recently opened a bank account?*

Answers
clean out / close / open a bank account
deposit / take out / transfer / withdraw money
default on / pay off / take out a loan

7
- Students work in pairs and discuss the questions.

Optional activity

Money matters
- Students work in pairs. Hand out another newspaper / magazine / internet article on the topic of finance to each pair. You can give the same article to more than one pair, or to everyone in the class.
- Tell the students: *Read through the article and underline all the examples of language connected with money that you can find. Check the meanings.*
- Students complete the task and then report back to the class. Write any useful language on the board for the students to copy down.

Speaking and writing

1
- Students read the tips. Check problematic vocabulary and emphasise that the language used here is formal.
- Draw attention to the phrases in bold. Elicit other phrases that can be used to give formal advice / warning and write them on the board. Examples could include: *It is advisable (not) to …   You are advised (not) to …
Be careful when you …   Make sure / Ensure (that) …*
- Ask students to think of more tips to add to the college list, using the phrases on the board. For example: *You are advised not to leave people alone in your room unless you know them well. Make sure that your windows are closed when you leave your room.*

2
- Read the instructions with the class and check that students understand the meaning of *mugged*.
- Divide the class into an even number of groups. Assign the topic of mugging to half the groups (A) and the topic of car crime to the other half (B).
- In their groups, students brainstorm ideas for tips on their topic.

3
- Students write their tips. Encourage them to use the phrases in Ex 1.
- A and B groups pair up and exchange their tips.

4
- Groups discuss the tips they receive and then give feedback to the students who wrote them.
- You could compile a class list of tips for each topic.

Example answers
Take care not to go out alone at night.
Beware of walking in unlit areas.
It is recommended that you lock your car at all times.
Avoid leaving anything valuable in your car.

Language study

Using modals to express real and unreal past situations

Note
The aim of this language study is to review the different forms used for modal verbs when referring to a real or unreal situation in the past. *Have to* is treated as a modal verb in this language study.
Note that 'unreal' situations in the past are situations that didn't actually happen, but which are speculated or hypothesised about. Situations expressed by the third conditional (eg *If I'd brought my credit card, I would have bought that shirt*) or some modal verbs (eg *It might have been Tom you saw, but I'm not sure*) are examples of 'unreal' past situations. 'Real' situations, in contrast, are situations that did actually happen.

1
- Read through the question and check that students understand the meaning of 'real' and 'unreal' situations.
- Students complete the task individually or in pairs.
- Check that students understand the meaning and use of the modal verbs as they are used in the extracts.

Answers
a 4, 6   b 1, 2, 3, 5, 7

2
- Students complete the rules.
- Refer students to the Grammar reference on page 59 if necessary.

Answers
unreal, real

3
- Students work individually or in pairs. They complete each text, using the modals in the box in the affirmative or the negative form.
- Check the answers. As students read out the verbs, help them with the pronunciation of the modals + *have*: /ˈʃʊdəv/, /ˈmʌstəv/, /ˈkʊdntəv/, etc.
- Ask: *Which are the two examples of modals expressing a real past situation?* (had to hand over, couldn't pay).

Answers
1 should have been	6 might have got away with
2 could have burst	7 couldn't pay
3 must have pulled	8 must have thought
4 had to hand over	9 could have known
5 couldn't have picked	10 might have looked

Optional activity

Passport to prison: dictogloss

- Tell the students: *Listen to a short news article and make notes – you are going to reconstruct it.* Then read out the following article.
  The fake passport looked so good that it <u>could have been</u> genuine, but there was one flaw. The forger <u>could not spell</u>. And as a result, Abdul Hameed was jailed yesterday for eight months for forgery after customs officials spotted the word 'Government' without an 'n' in the middle and 'ministry' spelled with an 'e' in the passport he was carrying. 'He <u>should have used</u> a spellchecker,' said his lawyer.
- In pairs or groups, students try to reconstruct the text. Read the text a second and possibly a third time, for the students to refine their versions.
- Students read out their versions and compare with the original.

4

- Read the instructions and give an example to model the activity, for example: *When I was 16, I had a trial for the national swimming team. I should've taken it more seriously than I did. If I had, I might've …*
- Give students time to think about what they are going to say. Encourage them to make notes if they want to.
- Students work in pairs and tell each other about their experience.
- Ask some students to report back on what their partner has told them.

Caught on camera

Listening and vocabulary

Background information

CCTV systems for use in public areas were pioneered in the UK in the 1980s under the government slogan 'Looking out for you'. The UK has by far the highest number of CCTV systems, covering most urban centres as well as other public areas, and it is estimated that the total number of cameras in the UK is around 4,000,000, or one camera for every 15 people.

1

- Ask: *Look at the photo. What does it show?* Students give their ideas.
- Discuss the questions with the class.

2

- 🔊 **23** Ask students to read the four viewpoints. Help with the pronunciation of *surveillance* (/sɜːˈveɪləns/) and *harassment* (/həˈræsmənt/ or /ˈhærəsmənt/).
- Students listen, complete the matching task and note down the evidence that the callers give.
- Check the answers with the class.

Answers

Caller 1, Jody: d. Evidence: there's less drug dealing and mugging on her estate.
Caller 2, Naseem: b Evidence: his mate was wrongly charged with a crime on the basis of CCTV images.
Caller 3, Lily: a. Evidence: camera operators were spying on a woman in her bathroom.
Caller 4, Alvin: c Evidence: a mugger was arrested because of CCTV evidence.

Listening script 23

(P = presenter, J = Jody, N = Naseem, L = Lily, A = Alvin)

P: Hello and welcome to *Young Britain*. Today we're looking at the question of video surveillance. According to statistics from Liberty, the UK human rights and civil liberties organisation, Britain is monitored by over four million CCTV cameras, making us the most-watched nation in the world. The government claims CCTV prevents crime and helps detect criminals after crimes have taken place. However, some people object to constantly being caught on camera. They think it's an infringement of their civil liberties. So, let's hear what you think. Let's take our first caller … Jody from Sheffield. Hello, Jody.

J: Hello … er, well, I just want to say that I definitely support having cameras everywhere. I've felt a lot safer in my area, particularly at night, since we've had cameras … and, er, I'm convinced they help stop people from committing crimes. You know, if their faces are going to be on camera, then people think twice about doing something illegal. There used to be a lot of problems on our estate, you know, like drug dealing and mugging, and now the situation's got a lot better. I don't think that could have happened without CCTV.

P: OK, thanks, Jody. And I have to say Jody's opinion does reflect that of the public at large. Most people firmly believe that video surveillance has made them feel safer. Right, on to our next caller. And it's Naseem from Birmingham.

N: Hi. You know, what I don't understand is why everyone is so positive about these cameras. I mean, it's just harassment, right? My mate was charged with a crime he didn't commit when there was a break-in at our local supermarket. The CCTV images were so unclear it could have been anybody. But they marched my mate off to the police station because he's got a police record and said he matched the person on the film.

P: And what happened then?

N: Well, it turned out he was at work when the break-in happened, didn't it? Just like he'd been saying all along. People are supposed to be innocent until proved guilty, aren't they?

P: OK, Naseem, thanks for that. Well, looking at the statistics, there have been a considerable number of misidentifications due to poor-quality images but the technology is improving all the time. Our next caller is Lily from Oxford. Hello, Lily.

L: Hello. Well, I should have thought privacy ought to be the main issue here. These cameras are totally in-your-face everywhere you go. You don't know who's watching through these cameras and what they do with the film they take. Remember the case last week? The camera operators were using a camera to spy on a woman in her bathroom, taking pictures of her in the shower. I've come to the conclusion that we can't be expected to have faith in video surveillance, you know, when things like that happen.

P: Well to be quite honest, Lily, how often does something like that happen? I mean, isn't it the case that if you've got nothing to fear, then why let the cameras bother you?

L: Well, I've got nothing to hide, but it's the basic principle, isn't it? Why should we accept people spying on us?

P: OK, Lily, let's turn that question over to the next caller and that's Alvin from London. Hello Alvin. How would you answer Lily's question?

A: Well, she's obviously never been in a situation like I have. I was mugged last month in broad daylight, out on the street, you know, on a Saturday afternoon. This guy just hit me in the face and took my mobile. The streets were packed but there were no witnesses because there was so much going on and it was all over so quickly.

P: But the crime was caught on camera?

A: That's right. And two weeks later, they got the guy that did it. So I've no doubt at all that we need CCTV.

P: Ok, thanks Alvin. We'll take a break now and then be right back. And if you want to call in with your opinion, remember our number is 021 …

3
- Students listen again and note down the phrases used for expressing opinions.
- Check the answers with the class.
- Brainstorm other phrases for expressing opinions. These could include:
  I'm all for …   I'm right behind …   I'm totally against …   To me, …   In my opinion, …   As far as I'm concerned, …   As I see it, …   If you ask me, …

Answers

1 definitely support	4 should have thought
2 'm convinced	5 've come to the conclusion
3 firmly believe	6 've no doubt at all

4
- Students discuss the questions in pairs or small groups. Encourage them to use the language for expressing opinions in Ex 3.
- Students report back to the class.

5
- Students look at the mind map. Elicit one or two items that can be added.
- Students work in pairs and complete their own mind map. Encourage them to look for vocabulary in the listening script (page 63) and the rest of the unit, and to consult dictionaries where necessary.
- Reproduce the incomplete mind map from the Coursebook on the board and elicit students' suggestions on how to develop it.

Optional activity

Pass it on
- As an alternative to compiling a class map on the board, students pass their completed mind map to the pair next to them, who add one new item to it. The maps are then passed on again with a further item being added each time. This continues until the mind maps return to their owners.

Speaking

1
- Divide the class into two groups or, with larger classes, into pairs of groups. They each read their own role card and discuss what they will say at the meeting.
- Students role-play the meeting. Encourage them to try to reach agreement.
- At the end, ask: *Were you happy with the outcome?*

Revision activity

could have, might have, should have
- Tell the students: *Think of some famous people who could have, might have or should have done something differently.* Give or elicit one or two sentences, for example: *Elvis might have lived longer if he'd had better advice. David Beckham shouldn't have gone to Real Madrid.* Students write their own sentences.
- Ask some students to read out one of their sentences without naming the person. The others try to guess who the person is.

Extra practice
Students complete the Extra practice material on page 57, either in class or for homework.

Extra practice answers

1 **Across:** 1 card details   7 loan   8 account   9 in   10 ATM   11 money   14 online   15 statement
Down: 2 balance   3 bank account   4 identity theft   6 interest   12 PIN   13 out

2 1 It is recommended that
  2 Take care not to
  3 You may also want to
  4 It is a good idea to
  5 Always beware of, always make sure
  6 Whatever you do, don't

3 (individual answers)

4 1 could afford   4 should have been done
  2 could have been   5 must have been
  3 might have been

5 (individual answers)

References
Grammar reference: Coursebook page 59
Wordlist: Coursebook page 60
Photocopiable resources: Teacher's Book pages 102–103
Test: Teacher's Book pages 138–139

CD-ROM
Unit 4 Safe and sound?
Language exercise: You really shouldn't have
Vocabulary activity: Bank information
CEF-linked activity: I can discuss crime prevention and civil liberties
Game: The big squeeze (banking vocabulary)

UNIT 5
Review

Before starting this unit, ask students to read the Grammar reference on pages 58–59 and study the Wordlist on page 60 of the Coursebook.

Ideas for preparation
- Dice and counters for the *Talk about it* game (see Vocabulary, p65)

Warmer
- Discuss the following questions with the class: *What defines a celebrity? Who are the biggest celebrities in your country / in the world? Why are they the biggest?*

Lead-in

Background information

At the time of publication this information is up to date. Check the media for any changes in the couples' circumstances.

Chris Martin was born in Devon, UK in 1977. He is the lead singer, rhythm guitarist and pianist of the band *Coldplay*. **Gwyneth Paltrow** was born in Los Angeles in 1972. She is an Academy Award-winning actress who was once engaged to actor Brad Pitt. She and Chris Martin were married in 2003 and have two children.

Tennis champion **Steffi Graf** was born in Mannheim, Germany in 1969. She won 22 Grand Slam singles titles, more than any other player. **Andre Agassi** was born in Las Vegas in 1970. He is the only male tennis player of the modern era to have won all four Grand Slam singles events. He was married to actress Brooke Shields from 1997 to 1999. He and Steffi Graf married in 2001 and have two children.

Tom Cruise was born in New York in 1962 and is one of Hollywood's most successful stars. He was married to actress Nicole Kidman for ten years. **Katie Holmes** was born in Toledo, Ohio in 1978. She is an actress who first came to fame when she starred in the teen drama *Dawson's Creek*. The couple got together in 2005. They had a daughter in 2006 and got married in the same year.

Jay-Z (real name Shawn Carter) was born in 1969. He is one of the most successful American rap performers of recent years. **Beyoncé** (full name Beyoncé Knowles) was born in Houston, Texas in 1981. She rose to stardom as a founding member of the group *Destiny's Child*, before embarking on a solo career in 2003. Her first single, *Crazy in love*, featured Jay-Z. The couple got together in 2002.

1
- Discuss questions 1–4 with the class. For question 4 you could list the pros and cons on the board.

Answers
1 Katie Holmes and Tom Cruise; Steffi Graf and Andre Agassi; Beyoncé and Jay-Z; Gwyneth Paltrow and Chris Martin

The world of celebrity

1
- Students read the article and choose the most natural form of the verbs. They can compare their answers with a partner.
- Check the answers with the class.

Answers
1 have shown	5 have lasted
2 has taken off	6 have been drinking
3 has met	7 has never lived
4 have been working	8 have had

2
- Discuss the question with the class, and ask: *What reasons does the article give for celebrity couples splitting up?*

3
- 🔵 **24** Check that students understand all the items in the list.
- Students listen and tick the topics.
- They listen again and make notes about the speakers' opinions.
- Check the answers with the class.

Listening script 25
(B = Ben, A = Anna)

B: ... and I think she's fantastic. All her films have been just brilliant.

A: You know it never ceases to amaze me just how much all these Hollywood stars get paid for a film. I think it's disgusting. I mean, 20 or 30 million dollars for just a few weeks' work. It just seems to be getting more and more ridiculous. Don't you think?

B: Well, yes, but the films do earn a vast amount, so as a percentage of the earnings the star's fee is probably not that great. And without a big name, the film wouldn't do nearly as well. That said, I do agree that it's maybe getting a little out of hand. And footballers too, getting, like, £150,000 a week! Now that *is* crazy.

A: Yeah. And another thing that really annoys me is all the ludicrous things that these stars spend their money on. You know, stuff like gold-plated bathroom taps, million-dollar barbeque sets, bottles of wine that cost thousands, diamond-studded collars for their irritating little pet dogs and so on.

B: Yes, I have to say it can be pretty gross. But as they say, if you've got it, flaunt it.

A: Speaking of 'flaunting it', did you see those hideous pictures the other day of what's-her-name from that girl band's wedding, you know, the one that's just married that footballer. They got paid a million, or so they say, by some celebrity magazine, just for a few wedding snaps.

It's madness. And I read that Elton John actually turned down $6 million to have his wedding televised in the States. But what I don't understand is who on earth is remotely interested enough in all that stuff to warrant the magazines paying such an obscene amount. After all, they're just pictures.

B: I agree, but the right one on the front cover of, let's say, *Hello!* magazine, or something like that, can boost sales massively. I think I remember reading somewhere that the issue with David Beckham's wedding sold three times the normal amount.

A: And the paparazzi – they're just as bad. They've got no real career of their own, so they just make a living out of other people's success. It's the fact that they can get tens of thousands of pounds just for taking dodgy snaps of someone doing their shopping or walking down the street that gets me. And if you ask me, I think the celebrities themselves are behind all this paparazzi stuff a lot of the time. You know, as a way of keeping themselves in the spotlight and on their terms. They might pretend they don't like it, but I wouldn't be surprised if most of the tip-offs come from the celebs themselves.

B: Mm, not sure about that. But as I was saying, I suppose any publicity is good publicity.

A: Well, I suppose so, but what I'd really like to know is who on earth buys these magazines. You always see them in dentists' waiting rooms and such places, but who is actually sad enough to go to the shops to buy a copy?

B: Erm, well ...

A: Don't say you buy them, please ... Erm, well, if you do, you wouldn't happen to have the latest issue of *Hello!* would you? Apparently, there's a really good feature on ...

Answers
1 celebrity magazines, celebrity weddings, earning money, spending money, self-publicity
2 Possible answers:

Celebrity magazines
Anna: They pay mad prices; she can't understand why people are interested in them.
Ben: The right cover photo can increase sales massively.

Celebrity weddings
Anna: Huge payment for celebrity wedding photos is madness, obscene.

Earning money
Anna: Payment to film stars is amazing, disgusting, ridiculous.
Ben: A star's fee isn't a big percentage of the profits, a big name is needed for the film to do well; however, it's getting out of hand; footballers get too much – it's crazy.

Self-publicity
Anna: Celebrities probably invite the attention of paparazzi, they want to keep in the spotlight.
Ben: Not sure about this theory.

Spending money
Anna: Stars spend their money on ludicrous things – it really annoys her.
Ben: It can be pretty gross, but if you're rich, it's normal to show off your wealth.

4
- Students complete the extracts with the correct form of *say* or *speak*. They can check the answers in the listening script on page 63.
- Check the answers with the class. Ask students to say what each extract is referring to in the listening.

Answers
1 said; commenting on the money stars are paid
2 say; commenting on the things that stars spend their money on
3 say; commenting on wealth / money
4 Speaking; commenting on flaunting wealth
5 say; commenting on a singer and a footballer at the time of their wedding
6 say; commenting on celebrity photos
7 saying; commenting on publicity

5
- Look at the example and invite students to respond to it.
- Give students time to prepare what they want to say. They could write down their sentences.
- In pairs, students express and discuss their opinions.
- Students report back to the class.

6
- Students complete the sentences. Explain that sometimes more than one answer is possible.
- Check the answers with the class.

Answers
1 must have been
2 couldn't bear, should have left
3 otherwise might / would have been
4 should / could have been listed
5 had to pause, wouldn't have made

7
- Look at the example with the class. You could give an example yourself to model the activity.
- Students work in pairs. They suggest and describe films that fit the comments in Ex 6.
- Students report their ideas to the class.

8
- Students write two summaries of two or three sentences each. Remind them to include at least one past modal verb in each summary.

9
- Students work in pairs. They take it in turns to read out their summaries and guess each other's films.
- Ask some students to read out one of their summaries. The other students guess the film and respond to the opinions.

Speaking

1

- In a large class, students work in two groups of eight or more. In each group there should be two or three speakers for the proposed law (anti-paparazzi), two or three speakers against it (pro-paparazzi), one chair and at least three audience members.
- A small class can work all together on one debate, with two to four speakers on each side, one chair and everyone else in the audience.
- Assign the roles and check that students understand the debate procedure.
- Students prepare their arguments / questions. Encourage them to use the comments in speech bubbles for ideas.
- Groups hold their debate, following the debate procedure. The audience then votes for the winning side.

Song

1

- Draw attention to the photo and ask: *Who's this?* (James Blunt) *What do you know about him?* Establish that James Blunt is a singer and songwriter.
- Students read the factfile to answer the question.

Answers

James Blunt was educated at Harrow School.
He studied Aerospace Engineering at Bristol University.
He completed his education at the Royal Military Academy in Sandhurst.
He was a captain in the British Army. His father had also been in the British Army.
He served as a tank commander in the NATO peacekeeping force in Kosovo.
He was part of the guard of honour at the funeral of the Queen Mother.
He lived in Los Angeles after leaving the army.
He lodged with the *Star Wars* actress Carrie Fisher.

2

- Students discuss the question in pairs.
- Discuss the questions with the class.

Answers

1 He followed in his father's footsteps by joining the British Army
2 In Kosovo he carried his guitar around with him and regularly entertained his fellow troops. Some songs from his debut album were inspired by his experiences in Kosovo.

3

- Students work individually or in pairs. They match each line in the song with its final word. Encourage them to think about the rhyming of words.

4

- 🔊 **25** Students listen to the song and check their ideas in Ex 3.

Answers

2 pure   3 angel   4 sure   5 subway   6 man
7 sleep on that   8 plan   9 beautiful   10 true
11 face   12 place   13 do   14 you   15 eye
16 by   17 face   18 high   19 think   20 again
21 moment   22 end   23 beautiful   24 true
25 angel   26 face   27 up   28 you   29 truth
30 you

5

- Students find the expressions in the song.
- Check the answers with the class. Note that for answer 1 the usual expression, expressed with the correct grammar, is *I won't lose **any** sleep **over** that.*

Answers

1 I won't lose no sleep on that   3 we walked on by
2 she caught my eye   4 face the truth

6

- Discuss the questions with the class. <u>Alternatively</u>, students can discuss them in pairs before reporting back to the class.
- Note that the song was in fact written about an ex-girlfriend. However, this is open to interpretation and students may assume that the woman on the subway was a stranger for whom the singer felt an attraction.

Possible answers

1 He is describing a time when he saw a woman in the subway/underground. She was with another man.
2 He is singing to the woman.
3 She is an ex-girlfriend.
4 He has mixed emotions. He feels uplifted by the experience of seeing her, but at the same time he feels a certain sadness that they are not together and never will be.

Vocabulary

1

- Read through the instructions and check that students understand the rules. Point out that someone will need to time each speaker with a watch to make sure they speak for 30 seconds. Also, the decision about whether a speaker is too hesitant or repetitive must come from a consensus of opinion from all the other players.
- Students play the game in groups of three or four.
- At the end, get some feedback from the class. Ask: *Did you find some questions easier than others? Was it difficult to speak for 30 seconds? What techniques did you use when you knew you were running out of things to say?*

References

Module 2 test: Teacher's Book pages 140–142

Living together

Topic	Language study	Vocabulary	Main skills
• Happy families (Britain's biggest family) • A social experiment (living in an alternative community)	• Ellipsis and substitution	• Family relationships • Community organisation	• **Reading:** understanding gist; understanding vocabulary in context • **Speaking:** discussing cultural values and family relationships; discussing the aims of non-traditional living communities • **Listening:** identifying key information • **Writing:** an online advert

Learning aims
- Can use ellipsis and substitution
- Can discuss cultural values and family relationships
- Can discuss the aims of non-traditional living communities

Warmer
- Ask: *What's a family tree?* You may like to draw a simple version of your family tree on the board.
- Students draw their family tree.
- Students work in pairs or small groups. They show each other their family tree and describe some of the people in them.

Lead-in

Background information
In the EU in 2005, 67% of households were without children. 29% were single-person households, 24% were couples without children and 14% were other all-adult households (eg houses shared by students). Of those households with children, 16% had one child, 13% had two children and 4% had three or more.

1
- Write *family* on the board. Ask students what they associate with this word and brainstorm ideas.
- For question 2 you could look at the photos and ask: *How would you describe each of these families?* (The photos show an extended family, a single-parent family and a foster family.)
- Elicit expressions for different family types, supplying vocabulary as necessary. The list could include:
  nuclear family: the parents and their children
  extended family: includes more distant relatives who play a large part in family life
  stepfamily: a family with one or more children from a previous relationship
  foster family: a family where adults look after other people's children for payment
  single-parent family: a family where one parent brings up the children
  same-sex family: a family where the parents are of the same sex (one partner may be the natural mother / father, or the child may be adopted)

- Ask: *Which of these types of family are common in your country?*
- Ask and discuss question 3.
- Read out the statistics in the Background information box above. Ask: *How do you think your country compares?*

Optional activity

Family expressions
- Ask some or all of the following questions and check that students understand the meaning of the expressions (in brackets below).
  Do you agree with the saying 'Blood is thicker than water'? (family relationships are stronger than non-family relationships)
  Do you agree that charity begins at home? (you should look after your family and the people closest to you before you start helping others)
  What characteristics run in your family? (recur in different generations of the same family)
  Who do you take after? (resemble in appearance and/or character – used to refer to an older family member)
- Students discuss the questions.

Happy families

Reading and vocabulary

Background information
The world average fertility rate was 3.4 births per woman in 1990 and 2.8 in 2000. It is forecast to be 2.5 in 2010 and 2.3 in 2020.
In 2006, average fertility rates were: Africa 5.1, Central and South America 2.6, Asia 2.4, Oceania 2.1, North America 2.0 and Europe 1.4.
In Europe there is a tendency towards fewer children. In 2006, Iceland (2.1) had the highest fertility rate, followed by Ireland, France and Albania (1.9), the Scandinavian countries (1.8) and the UK, Luxembourg and the Netherlands (1.7).
Other countries: Argentina (2.4), Australia (1.8), (Brazil (2.3), China (1.6), Germany (1.3), India (2.9), Italy (1.3), Japan (1.3), Russia (1.3), Saudi Arabia (4.5) Spain (1.3), Turkey (2.2)

1

- In pairs, students discuss the questions. They check ideas for question 2 with the information on page 93.
- Discuss the questions with the class.

2

- 🔊 **01** Students look at the photo on page 67 and the article headline. Ask: *What do you think the article is about?* Check the meaning of *brood* (a humorous word for a large number of children from the same family).
- Students read the article and answer the questions. They can listen to the article on CD.

Answers

1 Sue was extremely happy about the birth of her 15th child ('elated'). Ian said he was really pleased and that a new birth is always exciting.
2 Sue is already looking forward to her next child ('sweet sixteen') and she would love to have twins ('the icing on the cake'). Ian thinks Sue will have another baby and doesn't seem to mind.
3 Becky says she is thinking of having children after seeing Isabelle ('I'm getting broody'). Charlotte has changed her mind about children: previously she didn't want any but now she would like two.

Optional activity

More about the Poveys

- You could ask further questions about the article to check comprehension and/or to practise scan reading. For example: *How many children have Sue and Ian Povey got? What's their youngest called? When did Sue know she wanted number 16? How old was Sue when she had her first child? How many girls and boys do they have? Do all their children live at home? How many children did Sue originally want? What did Ian initially think of this? What did all the children want to be the first to do? What was Sue's job? Has Sue got any brothers or sisters? How does Sue describe Ian? What will be 'the icing on the cake'?*

3

- Students find and underline sentences 1–6 in the article.
- Students work in pairs and discuss the meaning of the expressions in bold.
- Check the answers with the class.

Answers

1 having a very strong bond
2 join in to get jobs done
3 give all our time
4 actively participates
5 endures difficult situations without complaining
6 behaving in an unacceptable way, get very angry, stares at them in an annoyed way

4

- Students work in pairs and write their lists.
- Check the answers with the class.

Suggested answers

very positive: be close, devote your life to
positive: muck in, be hands on, suffer in silence
negative: be out of line, give somebody a look
very negative: lose your temper

5

- Students add the phrases to their lists from Ex.4. Advise them to use a dictionary to check the meanings.
- Note the pronunciation of *squabble*: /skwɒbl/.

Suggested answers

very positive: the patience of a saint, get on like a house on fire
positive: stick up for, give and take
negative: squabbling, nagging
very negative: resents, neglects

6

- Students discuss the questions in pairs or groups.
- Students report back to the class.

Optional activity

- Ask: *What does 'babyaholic' mean?* Explain that this is an invented word from the noun *alcoholic* (someone addicted to alcohol). Give examples of this form that are in common use: *workaholic, shopaholic, chocoholic.*
- Tell the students: *Make up three -aholic words to describe yourself.* Provide some examples: *I'd say I'm a footballaholic* or *I'm definitely an internetaholic.*
- Students discuss in pairs and then share their ideas with the class.

Speaking

1

- Read out the questions and check that students understand the meaning of *demographic*.
- Divide the class into groups to discuss the questions. They could choose one person to make notes.
- Each group joins up with another and the two groups compare opinions.
- Ask some students to report back on their group's ideas and invite class discussion.

Language study

Ellipsis and substitution

1

- Students read the sentences and identify the words in bold as either ellipsis or substitution.
- Check the answers with the class.

Answers

a 2, 3   b 1

2

- Tell students to look back to the earlier part of each sentence to decide what has been omitted or substituted.
- Check the answers with the class.
- Refer students to the Grammar reference on page 90 if necessary.

Answers
1 *doing so* substitutes for *giving birth*.
2 *have lots of brothers and sisters* has been omitted.
3 *have another baby* has been omitted.

3

- Students complete the task individually or in pairs.
- Check the answers with the class.
- Ask: *What has been omitted or substituted in each item?* (Answers are in brackets in the answer key below.)

Answers
1 to do so (*to remain together for life* has been substituted)
2 were (*involved in raising their children* has been omitted)
3 are doing so (*are getting married* has been substituted)
4 not to (*get married in their 20s* has been omitted)
5 do (*work while their children are growing up* has been omitted)

4

- Discuss the statements in Ex 3, with reference to the students' own country.
- Ask: *What other changes in attitudes to marriage and the family have there been in recent times?*

5

- Students complete the task, working individually or in pairs. Ask them to write down each answer.
- Check the answers with the class.

Answers
2 *buy a house* is omitted.
3 *did* substitutes for *got on the property ladder*.
4 *do so* substitutes for *get on the property ladder*.
5 *taken time out* is omitted.
6 *I wonder if we should've* is omitted
7 *to see a bit more of the world and be a bit more adventurous* is omitted.
8 *we might* is omitted.
9 *do* substitutes for *have freedom and spontaneity*.
10 *so* substitutes for *we've made the right choices*.
11 *do so* substitutes for *marry and have kids*.
12 *be buying* is omitted

Note
The text contains two other examples of ellipsis:
We got steady jobs and (we) bought a house …
We do plan to marry and (we plan to) have kids …

6

- Students discuss the questions in pairs or small groups.

Optional activity
Substitution with *so*
- Write the following expressions on the board:
  *I think so.   I don't think so.   I hope so.
  I suppose so.   I expect so.*
- Elicit the point that *so* substitutes for previous information. Give an example: *Are you going to the party? I hope so. (= I hope I'm going to the party.)*
- Students think of five questions to ask each other that might require some of the responses on the board. For example:
  A: *Are you doing anything at the weekend?*
  B: *I expect so, but I'm not sure what yet. I might …*
- In pairs, students answer each other's questions, using the expressions with *so*.

A social experiment

Listening and speaking

1

- Students look at the photos. Ask: *What do you think this place is?*
- Discuss the question with the class.

2

- 🔘 **02** Students listen and complete the task.
- Check the answers with the class. Ask students to give evidence for their answers.

Answers
art, common childcare and healthcare, common ownership of property, democracy, eco-friendly practices, independence from Danish laws, no cars, unconventional housing

Listening script 02
(P = presenter, R = reporter
P: Today on *Your Travel* Lisa Alexander reports on the colourful and controversial living community of Christiania in Copenhagen.
R: Copenhagen seems to epitomise the modern European capital and in many ways it does so. But in the Christianshavn district lies a different kind of place – a motley group of hippies, artists and misfits have founded a home that shuns order, rules and conformity. The 'freetown' of Christiania has been conducting a social experiment for more than 30 years. Fiercely independent-minded, the Christianite squatters have established their own holidays, government and rules. The Christianites were determined to create a place where they could create art, let their children play in overgrown nature and live out untraditional lifestyles – and they did. Strange houses were erected. Cars were banned, and ecological experiments with wind and solar power, garbage recycling and water treatment took place before the rest of the country had even heard of the green movement. A consensus democracy was formed, wherein no decision could be made without the agreement of all participants. There were no laws, only a few rules – paramount amongst

them the prohibition on buying and selling property. Even now, Christianites do not own their homes. They have a close community and place a heavy value on community programmes – feeding the homeless, creating their own kindergartens, playgrounds and clinics.

But many outside Christiania see the community as a scourge on the city, a group of drug-smoking criminals trespassing on public land and ignoring the laws the rest of Denmark have to obey. Liberal governments in the past adopted a hands-off policy but now the government is demanding changes. The dirt streets are to receive official names; buildings are to receive house numbers; and residents will have to register where they live. In their words, the government wants to 'normalise' the area.

Government officials claim the plan seeks to preserve the cultural uniqueness of the area, which attracts close to a million tourists a year, but private ownership of the land will need to be arranged. Christianites are demanding that a system of common ownership remains. In their eyes, all the things that have made the area so special are rooted in the unique way they administer the area and prohibit the buying and selling of homes.

No matter what the outcome of the negotiations, no amount of normalisation could ever make Christiania normal. Lawless, elitist and dirty? Or progressive, inventive and free? Whatever your opinion is of Copenhagen's most unique neighbourhood, it always leaves a lasting impression on visitors.

3

- Students work in pairs and discuss the questions.

Answers

1 They see Christianites as drug-smoking criminals who trespass on public land and ignore Danish law.
2 The government wanted to 'normalise' Christiania. This meant Christianites would have to register where they lived and accept private ownership of their land.
3 (individual answers)
4 (individual answers)

Vocabulary

1

- Students listen again and complete the sentences.
- Students check the answers in the listening script.

Answers

1 order; rules; conformity
2 a social experiment
3 their own holidays, government and rules
4 on public land; the laws
5 a hands-off policy
6 where they live
7 the cultural uniqueness of the area
8 the area; buying and selling of homes

2

- Elicit a few ideas as examples for topics 1–4.
- Students brainstorm ideas and make notes.

3

- Students use their notes to write their advert.

4

- Groups exchange adverts. They read and discuss each advert they receive, and then give feedback to the group who wrote it.

Revision activity

... but I didn't

- Write these sentence endings on the board:
  1 ... but I wish I could.
  2 ... but I've decided not to.
  3 ... but I wish I had.
  4 ... but I wish I hadn't.
  5 ... but I didn't in the end.
  6 ... but I'll never do so again.
  7 ... but I haven't done so for ages.
  8 ... but I'd like to one day.
- Students complete the sentences to make true statements.
- Students read their sentences to each other. Encourage them to ask questions to find out more.
- Students report back one interesting fact from their discussions.

Extra practice

Students complete the Extra practice material on page 86, either in class or for homework.

Extra practice answers

1 1 muck   2 silence   3 temper, line, look   4 hands

2 2 of babies
   3 proportions of births outside marriage are found
   4 of households
   5 of households have
   6 children
   7 of single parent households
   8 marriage rate
   9 divorce rates

3 (individual answers)

4 1 learn from the experience of others
   2 produced immortal works
   3 thinking about his troubles

5 1 adopt   2 conduct   3 establish   4 prohibit
   5 preserve   6 register

References

Grammar reference: Coursebook page 90
Wordlist: Coursebook page 92
Photocopiable resources: Teacher's Book pages 104–105
Test: Teacher's Book pages 143–144

CD-ROM

Unit 1 Living together
Language exercise: Perfect harmony?
Vocabulary activity: Happy families
CEF-linked activity: I can discuss the aims of non-traditional communities
Game: Cats in hats (community organisation)

Talk talk

Topic	Language study	Vocabulary	Main skills
• World languages (Are fewer languages better?) • Language learning (attitudes to learning English and other foreign languages)	• Forming adjectives from verbs and nouns (adjective suffixes)	• Sensitive language (euphemisms)	• **Reading:** predicting; understanding main information and vocabulary in context • **Speaking:** evaluating the cultural and practical value of languages; using sensitive language and softeners to avoid offence • **Listening:** identifying key information • **Pronunciation:** sentence stress

Learning aims

- Can form adjectives from verbs and nouns using suffixes
- Can evaluate the cultural and practical value of languages
- Can use sensitive language and softeners to avoid offence

Warmer

- Ask students: *What are some of your favourite words in English, and why?* Elicit some ideas.
- Give students the list below. It is the top ten favourite words chosen by non-native English speakers in a British Council survey in 2004.

1 *mother*	2 *passion*	3 *smile*	4 *love*
5 *eternity*	6 *fantastic*	7 *destiny*	8 *freedom*
9 *liberty*	10 *tranquillity*		

World languages

Lead-in

Note

If you have internet access, students could research their own language by visiting http://www.ethnologue.com.

1

- Students look at the photo. Ask: *What's going on? How effectively do you think the people are communicating?*
- Students discuss the questions in pairs. In a multilingual class, organise the pairs where possible so that students have a different native language from their partner.
- Students share their ideas with the class.

Reading and speaking

1

- Discuss the question with the class.
- Students find the answer in the text.

Answer

About 6,000 according to the article. (3,000 languages are endangered, which represents 'half the world's languages'.)

2

- 🎧 **03** Students read the article and complete the task. They can listen to the article on CD.
- Check the answers with the class.

Answers

a 6   b 7   c 4   d 1   e 3   f 5   g 2

Optional activity

More questions

- You could ask further questions about the article to check comprehension and/or practise scan reading. For example: *How old is Marie Smith-Jones? Where does she live? What language does she speak? How does Unesco describe language extinction? What was the situation 10,000 years ago? What role does modern technology play in the decrease in the number of languages? What promotes linguistic diversity? How many people are needed to sustain a language? Which country has the most languages and how many? How does Unesco describe this country? Why? What does David Crystal say about the connection between language and biology? Does the writer of the article feel that dying languages can easily be saved?*

3

- Ask: *Which languages are spoken less than they used to be? Think about both minority languages and major languages.* Discuss this and the other questions with the class. Alternatively, students can discuss in pairs or groups before reporting back to the class.
- Make a list of languages on the board and ask students to decide which of these are in danger of extinction.

4

- Ask: *What steps can be taken to revive a language that seems to be dying?* Examples could include teaching the language or using it as the medium for learning other subjects in schools, encouraging parents to speak it at home, using it in the media, creating a computer interface for the language, promoting its literary / musical heritage, etc.
- Read out the questions and discuss them with the class.

Vocabulary

1

- Discuss the questions with the class. Explain that an expression like *pass away* is called a *euphemism*. Help with the pronunciation: /'juːfəmɪzm/.

Answers

pass away and *fall silent* = die
They are used to soften or distance a reality that is painful or unpleasant.

Note

Although in this context *fall silent* implies 'die', it is generally used more literally to mean 'stop speaking / stop making noise', for example: *The crowd fell silent as he stepped up to take the penalty*.

2

- Look at the example with the class and check that students understand the task. Explain the meaning of *tipple* (an alcoholic drink that you drink regularly).
- Students work in pairs and complete the task. Encourage them to think about whether any of the expressions have equivalents in their own language.
- Check the answers with the class.

Answers

1 He's fairly old.
2 She's mean.
3 His shoes are old / in a bad condition.
4 I need to use the toilet.
5 She's fat.
6 They're poor.
7 She's unemployed.
8 He drinks a lot / too much.

Note

Point out that euphemisms should be used with caution. Some may be seen as trivialising a serious issue (eg *He likes a tipple*) while others can be perceived to be almost as blunt as the more direct phrase they are replacing (eg *She's on the large side*). To avoid causing offence, the best advice is for speakers to use euphemisms only if they are 100% confident that they are using them appropriately.

3

- Students match the words with the euphemisms.
- Check the answers with the class. Note that these particular expressions are generally not used seriously, but are tongue-in-cheek, often used to poke fun at 'political correctness'. Ask if there are any similar euphemisms in the students' language.

Answers

bald – hair disadvantaged   short – vertically challenged
dishonest – morally different   stupid – mentally challenged
lazy – motivationally deficient

4

- Elicit from the students some areas where euphemisms are often used. Ask if they can think of any English euphemisms in these areas. If they need help with ideas, you could do the optional activity below.
- Elicit euphemisms in the students' language. If you have a mixed-nationality class, you can compare euphemisms from different countries.

Optional activity

- Write some or all of the following euphemisms in random order on the board. Ask: *What do you think they are euphemisms for? Put them into groups.*
  no spring chicken, a senior citizen, in her golden years (old)
  chubby, cuddly, big-boned, full-figured (fat)
  spend a penny, powder my nose, go to the loo / john / restroom (use the toilet)
  pass on, check out, bite the dust (die)
  dispatch, take out, bump off (kill)
- Check the answers (in brackets above). Ask: *Can you add any more euphemisms to each group?*

Language study

Forming adjectives from verbs and nouns (adjective suffixes)

Note

The main focus of the language study is the formation of adjectives from nouns and verbs using *-able*. It also looks at using the suffixes *-y*, *-ful*, *-ish* and *-ous* to form adjectives from nouns.

1

- Read the question with the students and check that they understand the two different uses of the suffix *-able*.
- Students complete the task.
- Check the answers with the class. Explain that *unspeakable* means 'really terrible' – the idea is that the thing described is too awful to be spoken about.

Answers

a 1, 2, 3, 6   b 4, 5

2

- Discuss the questions with the class.
- Elicit some general rules (eg *ir-* before words beginning with *r*) about the use of the negative prefixes *-ir*, *-il* and *-im*. See the Grammar reference on page 90.
- Refer students to the Grammar reference if necessary.

Answers

un- (extract 2), *ir-* (extracts 1 and 3)
Other negative prefixes for adjectives: *in-, non-, il-, im-*
(Note that *dis-* is also commonly used as a prefix, but rarely with adjectives ending in *-able*.)

3

- Look at the words in the box. Remind students that they will normally (but not always) need to drop a final *e* before adding *-able*. Also point out that the adjective form may be irregular (eg *appreciate / appreciable* – not *appreciatable*; *reputation / reputable* – not *reputationable*). Advise students to use a dictionary.
- Students complete the task individually or in pairs.
- Check the answers with the class. Check the word stress of the adjectives (underlined in the answer key below) and their meaning (those which are less straightforward have the meaning in brackets in the key).
- Note the meaning of *invaluable*. Students may think this means 'not valuable', whereas in fact it means the opposite: 'so important that you can't put a value on it'.
- Ask: *Do you agree with the statements in Exercise 3?*

Answers
1 inescapable
2 invaluable (extremely valuable), sizeable (large)
3 appreciable (will be noticed and considered important)
4 advisable, reputable
5 downloadable

4

- Students complete the task individually or in pairs.
- Check the answers with the class. Check the word stress (underlined in the key below) and draw attention to the irregular form of *explain / inexplicable*.

Answers
1 It was unstoppable.
2 It's justifiable in some cases.
3 It's incurable.
4 It's irreplaceable.
5 It's difficult, but it's doable.
6 It's inexplicable.

5

- Students work in pairs and complete the task. You could give or elicit one or two examples first, for example: *The feeling you get when you do a bungee jump is indescribable.*
- Ask students to share their ideas with the class.

6

- Read the instruction with the class. Tell the students: *There are no simple rules to help you decide which nouns take which suffixes. You have to learn each one individually.*
- Students write the adjectives in the table. Encourage them to use dictionaries.
- Check the answers. Give particular attention to the meaning of *sluggish* (very slow) and *sheepish* (ashamed or embarrassed about something you have done).
- Ask: *In which nouns do we double the final letter when forming the adjective?* (snobbish, sluggish), *In which ones do we drop the final 'e'?* (stylish, adventurous, famous), *Which adjective has an irregular form?* (numerous).

Answers
1 colourful, careful, meaningful, useful, thoughtful, harmful
2 childish, snobbish, sluggish, sheepish, stylish, foolish
3 rocky, dusty, misty, rainy, salty, roomy, mood, hairy
4 adventurous, dangerous, famous, numerous, advantageous

7

- You could elicit one or two examples for the table, for example: *cloudy, helpful, selfish, disastrous*.
- Students work in pairs and add more adjectives to the table. Encourage them to use dictionaries to check.
- Ask students to give their answers and build up lists on the board.

Optional activities

1 **Five-minute adjective game**
- Students work in pairs. They take turns to choose an adjective from the table for their partner, who has 20 seconds to talk about a person, place or thing using that adjective. For example:
  A: *Knowledgeable.*
  B: *My brother is the most knowledgeable person I know when it comes to computers and the Internet.*
- Students score 1 point for making a correct sentence within the time limit. The person with the most points after five minutes is the winner.

2 ***-ible* adjectives**
- Tell students that some adjectives can end in *-ible* and write the following on the board:
  visible   legible   audible   edible   tangible   credible
- Ask: *What do the adjectives mean? What are the negative forms?*

Answers
visible = you can see it. Negative: *invisible*
legible = you can read it. Negative: *illegible*
audible = you can hear it. Negative: *inaudible*
edible = you can eat it. Negative: *inedible*
tangible = you can touch it. Negative: *intangible*
credible = you can believe it. No negative prefix (we say *not credible*)

- Tell the students: *Name something that can be described by each of the adjectives, both the affirmative and the negative form.*

Language learning

Listening

1
- Students look at the comments in speech bubbles. Ask: *Does either of these comments apply to you?*
- Discuss the question with the class.

2

- ⊙ **04** Read the dictionary definition for *lingua franca* with the students and check that they understand the meaning. Ask: *Apart from English, what other languages are likely to be used as a lingua franca in different parts of the world?*
- Students look at the photos. Ask: *Where do you think these students are from?*
- Students listen to the recording and complete the task by making notes. They can compare their notes with a partner.
- Check the answers with the class.

Answers

Tatyana
Motivation: She thinks you can't get a good job without English.
Attitude: People have to accept that English as the *lingua franca* – it's unavoidable.

Lars
Motivation: In his job he needs English to communicate with people who speak different languages.
Attitude: It's sad that other languages are dying out but it's practical to have a *lingua franca* that breaks down obstacles to communication.

Paolo
Motivation: He needs English for his job, and he also enjoys learning languages.
Attitude: Knowledge of English is essential now, but it would be better if everybody spoke more foreign languages. Native English speakers are imposing their values on other people through their language.

Listening script 04
(T = Tatyana, L = Lars, P = Paolo)

T: My name's Tatyana, I'm from Russia and I've been learning English in Oxford for about a year now. I'm planning to study international business and administration at an English university. I think it's difficult to get a good job without English – English is the world's *lingua franca*. I realise that some people don't like that, but under the circumstances, I tend to think it's unavoidable. I can't get a good job in my country if I don't learn English. Perhaps all countries should teach children English when they are small, so they find it easy to learn. I found English easy to learn at first, but then it got harder because the tenses are so difficult.

L: My name's Lars and I'm from Germany. I'm doing a summer course in Oxford and I'm, er, very lucky because my company – I work for an engineering company – is paying for it. I work in the foreign trade department. We sell machine parts to countries all over the world and I have to go to trade fairs and be able to communicate with people who speak different languages. I have to negotiate deals and also talk to people socially in restaurants and things like that. Sometimes I can use German but usually we speak English to our customers. In a way I think it's sad that English has become a *lingua franca* and that other languages, you know, are dying out because English is getting more important. But on the other

hand, it's practical to have one language you can speak wherever you go. English is breaking down a lot of obstacles to communication. I suppose you can say that English doesn't belong to certain countries any more. It's just everybody's world language.

P: My name's Paolo. I work in an export company in Brazil and I need English for my job, so I'm trying to improve it now. I love learning English. I spend all my free time trying to get better. I watch films in English and go to the pub and talk to people. It's really interesting to meet so many different people and just talk to them. I listen to a lot of music in English too. Often I can't understand the lyrics, but I like the sound of the language. I've got a bit of a problem with English as a *lingua franca*. I know English is important, at any rate you can't get by without it nowadays, but I sort of think it would be better if everybody learnt more foreign languages. Native speakers of English are quite arrogant. They think they don't need to speak anybody else's language. They're kind of imposing their way of life and their view of the world on other people through their language, and a lot of people oppose that.

3
- Discuss the question with the class. Alternatively, students can discuss this in pairs or groups before reporting back to the class.

Speaking and pronunciation

1
- Check that students understand the task. Ask: *Can you remember any of the 'softeners' used by Tatyana, Lars and Paolo?*
- Students listen again and complete the extracts. They can compare their answers with a partner.

2
- Students check the answers to Ex 1 in the listening script.
- Find the extracts on recording 04. Students listen for and underline the stressed words.
- Check the answers with the class and check which of the 'softeners' have words that are stressed.

Answers
Tatyana
I realise some people don't <u>like</u> that, but under the <u>circumstances</u>, I tend to think it's <u>unavoidable</u>.
Perhaps <u>all</u> countries should teach children English when they are <u>small</u>, so they find it easy to <u>learn</u>.

Lars
In a <u>way</u> I think it's <u>sad</u> that English has become a *lingua franca* and that <u>other</u> languages are, you know, <u>dying out</u> because English is getting more <u>important</u>. On the <u>other</u> hand, it's <u>practical</u> to have one language you can speak <u>wherever</u> you go.
I suppose you can say that English doesn't <u>belong</u> to certain countries anymore, it's just <u>everybody's</u> world language.

> **Paolo**
>
> I've got a bit of a <u>problem</u> with <u>English</u> as a *lingua franca*. I know English is <u>important</u>, at <u>any</u> rate you can't get by <u>without</u> it nowadays, but I sort of think it would be <u>better</u> if <u>everybody</u> learnt <u>more</u> foreign languages.
> But they're kind of imposing <u>their</u> way of life and <u>their</u> view of the world on other people through their <u>language</u> and a lot of people <u>oppose</u> that.
>
> Softeners that are stressed: under the <u>circumstances</u>, In a <u>way</u>, On the <u>other</u> hand, at <u>any</u> rate

3

> **Note**
> Due to the sensitive nature of these role-plays, make sure that everyone in the class will respond positively before you do this activity.

- Students work in pairs. Ask them each to turn to their page, and read through the instructions (but not the actual roles) with them. Make it clear that they each have two role cards for two separate role-plays.
- Students read their own role cards and prepare what they are going to say in each situation. Encourage them to use appropriate euphemisms from page 70 and 'softeners' from page 73.
- Students role-play the two conversations with their partner.
- Ask some pairs to perform one of their role-plays for the class.

> **Revision activity**
>
> **Only one**
> - Students play in teams of two to four.
> - Tell the students: *Write down something or someone well known that can be described by the following. You get one point for each correct answer, but only if you are the only team to give that answer. You don't get a point if two or more teams have the same answer.*
> - Read out the following items, allowing students time to discuss and write their answers.
>   1 *a person who is or was unstoppable*
>   2 *a body part which is irreplaceable*
>   3 *something which is unpredictable*
>   4 *something in life which is unavoidable*
>   5 *something it is advisable to do every day*
>   6 *a company which is extremely reputable*
>   7 *a disease which is incurable*
>   8 *a phenomenon which is inexplicable*
>   9 *something in your school which is colourful*
>   10 *something advantageous in life*
>   11 *something which is sluggish*
>   12 *a car which is roomy*
> - Check the answers with the class. Give a point for each appropriate unique answer. The team with the most points is the winner.

Extra practice

- Students complete the Extra practice material on page 87, either in class or for homework.

Extra practice answers

1
1 careful with money
2 getting on a bit
3 on a low income
4 on the large side
5 has seen better days
6 likes a tipple

2
2 questionable   3 understandable   4 irreplaceable
5 laughable   6 knowledgeable   7 changeable
8 admirable

3
1 unthinkable   2 invaluable   3 watchable
4 recognisable   5 unstoppable   6 unspeakable
7 preventable, questionable
8 sizeable, unacceptable, inexcusable, reputable

4 Suggested answers:
2 a pop group
3 a film / TV programme / play
4 a celebrity / world leader
5 a tennis match
6 a film / play
7 a terrorist attack
8 illegal football transfer payments

5
2 childish   3 harmful   4 careful   5 advantageous
6 harmful   7 dusty   8 misty   9 meaningful
10 foolish   11 hairy   12 snobbish   13 moody
14 rocky

6 1 dangerous   2 sluggish   3 thoughtful   4 roomy

References

Grammar reference: Coursebook page 90
Wordlist: Coursebook page 92
Photocopiable resources: Teacher's Book pages 106–107
Test: Teacher's Book pages 145–146

CD-ROM

Unit 2 Talk talk
Language exercise: A world language
Vocabulary activity: Responses to euphemisms
CEF-linked activity: I can form adjectives from verbs and nouns using suffixes
Game: Crossword (adjectives)

Net value

Topic	Language study	Vocabulary	Main skills
• Is the Internet a good thing? • Are you addicted to email? (survey report)	• Using vague language	• Phrasal verbs: communication • Surveys	• **Listening:** understanding gist and key information; understanding vocabulary in context • **Speaking:** discussing the Internet; clarifying information and checking understanding; talking about email addiction; conducting a survey • **Pronunciation:** stress and weak forms • **Reading:** understanding key information • **Writing:** a survey report

Learning aims
- Can use vague language in informal communication
- Can evaluate the importance and dangers of electronic media
- Can clarify information and check understanding

Ideas for preparation
- Newspaper / magazine / internet articles of surveys (see Optional activity p78)

Warmer
- Ask: *What do you know about the history of the Internet?* Brainstorm a few ideas with the class.
- Write these lists on the board and ask students to match the 'internet firsts' with their dates.

  1 *www* 2 *music file sharing* 3 *email*
  4 *half a billion regular users* 5 *domain names*
  6 *online retail ordering* 7 *Google*

  a *1972* b *1983* c *1993* d *1994* e *1998*
  f *1999* g *2003*

Answers
1 c 2 f 3 a 4 g 5 b 6 d 7 e

Lead-in

1
- Students work in pairs and discuss the questions.
- Students report back to the class. How similar or different are their internet habits?

Is the Internet a good thing?

Listening and speaking

1
- Look at the photos and discuss the question with the class. <u>Alternatively</u>, students can discuss this in pairs or groups before reporting back to the class.

2

Background information
Nineteen Eighty-Four is a novel, first published in 1949, written by the English writer Eric Blair (1903–1950) under his pen-name George Orwell. The book tells the story of Winston Smith and his attempt to rebel against the totalitarian state in which he lives and which regulates and censors nearly every aspect of public and private behaviour, even people's thoughts. The state is led by Big Brother.

- 🔊 **05** Students listen to the adverts. They note down key words that illustrate what each photo represents and check their answers to Ex 1.
- Write the name *Orwell* on the board and ask: *Do you know anything about George Orwell?* Elicit or supply some information about Orwell's vision of the future in the novel *Nineteen Eighty-Four*.

Listening script 05
Some people think the Internet is a good thing.
The most powerful educational tool the world has ever known. It's preserving our history, making sure that in the future we never forget the past.
The Internet is a place that is free from state intervention, censorship and control. The only place where freedom of speech truly exists.
Orwell was wrong. It is not the state that holds all the power. It is us.
Some people think the Internet is a good thing.
What do you think?

Some people think the Internet is a bad thing.
Somewhere your identity can be stolen, your home invaded and your savings robbed without anyone setting foot inside your door.
It is one of the most dangerous weapons ever created. A way for the unhinged to spread evil, free of supervision or censorship.
A place for mankind to exercise its darkest desires.
An open market where you can purchase anything you want.
Orwell was right. The Internet has taken us to a place where everything we do is watched, monitored and processed without us ever realising.
Some people think the Internet is a bad thing.
What do you think?

3

● Students listen again and make further notes on the arguments put forward by each advert.

Suggested answers
Is the Internet a good thing?
Freedom of speech, freedom from state intervention, censorship, control – people have power.
Preserving our history so we never forget the past.
A powerful educational tool.

Is the Internet a bad thing?
Everything is watched, monitored, processed.
An open market, you can purchase anything you want, people can exercise dark desires.
Your identity can be stolen, your home invaded, your savings robbed.

4

● Divide the class into two groups or, for larger classes, into pairs of groups.
● Read the instructions with the class and check that students understand the task. Allow them plenty of time to prepare their arguments.
● Students hold their debate(s). At the end, the class can vote on whether the Internet is a good or bad thing.

Listening and vocabulary

1

● ◉ 06 Students listen and make notes summarising the views of the speakers.
● Check the answers with the class.

Suggested answers
Layla finds the Internet useful for downloading music and shopping and she values the access to information. She thinks that on balance the Internet is a good thing although she recognises that there are risks. She believes it gives poor countries a way of making their problems known and leads to increased cooperation and tolerance.

Graham is sceptical about the value of the Internet. He thinks a lot of the information is useless or unreliable and he is worried about security risks. He is concerned about the domination of the Internet by English speakers and he feels that internet communication is impersonal.

Listening script 06
(G = Graham, L = Layla)
G: Have you seen those ads for the Internet? You know the ones about whether the Internet is a good or bad thing?
L: Oh yeah, they're clever, very dramatic. They really get the message across.
G: Yes, they are good, but I couldn't figure out what it was all about at first. Isn't it a bit strange for an internet company to be questioning its own product?
L: They've got everybody talking, though. I think most people will say the Internet is a good thing, on balance. All that information and stuff, and it's free! The Internet's, like, a part of life now. I can't imagine not having the Internet for downloading music, shopping and whatever.

G: Yeah, there's lots of information, as you point out, but how much of that is useable? The Net's like a huge rubbish dump, anybody can chuck things in there. You can search forever and you never know how accurate things are, things disappear as soon as they're not news ... and what do you mean by 'it's free'? All the articles I've tried to access recently had to be paid for. Give me a decent library any day!
L: So in other words, you'd rather live in the good old days. Come off it!
G: Well, what about credit card fraud and identity theft and that sort of thing? Do you know what I mean? Don't you worry about things like that?
L: Not really. If people want to, er ... if they want to take you for a ride, they'll always find a way, they don't need the Internet to do it. What it boils down to is being careful. You can't stop using something because it has a couple of risks.
G: Yeah, fair enough but, er ... so you're not really bothered about the risks?
L: No, what I'm getting at is that it isn't an open-and-shut case but the pros definitely outweigh the cons.
G: I'm not sure you're right there. I mean you were on about music and shopping. Yeah, great but there are so many other aspects. Information equals power nowadays, it's the key to everything – information society and all that. Are you with me? Most of the Internet is dominated by English-speaking websites and American companies. I think I read that 75% or so of websites are in English and ...
L: Not true. It's 50%, or 50-ish anyway. People are waking up to the fact that customers want websites in their own language ... And the Internet actually helps countries that ... er, countries with few resources because it gives them, you know, a kind of platform to make their problems known, and that, well that can lead to increased cooperation and tolerance between countries.
G: Yeah, that's the rose-tinted view, the Internet strengthens social bonds and all that. But the reality is the Net alienates people. What I mean is, look how many people send emails instead of using the phone. It's so impersonal.
L: Ah, but you can always telephone over the Internet with video. That's even better than the phone!
G: OK, OK ... why did I start this?

2

● Students work in pairs and answer the questions.

3

● Students listen again and check their answers in Ex 2.
● Check the answers with the class.

Answers
1 She thinks they are clever and dramatic and convey their message well. She says everyone is talking about them.
2 He thought it was strange for an internet company to question its own product.
3 He talks about the fact that searches can take a long time, that a great deal of the material is rubbish and that you often have to pay for the information you want.
4 She says the most important thing is being careful and being prepared to take some risks.
5 She says the advantages outweigh the disadvantages.
6 He was saying that information technology is power – but it gives power to certain parts of the world's population, not everyone.

4
- Students complete the matching task and discuss the question.
- Check the answers with the class.

Answers
1 convey   2 understand   3 focus on   4 amount to
5 talking about   6 trying to say
The original sentences contain phrasal verbs, which are more informal than the ones in the box.

5
- Students complete the sentences with their own ideas. You could model the first one or two to help clarify the task.
- Explain that the phrase *always on about* is normally used when you are being critical or negative about someone. For example, *He's always on about how much he earns* – this implies that he's boring and tiresome on the subject.
- In pairs, students read their sentences to each other. Encourage them to comment on and discuss each other's ideas.

Optional activity

More phrasal verbs
- Write the following phrasal verbs (without the meanings in brackets) on the board:
  talk through (discuss in a detailed way)
  bring up (introduce an idea)   *sort out* (solve)
  look into (investigate)   *see through* (see the truth)
  rule out (stop considering something as a possibility)
  put forward (suggest, propose)   *think over* (consider)
- Tell students: *The verbs are all connected with discussion.* Ask them to work in pairs and discuss what the verbs mean.
- Students think about some recent news stories and prepare one-sentence summaries of them using some of the phrasal verbs. For example: *Senior police officers and ministers met yesterday to **talk through** the latest terrorist threat.*
- As a class or in groups, students read out their summaries and discuss what they know about the news stories.

Speaking and pronunciation

1
- Check that students understand the difference between the three categories in the table.
- Students put the phrases in the table.

2
- Students add the new phrases to the table.

3
- 07 Students listen and check their answers.
- They listen again and repeat after each phrase. Give special attention to weak forms and stress (syllables with the main stress are underlined in the key below).

Answers and listening script
Speaker clarification
What I'm getting at is ...
What I mean is ...
I suppose I'm really saying ...
To put it a different way ...

Speaker checking
Do you know what I mean?
Are you with me?
Do you follow?
Do you get me?

Listener checking
What do you mean by ...?
In other words, you ...
If I've understood you correctly, ...
So what you're trying to say is ...

4
- Read through the instructions and check that students understand the topics in the box.
- Students choose three topics and note down their opinion about each.
- In pairs, they take it in turns to state their opinions and to respond. Encourage them to use appropriate phrases to clarify and check understanding.
- Ask some students to give their opinions to the class and invite discussion of the topics.

Language study
Using vague language

Note
The language study presents phrases that can be used to express a vague idea to add to what has been said, or to make an approximation.

1
- Discuss the function of the phrases with the class. Elicit or explain the following points:
  - *and stuff, and whatever, and that sort of thing* and *and all that* are added on to specific information, and all express the idea 'and other similar things'.
  - *whatever* expresses 'it doesn't matter what'.
  - *a kind of* (or *a sort of*) comes before a noun and expresses 'something similar to'.
  - the suffix *-ish*, meaning 'approximately', can be added to numbers and also some adjectives (eg *biggish, brownish*).
- Ask students: *Do you have phrases like this in your language?*
- Refer them to the Grammar reference on page 91 if necessary.

Answers

The phrases in extracts 1, 2, 3, 6 and 7 are ways of being vague and express the idea of 'similarity'.
The phrase in extract 4 and the suffix -ish in extract 5 are ways of approximating.

2

- Students work individually or in pairs and add the phrases to the sentences.
- Check the answers with the class.
- Ask: *Which of the sentences reflect your own opinions?* Students discuss this in pairs and report back to the class.

Answers

1 When you're chatting or sending emails *or whatever*, …
2 The danger of the Net is that you can become trapped in a *kind of* vicious cycle …
3 Sites such as ebay *and the like* are just fantastic.
4 … jokes, quizzes, funny pictures *and that sort of thing*.
5 It's just the best thing ever – information, people, gaming, music, shopping *and so on* …
6 It's made the Net a *sort of* global music collection – you think of a song and two minutes later *or however long* it's on your MP3 player *or whatever*.

3

- Look at the example and check students understand the function of *wherever* (= it doesn't matter where). Brainstorm other words that can be formed with -*ever*, such as *whoever, whenever*, etc.
- Students complete the task individually or in pairs.
- Check the answers with the class.

Answers

1 whatever   2 wherever   3 whoever   4 whenever
5 whatever

4

- Ask the question and invite different students to respond.

Optional activity

whatever
- Write the following on the board:
   … , *whatever*.   … , *whoever*.   … , *whenever*.
   … , *wherever*.
- Students complete the first part of each sentence, for example: *We can stay here, go for a coffee, have lunch, whatever.* They compare their ideas in pairs or groups and report back to the class.

5

- Read the instructions with the class.
- Look at the phrases in the box. Explain that most of them mean 'approximately' – the actual figure could be higher or lower. However, the phrase *getting on for* means 'almost'.

- Students prepare a few questions, then ask and answer in small groups.

Reading and vocabulary

1
- Students look at the title and discuss the question.

2
- Students work in pairs. They read the article and discuss what the missing figures might be.

3
- 08 Students check the answers on page 96, or they can listen to the complete article on CD. Ask: *Which findings surprised you the most?*

Answers

1	two or three	5	About a quarter
2	an hour	6	60%
3	41%	7	About half (45%)
4	five times	8	43%

4
- Write the answers from Ex 3 on the board and add the examples in Ex 4.
- Brainstorm other phrases with the class and add them to the list on the board. For example:
   the (vast, overwhelming) majority   a minority
   33%   one in three   a third   three times as many
   +   more than   (just) over   five times   in excess of
   −   less than   (just) under   almost   getting on for
   +/−   approximately   roughly   in the region of

Optional activities

1 **Survey search**
- Give the students copies of other newspaper, magazine or internet articles which report surveys. Ask them to find words / phrases similar to those in Exs 3 and 4. Add these to the list in Ex 4.

2 **What can you see?**
- Tell the students: *Look around you and give some statistics using phrases in Ex 4.* For example: *There are **more than** 20 cars in the car park and **roughly one in three** is red. I'm **just over** 1.6 metres tall. It's **getting on for** 11.30.*

5
- Students work in pairs. They look at the words in their context in the article and decide on their meaning.

Answers

1 addicted to   2 carried out (a survey)   3 ordinary
4 people who answer questions for a survey   5 get back
6 follow

6
- Students work in pairs and discuss the questions.
- Ask some students to report back what their partner told them.

Speaking and writing

1
- Tell the class: *You are going to conduct your own survey about addiction.* Read through the procedure (1–5) with the students and check that they understand the task.
- Students work in groups and decide on a topic for their survey.

2
- Groups prepare their survey questions.

3
- The members of each group agree on who they are going to interview.
- They conduct the survey, writing down the answers.

4
- Students return to their groups. They pool their results and write up their findings. Encourage them to use language from the Reading and vocabulary exercises.

5
- One or more members of each group read out their reports. Invite comments or questions from the rest of the class.
- Have a class vote on the most interesting report.

Revision activities

1 Approximation quiz
- Students work individually or in teams. Ask the following questions and students write down the answers.
- Check the answers (in brackets below). Students get one point if the answer is close (at your discretion) and a bonus point if they use an appropriate approximation phrase, for example *or so, more or less, in the region of* etc. The winner is the student / team with the most points out of a possible 20.
  1 *How many countries are there in the world?* (192)
  2 *How high is Mount Everest?* (8,850 m)
  3 *In what year was the Empire State Building opened?* (1931)
  4 *How far is the moon from the earth?* (384,402 km)
  5 *What is the diameter of the earth?* (12,756 km)
  6 *What is the average life expectancy of a British female?* (78)
  7 *How tall was Robert Wadlow, the tallest person ever?* (2.72 m)
  8 *What is the highest total of languages spoken fluently by one person?* (32)
  9 *How long is the Nile?* (6,695 km)
  10 *How many phone calls does the average American make each year?* (1,140)

2 Vague chains
- Students can play this game as a whole class or in small groups. Write the following on the board: *I love … and that sort of thing.* Ask a student to complete the sentence and say it to the class, for example: *I love clubbing and that sort of thing.*

- The next student then adds something else to the sentence so that it makes sense, for example: *I love clubbing, going to parties and that sort of thing.*
- The chain continues until a student cannot think of anything appropriate to add.
- Then start a new chain using any of the following: *I'm interested in …and all that. I like listening to … and the like. I don't like … and stuff.*

Extra practice
Students complete the Extra practice material on page 88, either in class or for homework.

Extra practice answers

1 1 point out   2 figure out, were on about
3 get across, boils down to

2 2 a   3 e   4 d   5 b   6 h   7 f   8 g   9 j
10 i

3 speaker: 4, 6, 7, 8, 9   listener: 2, 3, 5, 10

4 1 whatever   2 wherever   3 however / whatever
4 whoever   5 whenever   6 whatever

5 1 She said I needed some **sort of** 'unzipper' program and emailed it to me, but I just don't know what I'm doing with this **kind of thing**.
2 Most of the time it's sorting out error messages **and the like**. It's just the **kind of** challenge I really enjoy.
3 You're welcome to come and stay one or two nights **or whatever** anytime you like. We've got a **sort of** spare room-cum-study you can stay in.
4 … watching all my old favourite DVDs, you know, 101 Best World Cup goals, 101 Funniest TV moments **and that sort of thing**. You should come round **sometime** before she's back.

6 (individual answers)

References
Grammar reference: Coursebook page 91
Wordlist: Coursebook page 92
Photocopiable resources: Teacher's Book pages 108–109
Test: Teacher's Book pages 147–148

CD-ROM
Unit 3 Net value
Language exercise: World wide wait
Vocabulary activity: The joys of email
Vocabulary activity: I can clarify information and check understanding
Game: Neighbourhood (clarifying, checking and vague language)

UNIT 4
Team spirit

Topic	Language study	Vocabulary	Main skills
• Team building • Are you a team player?	• Dependent prepositions	• World of work	• **Reading:** predicting information; checking key information and vocabulary in context • **Speaking:** discussing work practices and leadership styles; describing college- or work-related problems and giving advice • **Listening:** identifying key information; understanding vocabulary in context • **Writing:** a programme script

Learning aims
- Can use dependent prepositions with verbs, nouns and adjectives
- Can discuss work practices and leadership styles
- Can describe college- or work-related problems and give advice to others

Warmer
- Write the following on the board:
  well-paid   badly paid   varied   repetitive   dangerous   worthwhile
- Divide the students into groups and ask them to write down two or three jobs for each adjective.
- Students report back to the class and write the jobs on the board.

Lead-in
- Discuss the questions with the class.

Team building

Reading

1
- Students look at the photos and discuss the questions.

Suggested answers
They are taking part in team-building activities.
These are designed to help employees get to know and bond with each other. Companies are prepared to pay for this because they believe it improves employees' motivation and performance, which in turn is good for the business.

2
- 09 Students read the article and then work with a partner to decide if the statements are true or false. Ask them to underline the parts of the text that give the answers. They can listen to the article on CD.
- Check the meaning of *not be seen dead with* (emphasises that you wouldn't normally associate with someone), *bargain for* (expect), *a tight ship* (an efficiently run organisation), *eclectic* (varied), *a knees-up* (a fun time / party), *tandem bike* (a bicycle for two people).

Answers
1 True ('folks you may never be seen dead with')
2 False ('the annual team-building event')
3 False (this image is 'outdated', management 'has to show a return on the investment')
4 True ('the employee's responsibility to ... contribute proactively')
5 True (Caroline Barber 'suggests leaving their preconceptions at the door')
6 False ('increasingly innovative programmes')
7 True ('an all-expenses trip')
8 False (on Joe Thorne's trip, 'the buzz, the memories and the experience lasted for months')

Vocabulary and speaking

1
- Students work in pairs and work out the meanings of the words / phrases. Encourage them to look at the context in which the phrases occur.
- Check the answers with the class.

Answers
1 force oneself to deal with the challenge
2 use skills
3 be receptive to different possibilities
4 take part in tasks
5 attempt to deal with problems
6 improve performance
7 learn to give work or responsibility to other people
8 acquire feelings of trust and friendship among team members

2
- Students work individually or in pairs and complete the sentences. Point out that they will need to change the form of some of the verbs.
- Check the answers with the class.

Answers
1 with an open mind
2 bonded
3 participated
4 utilise
5 tackle
6 delegates
7 faced up to
8 enhanced

3
- Students rate the statements and then compare their ideas with a partner.
- Students report back to the class. Encourage discussion where they have different opinions.

4
- Discuss the questions with the class.
- Ask if anybody has been on a team-building course. If so, ask them to tell the class about it.

> ### Optional activity
> **Class team-building day out**
> - Tell the students to imagine that the class is going on a team-building day out.
> - Decide what the financial limit should be: eg £20, £50 or £100 per person.
> - Students work in pairs or small groups and plan the day. It must include a destination, food provision and at least two team activities.
> - Students present their ideas to the class. The students vote for the best idea.

Language study

Dependent prepositions

> ### Note
> The language study reviews dependent prepositions and presents a number of examples. Students should be made aware that the prepositions are essentially grammatical links and contribute no meaning. As such, they are sometimes difficult to predict and may seem illogical.

1
- Read the explanation and instruction with the class.
- Students work individually or in pairs and complete the task.
- Check the answers with the class. Establish the collocations (*specialise in*, *aware of*, etc) and write them on the board in three lists for students to copy down.

> ### Answers
> verb + preposition: 2, 4, 6, 8
> noun + preposition: 1, 3, 5, 7
> adjective + preposition: 9, 10

2
- Students answer the question. Refer them to the extracts in Ex 1 and ask them to find four examples (*specialises in improving*, *excuse for having*, *aware of timing*, *interested in trying*).
- Refer students to the Grammar reference on page 91 for other examples of verb, noun or adjective + preposition.

> ### Answer
> The *-ing* form of the verb.

> ### Optional activity
> **What's the preposition?**
> - Give students a few minutes to look at the examples of verb, noun or adjective + preposition in the Grammar reference on page 91. They then close their books.
> - Say one of the verbs, nouns or adjectives. The student who is first to call out the correct preposition gets a point.
> - Students could play in teams amongst themselves.

3
- Students work individually or in pairs and choose the correct preposition to complete each question. Tell them to use each preposition at least once.
- Check the answers with the class. Once again, establish the collocations (*responsible for, entitled to*, etc) and ask students to add these to the three lists they wrote down in Ex 1. Point out that *translate* can be followed by either *into* or *from*.

> ### Answers
> | 2 in | 3 to | 4 to | 5 from |
> |---|---|---|---|
> | 6 with | 7 into | 8 with | 9 of | 10 about |

4
- Students work in pairs or small groups and ask and answer some of the questions in Ex 3. Make sure that each pair / group has a least one student who has or has had a job.
- You could invite the students to ask you some of the questions, either to model the activity or after they have completed it.

5
- Read through the headlines with the class and check any problematic vocabulary.
- Students work individually or in pairs or groups and complete the task.
- Check the answers with the class. Establish the collocations (*focus on, eligibility for, depend on*, etc) and ask students to add them to their lists from Exs 1 and 3.
- Ask: *What news stories could each of the headlines be about?* Discuss this with the class.

> ### Answers
> | 1 on | 2 for, on | 3 of / about | 4 to | 5 between |
> |---|---|---|---|---|
> | 6 into | 7 with | 8 of, for | | |

> ### Optional activity
> **Preposition search**
> - Students work individually or in pairs. Ask them to look at one of the texts they have already read in the Coursebook and to find and underline any examples of dependent prepositions.
> - Students compare with other students and report back to the class.
> - Students write down the collocations, adding them to the lists they have made in Exs 1, 3 and 5.

Are you a team player?

Listening

1

- Discuss the questions with the class.

2

- Tell students that they are going to listen to a radio phone-in programme where people seek advice for their problems.
- 🔘 **10** Students listen to the radio programme and answer the questions. They can compare their answers with a partner.
- Check the answers with the class.

Answers
Maria works for an advertising agency. She has a problem with a colleague who ignores her ideas.
Ethan works in a call centre. He has a problem with a new supervisor who is making his life difficult.

3

- Explain to the students that they need to listen for exact phrases from the conversations. You could pause the recording after the first item to model the activity.
- Check the answers with the class.

Answers
Maria
1 The problem is that
2 had enough
3 tired of, getting me down
Ethan
1 your advice on a problem, make my life a misery
2 out of order
3 in a real dilemma, can't stand working there now

Listening script 10
(L = Liz, M = Maria, E = Ethan)
L: Hello and welcome to *Dear Liz*. I'm Liz Cooper, here to help you with all your work problems. Today our topic is difficult colleagues. And our first caller is already on the line. Maria. Hello, Maria. What's your problem?
M: Er well, I started working at an advertising agency a few months ago – it's my first job and I really like the work. The problem is that I work with someone who is always really rude when I ask a question or make a suggestion. Her whole attitude is one of non-cooperation and I've had enough of it.
L: Is this person part of your team?
M: Yes – theoretically anyway. In reality she seems to think her ideas are the best and she completely ignores whatever ideas I put forward. I'm tired of all the friction. It's really getting me down.
L: Hmm, yes, I can see your difficulty. What's interesting is that difficult people rarely see themselves as the difficult one. If you're willing to talk with this person – and I think you should do so – then, it's a good idea to consider an approach that won't put your colleague on the defensive.
M: What do you mean?

L: Well, first of all, talking away from your work environment might help. And rather than making assumptions or placing blame, I recommend you begin the conversation by asking questions. Ask about ways you may be contributing to the problems you've identified. Perhaps you make too many suggestions or ask questions in a manner that seems impertinent from someone who is new to the company.
M: Mmm, OK, well, I'll give it a try. Thank you.
L: You're welcome. Good luck, Maria. Right, on the line now is Ethan. Hi, Ethan, how can I help?
E: Hi, Liz. Well, I'm a student and I work at a call centre at weekends to pay for my studies. Anyway, I'd like your advice on a problem with my new supervisor. She's determined to make my life a misery.
L: What does she do exactly?
E: Well, she talks down to me and she constantly has to know my whereabouts and what I'm doing. I think she's out of order.
L: So you haven't had this problem with other supervisors?
E: Never. It's put me in a real dilemma. I can't afford to leave because like I said, I need the money for my course, but I can't stand working there now.
L: Have you tried approaching your colleague directly?
E: No, I haven't. To tell the truth I'm a bit scared of her and I don't want to cause a scene.
L: Hmm, but as long as you fear her, you surrender to her. When you're not afraid of her, the dynamics of your relationship will change. Stand up to her.
E: Right, but how do I do that?
L: My advice is, speak to her and ask her about the issues she has with you. You don't have to meet with her alone; ask her manager or someone from the personnel department to be present. Then if nothing changes, you should think about going to the company's legal department.
E: OK, thank you for your advice.
L: Thank *you* for calling, Ethan.

4

- Students identify which person each piece of advice is offered to. You could ask them to do this from memory first and then to check with the script on page 95.

Answers
1 Ethan	2 Ethan	3 Maria	4 Ethan	5 Maria	
6 Maria	7 Ethan				

- Students underline the 'advice' phrases. Do the first one with the class as an example.
- Check the answers with the class.
- Draw attention to the common use of *-ing* with some of the phrases: *Have you tried -ing? You should think about -ing. -ing might help.* Point out that we can also say *I recommend -ing* and *It's a good idea to consider -ing.*

Answers
1 Have you tried ...   2 you should ...   3 I recommend ...
4 You don't have to ...; ask ... (as an imperative)
5 I think you should ...; it's a good idea to ...
6 ... might help.   7 My advice is ...

5

- Discuss the questions with the class.

Writing

1
- Brainstorm a few ideas for problems that could be caused by difficult colleagues at work.
- Students work in groups. Give them plenty of time to prepare and write their radio programme in the form of a script with at least two callers.

2
- Students give their script to another group. Give the groups time to assign and quickly practise their parts. They then act out the programme for the class.
- Discuss which programmes gave the best advice.

Speaking

1
- Students work in pairs. They ask each other the quiz questions and record their partner's answers.

2
- Students calculate their partner's score. Together they read and discuss the analysis for each of their scores. Encourage them to use a dictionary where necessary.
- Check students' understanding and pronunciation of the key vocabulary in the analyses.
- Ask: *Is the analysis of you accurate?*

3
- Discuss the meanings of the phrases with the class.
- In pairs, students ask and answer the questions. Encourage them to give examples and to ask each other further questions.
- Students report back to the class.

Answers
1 make decisions and take action before other people do
2 look for confirmation that you are doing the right thing
3 actively deal with disagreement between people
4 expect that what you do you will be very good
5 achieve as much as they can
6 make decisions work / carry out decisions

Optional activity

Positive and negative adjectives
- Students underline all the adjectives referring to leadership and team player qualities in the quiz analyses on page 96. Ask them to decide whether each adjective has a positive or a negative meaning.

Answers
Positive: natural born, strong, decisive, wise, professional, creative, assertive, empathetic, forceful, smart, solid, reliable, loyal
Negative: authoritarian, arrogant, autocratic, old fashioned, punitive, sycophantic
- In pairs or groups, students decide which six of the positive adjectives are most desirable in a good team leader, and rank the negative adjectives 1–6 according to how undesirable they are (6 = worst).
- Discuss the results with the class.

Revision activity

Preposition noughts and crosses
- Draw the following noughts and crosses grid on the board:

in	of	into
with	on	to
for	about	from

- Divide the class into two teams, team O and team X.
- Teams take it in turns to choose one of the prepositions and make a sentence that includes a verb, noun or adjective that collocates with it. For example, *I want to **specialise in** business law at university*. If the sentence is correct, write the team's symbol (O or X) in the square.
- A team wins if they can get three Os or Xs in a horizontal, vertical or diagonal row.
- Students can then play in pairs or smaller groups. They make their own grids, with the prepositions in a different order. They must not repeat a verb, noun or adjective from a previous game.

Extra practice
Students complete the Extra practice material on page 89, either in class or for homework.

Extra practice answers

1 1 running   2 implementing   3 bonds   4 enhancing
5 utilise   6 realise   7 face up to   8 tackle
9 take   10 setting   11 perform

2
worry (etc): about   benefit (etc): from
comply (etc): with   be aware (etc): of
adapt (etc): to   translate (etc): into
have impact (etc): on   apologise (etc): for

3 (individual answers)
Prepositions: 1 of   2 in   3 to   4 from   5 about
6 about   7 for   8 of

4 1 f   2 d   3 c   4 g   5 b   6 a   7 e

References
Grammar reference: Coursebook page 91
Wordlist: Coursebook page 92
Photocopiable resources: Teacher's Book pages 110–111
Test: Teacher's Book pages 149–150

CD-ROM
Unit 4 Team spirit
Language exercise: All work and no play
Vocabulary activity: Project manager
CEF-linked activity: I can describe college or work problems and give advice to others
Game: Swamp disaster (prepositions)

Before starting this unit, ask students to read the Grammar reference on pages 90–91 and study the Wordlist on page 92 of the Coursebook.

Ideas for preparation
- Photos from magazines or the Internet of music fans dressed to reflect the music they like
  (see *You are what you listen to* Ex 1 below)
- One counter for each team of students for the game on p86

Warmer
- Tell the students: *Write down as many different music genres as you can in one minute.*
- Elicit the different genres and write them on the board. Ask: *What are the biggest artists in each genre?*

Lead-in
1
- Look at the photos. Ask: *Do you know any of these artists? What kind of music do you associate with them?*
- Discuss questions 1 and 2 with the class.
- For question 3, give students time to think about what they want to say, making notes if they want to. They tell each other about their favourite group or artist.
- Find out which musicians are the most popular.

Speaking
1
- To model the activity, choose one of the attributes from box A and elicit the adjectives that can describe it. Tell the students: *A lot of the adjectives can describe more than one of the attributes.*
- Students work in pairs or small groups and complete the task. Encourage them to use dictionaries to check the meaning of any unfamiliar language.
- Check the pronunciation of the adjectives. The main stress is underlined in the key below.

Suggested answers
appearance and image: charis<u>ma</u>tic, <u>co</u>lourful, <u>gla</u>morous, <u>me</u>morable, <u>o</u>riginal, out<u>lan</u>dish, out<u>ra</u>geous
lifestyle and attitude: charis<u>ma</u>tic, colourful, ex<u>tra</u>vagant, glamorous, outlandish, outrageous, unpre<u>dic</u>table
live performance: charis<u>ma</u>tic, <u>cap</u>tivating, dy<u>na</u>mic, in<u>i</u>mitable, inspi<u>ra</u>tional, memorable, <u>noi</u>sy, original, outlandish, outrageous, unpredictable
lyrics: e<u>mo</u>tive, inimitable, inspirational, <u>mea</u>ningful, ob<u>scure</u>, original, outrageous, re<u>la</u>table, <u>up</u>beat
voice / singing: captivating, dynamic, emotive, inimitable, inspirational, mellow, memorable, original, <u>skil</u>ful, <u>soul</u>ful
music: <u>dance</u>able, dynamic, emotive, mellow, memorable, noisy, original, soulful, upbeat
musicians and musicianship: dynamic, inspirational, irre<u>place</u>able, <u>re</u>putable, skilful, <u>ta</u>lented,

2
- Students work in small groups. They agree on a ranking of the attributes and prepare reasons and examples.

3
- Groups present and explain their final ranking to the class.

You are what you listen to
1
- Look at the photos with the class. If possible, add to these by holding up more photos showing fans of different styles of music, for example, punk, skate, jazz, country, world music, etc. Ask: *What type of music do you think these people like?*
- In pairs, students discuss questions 2 and 3.
- Students report back to the class and compare ideas.

2
- 🔘 **11** Students listen to the first part of the radio programme and make notes in answer to the questions.
- Check the answers with the class.
- Ask: *Do you agree that someone's taste in music may reveal their personality?* Refer back to some of the music genres mentioned earlier and discuss the possible types of people who like them.

Answers
1 By psychologists at various universities in the UK and the US.
2 Around 5,000.
3 Volunteers created a 10-track CD of their favourite songs. Strangers then judged what the compilers were like from listening to the CD.
4 a They are likely to be reflective and generally very well-read and knowledgeable people.
   b They tend to be quite straightforward and conventional – they're generally dutiful and reliable.
   c They are generally a bit more socially liberal, rebellious and more image-conscious.
5 People may select music to send out signals to establish how they like to be seen.
6 Music.

Listening script 11
(P = Presenter, AW = Professor Alistair Watson)
P: A recent survey conducted by psychologists at various universities in the UK and the US has found that a person's taste in music, and how it's organised, may help predict which personality groups he or she belongs to, and that if you want to assess a person's character, a quick look through their music collection is one of the most reliable ways of doing so. With me here today to tell us more is Professor Alistair Watson. Professor Watson.
AW: Hello. Around 5,000 volunteers participated in the research. And yes, it does seem that taste in music does broadly speaking correlate with a person's personality.
P: And how was the research carried out?

AW: The key element was getting the volunteers to create a 10-track CD of their favourite songs. Strangers then judged what the anonymous compilers were like. We found that the CD assessment proved significantly more reliable than any other ways of quickly assessing people such as by looks, clothes, taste in films, and so on. For example, people who listen to classical music are more likely to be, and be seen as, quite reflective and generally very well-read and knowledgeable people. Looking at more contemporary music, pop and chart music fans tend to be quite straightforward and conventional – they're generally pretty dutiful and reliable sort of people. Whereas rap and hip-hop fans, on the other hand, are generally a bit more, let's say, socially liberal, rebellious and more image-conscious.

P: So, do we know why musical likes and dislikes are so closely linked to personality?

AW: Well, it seems there's much more to listening to music than, well, just enjoying it. It's thought that individuals select music to send out signals to establish how they like to be seen. For some, music can be central to their way of life, and is why they dress, have their hair and generally look the way they do.

P: But isn't that, particularly with younger people, just a way of asserting your identity?

AW: Well, to a certain extent, yes, I think it is. But at the same time, and as we were saying, a person's musical likes and dislikes can reveal a lot more about a person.

3

- 🔊 **12** Students listen to the second part of the radio programme and answer the questions.

Answers
a could have an obsessive-compulsive personality, extremely organised and reliable, the kind of person who doesn't get parking tickets
b more artistic, open to new experiences and ideas
c use music to check each other out and to communicate their character types

Listening script 12
(P = Presenter, AW = Professor Alistair Watson)

P: … And you also found that how a person organises their music is a reflection of their personality.

AW: Yes. People organise their CD and MP3 collections in different ways and this certainly indicates personality types. Some are alphabetised or divided into genre and so on, or, and this is much more common we found, more randomly arranged. If your CDs are stored in no particular order, then you are probably more artistic and open to new experiences and ideas. The opposite – religiously following a strict organisational formula – is a sign of an obsessive–compulsive personality. One of the volunteers in the research springs to mind. She and her fiancé live together and they have a sort of music room, which has two walls totally filled with shelves of CDs. I think they must have about a thousand between them, or thereabouts. Her CDs are very carefully organised by genre and then within this by artist and then alphabetised yet again by album title within that. Now, she is clearly an extremely organised and

reliable person, the kind who doesn't get parking tickets and that sort of thing. But what is really quite interesting is that she and her boyfriend, and I think they've been together for a couple of years now, have not yet combined their collections. Why they haven't done so, I don't know. His CDs are stacked completely randomly, by the way.

P: Mm, maybe it would be interesting to follow that up – see where they, and their CDs, are in another two years or so. And I understand that some of the research looked at how music plays a part in the way couples interact.

AW: Yes. We monitored 'new' couples' first six weeks of conversation, and discovered that they used music to 'check each other out' nearly twice as much as books, television, sport or whatever. Essentially, they were using music to communicate their character types.

P: So, next time you're trying to size somebody up, a quick look through their CD collection really does seem to be as good a place to start as any. Thank you, Professor Watson.

4

- Students listen again and complete the extracts with the phrases.
- Check the answers with the class.

Answers
1 and so on	3 or thereabouts	5 or so
2 sort of	4 and that sort of thing	6 or whatever

5

- Students work individually or in pairs. They identify examples of ellipsis and substitution in the extracts and say what has been omitted or substituted.
- Check the answers with the class.

Answers
1 doing so – substitution (it substitutes for *assessing a person's character*)
2 do – substitution (it substitutes for *dress, have their hair and generally look*)
3 is – ellipsis (*a way of asserting your identity* is omitted)
4 done so – substitution (it substitutes for *combined their collections*)

6

- Students work in pairs and discuss the questions.
- Students report back to the class.

7

- Give students time to choose their ten favourite songs.
- Students work in pairs or small groups. They tell each other which songs they have chosen and why.
- Students report on their discussions.

Song

1

- Ask: *Do you know the band The Dandy Warhols? What do you know about them?*
- Students read the factfile and answer the questions.
- Check the answers with the class.

Answers

1 a The band released their debut album.
  b They released their second album, had their first hit single and attained more widespread success.
  c They released their third album to much acclaim; the track *Bohemian like you* received massive radio airplay and became a hit in several countries
  d *Bohemian like you* was used in advertising campaigns for Chrysler and Vodafone.
2 The original drummer left and was replaced by Brent DeBoer.
3 They throw their parties in an apartment block in Portland. They bought part of the block with the money that *Bohemian like you* earned from the adverts.
4 It used synthesisers a lot ('synth-heavy') and was 80s-influenced. The other albums were more guitar-driven.
5 They have a large cult following in some countries, but are not very well known worldwide.

2
- 13 You may want to pre-teach the following informal language from the song: *hairdo* (hairstyle), *vegan* (someone who eats no animal products at all, including dairy products and eggs), *pad* (apartment / flat), *kinda* (= kind of), *break up* (separate), *bummed* (annoyed / upset), *get bent* (get angry / upset).
- Students listen, read and answer the questions. They can compare their answers with a partner.

Answers

1 The singer is talking to a woman he would like to have a relationship with.
2 a It is a great car, but there is something wrong with it at the moment.
  b Her hairdo looks good. The singer likes it.
  c She is a waitress.
  d She is in a new band.
  e She is a vegan.
  f She still lives with her ex-boyfriend.

3
- Discuss the question with the class. Alternatively, students can discuss this in pairs / groups before reporting back to the class.

Answers

He used to have the same car as hers.
They like each other's hairstyles.
He thinks they both look pretty cool.
He's a waiter and she's a waitress.
She's a vegan and he works in a restaurant that cooks vegan food.
He thinks they are both 'bohemian'.

4
- Students discuss the question in pairs. Ask: *Which famous people would you say have a bohemian lifestyle? Does your town / city have a bohemian area?*

Vocabulary

1
- Read through the instructions. Explain that if a team lands on a square where one of the questions has already been asked, they must answer the other question. If teams are not sure whether an answer is right or wrong, they can ask you.
- Students play the game in teams, with two or three players in each team. The first team to reach the 'Finish' square is the winner.

Possible answers

1 tackle: a problem, an issue, an intruder / burglar, a football / rugby player, etc
  shun: society, your neighbours, the limelight, publicity, violence, etc
2 bonding with someone: developing a close relationship with someone
  having a knees-up: having a lively party, often with dancing
3 utilise: a room, a skill, equipment, etc
  enhance: your quality of life, your reputation, etc
4 (dis)reputable   (un)stoppable
5 focus on   translate into / from
6 adopt: a proposal, an attitude, a pose, a child, etc
  implement: a plan, a law, change, a system, etc
7 (dis)advantageous   roomy
8 causing a scene: having a noisy argument or creating a disturbance
  giving someone a look: looking at someone to show annoyance / disapproval
9 figure out: the answer / solution, what's going on, etc
  get across: a message, a viewpoint, an idea, etc
10 specialise in   participate in
11 be hooked on: coffee, chocolate, shopping, drugs, etc
  face up to: difficulties, problems, etc
12 comply with   benefit from
13 enduring something: suffering something unpleasant over a long period
  mucking in: joining in an activity, usually to help someone
14 (in)explicable   (in)curable
15 be entitled to   be aware of
16 conduct: business, research, a survey, an interview, your life, yourself, etc
  administer: a test, justice, medicine, drugs, etc
17 delegating: handing over some of your work duties to someone else
  confronting someone: facing and challenging someone
18 (in)valuable   sizeable
19 being hands on: doing something practical yourself
  out of line: behaving in an unacceptable way
20 sluggish   numerous / innumerable

References

Module 3 test: Teacher's Book pages 151–153

Additional material

Photocopiable resources

Everyone's different

Module 1

1   If you shared a house with someone, what kind of behaviour would you expect from them?
    What kind of behaviour would you find unacceptable? Discuss your ideas.

2   Imagine you are going to share a house with one of these five people. Read about each person's personality and
    behaviour, and give them a mark on each scale. Work with a partner and compare your answers.

1	2	3	4	5

eccentric behaviour ●━━━━━━━━━━━━━━━━━● 'normal' behaviour

likeable / interesting ●━━━━━━━━━━━━━━━━━● annoying / boring
person   person

1 Gemma likes to spend almost all of her time at home. She always finds the best place to sit in the lounge and watches reality TV shows almost every evening. She's a celebrity magazine addict and likes to tell everyone about the latest celebrity gossip. If you get caught in a conversation with her you'll be there for hours because she doesn't pick up the signals that you are trying to escape. She doesn't go out much apart from to the supermarket to buy microwave food, but she seems really happy, and laughs out loud a lot in front of the TV.

2 You'll know when Grant's around. In the morning he rushes into the kitchen in a mad panic, desperately looking for something he's lost while putting on his jacket. He drinks a cup of coffee in 10 seconds and rushes out of the door, late. Grant spends most of the day making business deals on his mobile phone while walking between offices, but if you go out with him he's always agitated and never has any money to buy you a drink. He's always on the move, but leaves his things lying around because he never has time to tidy up.

3 Julian keeps himself to himself most of the time. He always dresses in somber, dark colours and listens to dark, pessimistic grunge music alone in his room and plays his bass guitar incessantly. Occasionally he surfaces to cook some simple food but he hardly says a word to anyone, though he does mutter to himself quite a lot.

4 Charlotte spends 18.5 minutes in the bathroom every morning and then carefully sets the table so that she can enjoy a healthy orange juice and yoghurt breakfast. She eats salad for lunch and goes to the gym every day. She has an exercise bike in her room. She can't abide people who eat fast food and makes a point of letting you know how bad it is for you. She will give you a look if you so much as leave an unwashed cup on the coffee table. Don't even think about smoking anywhere near her. Her room is kept spotlessly tidy.

5 Grace has nine cats, two rabbits and a hamster, and she has names for all of them. She also has a huge collection of cuddly toys. She spends all of her free time looking after her pets and talking to them. Her room is unkept and frequently smelly. She seems to live in a world of her own, blissfully unaware of what other people think.

3   Write a short text about an imaginary housemate and give him / her marks.

4   Work in a group and discuss these questions.

1   What marks did you give your character and why?

2   What could you learn from each person?

3   For each person, what behaviour (if any) would you try and change? How would you go about it?

5   Discuss which imaginary housemate you would most / least like to share a house with.

The office

Work with a partner. Complete the plan with the names and character adjectives. Where does Ms Francis sit?

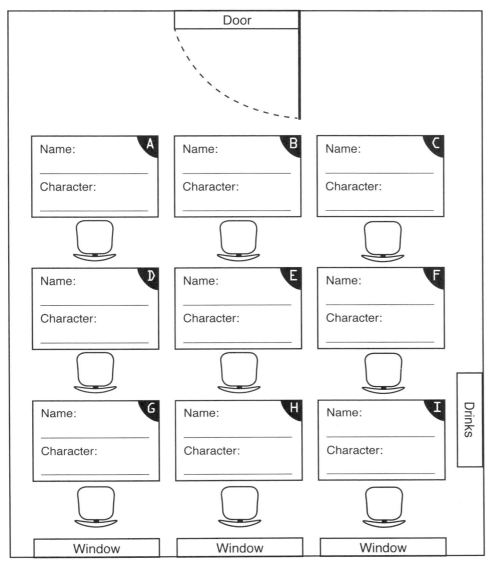

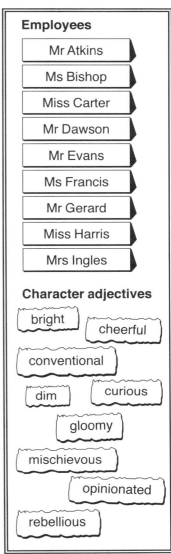

Student A

The person who's inquisitive has a desk next to the door.

Mr Evans has a desk above the bright person, closer to the door.

Mrs Ingles is a bit stupid.

The orthodox person is in the middle.

Mr Evans is miserable.

The cheerful person sits next to the window.

Mr Dawson sits between Mr Atkins and Mr Gerard.

Miss Harris is conventional and sits to the left of Miss Carter.

Student B

The curious person has a desk between Mr Atkins and Mr Evans.

The dim person sits next to the drinks machine.

Miss Carter is intelligent and sits below Mr Evans, further away from the door.

The disobedient person sits next to Mrs Ingles.

The playful person sits next to Miss Harris.

The pig-headed person has a desk in a corner without a window.

Ms Bishop sits next to a window.

The gloomy person has a desk in a corner.

UNIT 2
Energy-efficient house

1 Work in pairs and discuss these questions.

 1 What renewable energy sources can you think of?

 2 Which are suitable for domestic use?

 3 Why do people use them?

 4 Do you use any renewable energy sources in your home? What about other people in your country?

 5 What do you predict for the future?

2 Read these texts about four renewable energy technologies in the UK. Which do you think is the best idea? Why?

 Glossary: carbon saving* = the amount of carbon that is not used (thus reducing carbon emissions and global warming).

 CO_2 = carbon dioxide

3 Read the texts again and make notes under the following headings: initial cost, how it works, energy saved annually and the environmental benefit.

4 Work with a partner. You are building a new house and have been given a special grant of £12,000 to spend on renewable energy sources. Discuss which of the renewable energy technologies you will invest in.

5 Explain your choices to another pair.

Wind turbines

Wind speeds of 20kph or more are needed for this technology to be effective. Small turbines are 1.75m in diameter and supply 1kW of power. Large turbines are 2m in diameter and generate 1.5kW worth of electricity. They generate 35% / 70% of your electricity needs. The cost? £1,500 for the small turbine, £4,500 for the large, but government grants are available of £500 and £1,500 respectively. The CO_2 saving* for small turbines is 15% and for large ones 30%.

Ground source heat pumps

This technology draws heat from the ground, which is piped underground to your home. This can supply under-floor heating or power radiators. You need power to run the system, and you get 4 units of power for every 1 unit of input. A 10kW unit should save all the gas you would have used, but depending on your electricity use the annual energy saved is variable. The initial cost is in the region of £10,000, with government grants of £1,200 on offer. The annual carbon saving* is around 33%.

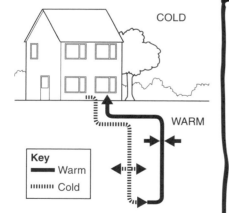

COLD

WARM

Key
— Warm
······· Cold

Wood-burning boilers

Like gas boilers, wood-burning boilers burn carbon-based fuel, but because trees absorb carbon, they are carbon-neutral. They cost more to run than gas, so there is no annual saving, and the initial investment will be at least £5,000. Government grants are available of up to £1,500. They heat both your house and your water and should save you all the money you spend on gas. These boilers effectively save nearly 70% of your annual CO_2 emissions.

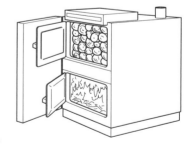

Solar water heaters

Solar panels are a familiar sight, particularly in hotter countries. Essentially they heat water which is piped round the house. Technology has been improving over the past few years and you should expect to pay about £2,500 for a medium-sized system. A government grant of £500 is currently available and you should expect to save around 8% on your heating bill. The annual carbon saving* is also 8%.

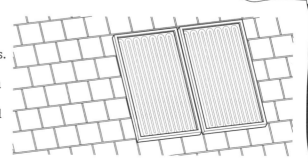

Adjective dominoes

-made	much-	-made	third-
-floor	non-	-catching	all-
-day	expensive-	-saving	child-
-friendly	south-	-shaped	UK-
-based	environment-	-floor	time-
-saving	well-	-looking	sea-
-facing	time-	-shaped	internet-
-based	cheap-	-night	hand-
-loved	well-	-friendly	top-
-smoking	eye-	-known	good-
-looking	energy-	-saving	odd-
-facing	heart-	-looking	all-

UNIT 3
Two sides to everything!

1 Match the headlines to the newspaper articles.

A
Superhero arrested!

B
War on pirates!

C
What's the colour?

1 _____

Two men have each received £1,000 fines for copying music from the Internet and selling it to family and friends. Paul Hunter, 23, and Hamid Kahn, 19, were found guilty of music piracy at Ipswich Crown Court. The music company at the centre of the case said 'Illegal downloads are by far the biggest problem facing the music industry. In the past people copied tapes or made bootleg tapes of concerts, but these were both expensive and of relatively poor quality. But nowadays, with computer technology almost anything is possible at a fraction of the cost and with almost no loss in quality.' The case is seen as a landmark in the fight against illegal downloading of music.

2 _____

A government policy document outlining new guidelines for the fight against obesity goes further than ever before. The policy recommends that the government should force the food industry to follow strict labelling on all food products. A new colour code will be introduced with a simple traffic light system to indicate whether a food item is regarded as healthy or not. Products with high fat, salt or sugar levels will be given a red sticker, foods that have medium levels of one category will be given an orange sticker, while only foods that have low levels in all three areas will be awarded a green sticker. The measures are to be introduced early next year.

3 _____

Two men dressed in superman outfits were arrested after handcuffing themselves to the railings outside the Houses of Parliament in London. The two, Peter Watson, 43, and Derek Wilcott, 28, were protesting against their lack of access to their children. They are both members of the 'Fathers for Justice' group that campaigns for the rights of fathers who have been denied access to their children after divorce. The protest caused severe delays in central London as traffic was brought to a standstill and the area around the building evacuated. One woman said 'I can understand why they are upset, but they should do things through the proper channels. It's an absolute disgrace that they can cause so much disruption.'

2 Look at these statements. Match them to the newspaper articles in Ex 1 and say which support the actions of the music company / the government / the protestors, and which oppose them.

a
It's ridiculous that people can download music for free from the Internet. They are stealing from the artists.

b
The only way we can get publicity is to protest in public places. I think we have a right to do that!

c
Unless the government brings in legislation, companies won't have to tell people what their products contain and people will keep on getting fatter.

d
Why should we suffer because people disrupt the traffic? Surely there are better ways of protesting.

e
Have you seen the prices of CDs and DVDs? It's daylight robbery! Why should I pay so much when I can get it for free?

f
Governments should stop interfering in people's lives by passing silly laws.

3 Write two more sentences, one in support of and one in opposition to each article.

4 Choose one of the issues to debate as a class.

Just a minute

'Just a minute' on … *the most exciting moment in your life* **without doubt** **single**	**'Just a minute' on …** *the worst you've ever felt physically* **by far** **whatsoever**	**'Just a minute' on …** *the thing you hate the most* **at all** **just**	**'Just a minute' on …** *the most stupid thing you've ever done* **total** **just**
'Just a minute' on … *the biggest disaster you've experienced* **total** **from start to finish**	**'Just a minute' on …** *the most interesting place you've visited* **well worth** **completely**	**'Just a minute' on …** *the most frightening experience you've ever had* **by far** **terrible**	**'Just a minute' on …** *the most bored you've ever been* **absolute** **simply couldn't** **believe it**
'Just a minute' on … *the biggest problem in the world* **at all** **just so**	**'Just a minute' on …** *the most wonderful person you've ever met* **without doubt** **absolutely**	**'Just a minute' on …** *the most stressed you've ever been* **even** **from start to finish**	**'Just a minute' on …** *the funniest thing you've ever seen* **really** **so totally**
'Just a minute' on … *the most important thing that's happened to you* **such** **single**	**'Just a minute' on …** *the most beautiful thing you've ever seen* **you know** **just stunning**	**'Just a minute' on …** *the best meal you've ever eaten* **well worth** **just incredible**	**'Just a minute' on …** *the strangest thing that's ever happened to you* **my entire life** **such**
'Just a minute' on … *the angriest you've ever been* **simply couldn't** **believe it** **terrible**	**'Just a minute' on …** *the most disappointed you've ever been* **absolute** **my entire life**	**'Just a minute' on …** *your most treasured possession* **even** **totally**	**'Just a minute' on …** *the loneliest you've ever been* **you know** **whatsoever**

How motivated are you?

1   Complete this questionnaire. Choose one answer for each question. Be honest!

1   When your alarm clock goes off in the morning, do you …
   a   jump out of bed immediately and do some exercise?
   b   press the snooze button and get an extra 10 minutes?
   c   rack your brains as to why you set it in the first place?

2   You have been asked to do something you really don't enjoy. Do you …
   a   grumble about it to anyone who will listen and get it over with as quickly as you can?
   b   get on with it to the best of your ability, giving it as much time and effort as it needs?
   c   keep putting it off hoping that someone else will do it?

3   Your New Year's resolution is to keep a diary but the entries turn blank by the middle of January. This is because …
   a   no-one's going to read it anyway.
   b   you just don't have enough to say.
   c   you don't have enough time in your busy schedule.

4   Work is mounting, deadlines are looming and the pressure is on. Do you …
   a   do as much as you can?
   b   go for a drink and come back to it later?
   c   remind yourself why you're doing it and what you'll learn from it, and get on with it?

5   Which of the following most motivates you?
   a   success   b   failure   c   fear of failure

6   On a normal work or study day, do you arrive …
   a   in plenty of time in order to get organised?
   b   at the last minute – as long as you're not late?
   c   ten minutes late and spend the whole morning yawning?

2   Exchange your completed questionnaire with a classmate and calculate each other's scores. Read what the score means and tell each other.

Scoring and analysis

1   a 4   b 1   c 0
2   a 2   b 4   c 0
3   a 1   b 0   c 4
4   a 2   b 0   c 4
5   a 3   b 2   c 1
6   a 4   b 2   c 0

17–23 points
There's no stopping you! What's important is that you know that motivation has to come from within. You're able to maintain momentum when the going gets tough. Make sure you're not always too busy whizzing through your *To do* list (for the week after next) to spend time on the fun things in life.

9–16 points
So-so! You are averagely motivated. You know you could be more motivated at times but your bottom line is keeping yourself interested and enjoying things. You're likely to be the kind of person who starts something motivated and full of enthusiasm, but once it becomes routine you lose interest and drive.

1–8 points
Oh dear! How do you manage to motivate yourself to wake up in the morning? You probably think that motivation is something that we get from others. You need to realise that motivation can only come from within. Maybe it's time to find something new to get excited about.

3   Discuss these questions.
   1   Do you agree with the analysis?
   2   What things do you find it easy and difficult to get motivated about in (a) your everyday life, and (b) your work or studies?

4   Look at the 'Seven rules for success'. Give yourself a score of 1 (lowest) to 5 (highest) for each according to how well you do them.

5   Discuss your scores in Ex 4 with a partner, giving examples to illustrate. What other rules for success would you add? What does it mean to be 'successful'?

Seven rules for success
- Set yourself short-term and long-term goals.
- Always finish what you start.
- Play to your natural strengths, talents and abilities.
- Take risks.
- Accept criticism and learn from failure.
- Be self-confident and trust your instincts.
- Make the most of learning environments.

Phrasal verb game

START →

1
Tell the group about the biggest thing you've ever got away with.

2
In business, what do you need to keep up with?

3
Tell the group two things you are looking forward to and why.

4
What's the best / worst idea you've ever come up with?

9
What things do you need to cut down on and why?

8
Tell the group what you got up to last night.

7
GO BACK 3

6
Who do / did you look up to and why?

5
Give three pieces of advice to students who want to get off to a flying start.

10
Explain what you do if you think you're coming down with something.

11
What's the most stupid thing you've ever come out with?

12
Tell the group three things you put up with in life that you don't like.

13
Why do some people look down on other people?

14
Describe a situation in which you had to face up to not being good enough.

19
Do you get back to people immediately or does it take you a bit longer?

18
What facts have you had to face up to in life?

17
Tell the group three things people can catch up with.

16
How do you make up for forgetting birthdays / anniversaries etc?

15
Do you generally just get on with things or do you tend to put them off?

20
Give three reasons why people drop out of university or courses.

21
Did you / will you go on to university after school? Why / Why not?

22
GO BACK 3

23
When do you have to stand up for yourself?

24
Describe the qualities you need to come back from defeat.

FINISH

28
Do you stand up to people or do you try and avoid conflict?

27
Tell the group two things you'll get round to doing one day.

26
When did you come up against a major obstacle?

25
Tell the group five things you can run out of.

UNIT 1
Important books in history

1 These books are taken from recent surveys on books that have changed the world.
Work in groups and discuss what you know about them and why they might be important.

- *The Holy Bible*, various

- *Book of Rules of Association Football* (1863), English ex-public schoolboys

- *Das Kapital* (1884), Karl Marx

- *The Female Eunuch* (1970), Germaine Greer

- *The Koran* compiled by Uthman

- *On the Origin of Species* (1859), Charles Darwin

- *The Interpretation of Dreams* (1900), Sigmund Freud

- *Relativity: The Special and the General Theory* (1918), Albert Einstein

2 What books would you add to or remove from this list?
Work in groups and create a list of the three most important books.

3 Quickly read these texts and decide which books from Ex 1 are being described.

This book explores the way that economic systems evolve and change. The author describes the capitalist system, where wealth is owned by individuals, as involving two groups of people. The first group owns the capital (land, machines etc) and buys the labour of workers to produce goods. The second group sells its labour in order to get money to survive. The author argues that within this system there are a number of unsolvable problems. In particular, economic power becomes controlled by fewer and fewer people, and this, together with changes in technology leads to periods of rapid economic growth followed by increasingly severe crises as profits fall. This work, along with the author's *Communist Manifesto*, was immensely influential in inspiring revolutionary movements throughout Europe, and in particular the Russian revolution of 1917.

Before writing this book, the author spent five years traveling around the world documenting the differences between animal species and collecting animal fossil samples. As a result of his voyage and further detailed research, the author concluded that animals evolve through a process of natural selection. This theory argues that the strongest members of a species are more likely to survive and reproduce. The characteristics that make these members strong will be inherited by their offspring. From one generation to the next, this species will evolve and may eventually become a new species. This theory provoked a lot of opposition, particularly from religious groups, because of the implications it had for the origin of mankind and for the suggestion that humans are, in fact, no different from other animals.

4 Work in groups and discuss these questions.

1 What new information did you find out about these two books?

2 Do you think the books were controversial when they were first published? Why / Why not? Are they controversial now?

3 Do they contain any ideas you strongly agree or disagree with?

5 Read this short text and then discuss the questions.
Some famous books in history were censored.

- *Lady Chatterley's Lover* (1928), by D. H. Lawrence, was not printed in the United Kingdom until 1960 because it contained descriptions of sexual acts.

- *The Adventures of Huckleberry Finn* (1885), by Mark Twain, was removed from many school reading lists in the USA because it contained many examples of a derogatory term for African-Americans.

1 Do you know about any books that have been censored? Why were they censored?

2 Do you believe in total freedom of self-expression or censorship in some cases?

3 What should the rules of censorship be? What is acceptable to put into print and what isn't?

4 How is censoring writing different to censoring other media? Is there a case to be made for having tighter controls on TV, film and music than on books?

Can you hide your feelings?

Oh no! What have you done?	What the hell did you do that for?
I'm sorry, but it's true.	I know you can't accept it, but you'll have to.
I'm not sure I want to ...	Do you really mean it?
What are you talking about?	Take it easy!
I don't understand! I ...	Are you absolutely sure about that?
You're joking, aren't you?	What are you doing?
Come on!	Just give me one more chance!
Why did you do that?	Watch out!

UNIT 2 Future forecasts

1 Work in pairs. Read one text each and answer the questions for your text. Write down your answers.

Text A

1 What's the general idea of the text?

2 What predictions about computers and machines are mentioned?

3 Which of the predictions do you think are likely and unlikely?

Humans RIP *posted by Hussey*

In the not-too-distant future, humans will have been replaced by machines. Super-powerful computers with human-like intelligence will be able to replicate themselves and will have developed their own autonomy. People will have become superfluous and the human race as we know it will be at risk of becoming extinct.

As society becomes more complex, computers will become more intelligent and increasingly they will do most of the decision making. Machine-made decisions will bring faster, better and more consistent results than man-made ones and human error will be a thing of the past.

Eventually a stage will be reached where the decisions necessary to keep the systems running will be so complex that humans will be incapable of making them. People won't be able to simply turn the machines off and reboot because they will be so utterly dependent on them. At that stage the machines will in effect be in control.

It will also be possible to download human consciousness into a computer. These hybrid organisms, part-human, part-computer will be able to use instinct and intuition and draw on ethical and moral codes, but with the ability to override the frailties and inconsistencies of the human psyche.

They will be the next dominant species on earth and their evolution has already begun.

Text B

1 What forecasts were made 50 years ago about life today?

2 What forecasts are being made today about medicine, ageing, the animal world and extraterrestrial matters?

3 Which of the forecasts do you think are likely and unlikely?

Aliens on earth? Forecasts for the next fifty years

FIFTY YEARS AGO IT WAS predicted that by now we would be living entirely on pills, there would be a world market for about 1,000 computers and that several generations would pass before humans ever landed on the Moon. Today, some of the world's top scientists are forecasting a world 50 years from now.

In medicine, there will be routine regrowing of body parts through regenerative drugs. 'Treatments will first be developed to regrow damaged fingers and toes and this will advance so that whole limbs, organs and even the spinal cord can be repaired,' said Professor Swinburn of the Bio-Research Institute.

Our life-span will increase so that 50 years from now living to be 100 will be the norm. Thanks to anti-ageing drugs life expectancy will have increased by about 40% by the year 2050.

Communication with the animal world will be made possible by the 'translation' into human terms of animals' thoughts and emotions. A huge rise in vegetarianism is expected to follow.

In 50 years we will have started colonising Mars as insurance against catastrophes on Earth. But the general consensus among futurologists is that the discovery of alien life will be the biggest advance. And it's likely that we will first find alien life forms here on Earth in the form of microbes that have been with us for millions of years.

---

2 Explain the main message of your text to your partner. Use your answers in Ex 1 to help you. Compare and discuss your ideas about which future scenarios are likely and unlikely.

3 What's the meaning of these words and phrases from the texts? What does each refer to?

1 regenerative 2 the norm 3 consensus

4 catastrophes 5 replicate 6 autonomy

7 superfluous 8 automated 9 frailties

10 inconsistencies

4 Work in groups and discuss the possible advantages and disadvantages of some of the scenarios in the box. Try to use some of the sentence beginnings below.

communicating with animals	invisibility
discovering alien life	living entirely on pills
dependency on computers	living to over 100
	regrowing body parts
	time travel

What worries / frightens / amazes / fascinates me is …

What I think / don't understand / can't get my head round / worry about is …

The key issue / greatest benefit / problem / main worry / danger is …

Quiz time!

Student A

1 You are going to do a general knowledge quiz with student B.
Make questions using the prompts and *Is /Was it …* + relative clause.

2 Ask student B your questions.
Listen to his / her answers and give him / her one point for each correct answer. (The correct answer is in brackets.)

1 George Harrison / sang Imagine ? (John Lennon)
Was it George Harrison who sang 'Imagine'?

2 Alexander Fleming / invented the telephone ?
(Alexander Graham Bell)

3 1990 / the Berlin Wall came down ? (1989)

4 Oxford Street / the British Prime Minister lives ?
(Downing Street)

5 the French / invented modern football ? (English)

6 Washington / John F Kennedy was assassinated ? (Dallas)

7 Madonna / sang Beautiful ? (Christina Aguilera)

8 Tom Cruise / stars in the Pirates of the Caribbean films?
(Johnny Depp)

9 Rubens / painted The Mona Lisa ? (Da Vinci)

10 Namibia / is totally surrounded by South Africa ?
(Lesotho)

11 Your question + give Student B 3 alternative answers.

12 Your question + give Student B 3 alternative answers.

3 Listen to student B's questions and choose the correct alternative.
Give your answer using *No, it isn't / wasn't. It is / was …*

1 Ricky Martin   Robbie Williams   James Blunt
No, it wasn't. It was Robbie Williams.

2 Italy   Germany   Brazil

3 2000   2001   2002

4 the Egyptians   The Chinese   The Aztecs

5 Tim Burners-Lee   Bill Gates   Michael Dell

6 Picasso   Dali   Van Gogh

7 The Nou Camp   The San Siro   The Bernabeu

8 the Baltic Sea   The Berents Sea   The Bering Sea

9 Apollo 11   Apollo 12   Apollo 13

10 Michael Crichton   Dan Brown   John Le Carré

- - - - - - - - ✂ -

Student B

1 You are going to do a general knowledge quiz with Student A.
Listen and choose the correct alternative. Student A will also ask two extra questions.

1 Ringo Starr   John Lennon   Paul McCartney
No, it wasn't. It was John Lennon.

2 Thomas Edison   Lars Magnus Ericsson
Alexander Graham Bell

3 1987   1989   1991

4 Park Lane   Regent Street   Downing Street

5 The English   The Brazilians   The Italians

6 Miami   Memphis   Dallas

7 Christina Aguilera   Jennifer Lopez
Britney Spears

8 Brad Pitt   Johnny Depp   Jude law

9 Rembrandt   Da Vinci   Renoir

10 Lesotho   Swaziland   Botswana

2 Make questions using the prompts and *Is /Was it …* + relative clause.

3 Ask student A your questions.
Listen to his / her answers and give him / her one point for each correct answer. (The correct answer is in brackets.)

1 Eminem / sang Angels ?(Robbie Williams)
Was it Eminem who sang 'Angels'?

2 France / won 2006 football World Cup ? (Italy)

3 2003 / World Trade Centre was attacked ? (2001)

4 the Romans / invented sunglasses ? (The Chinese)

5 Steve Jobs / invented the World Wide Web ?
(Tim Burners-Lee)

6 Monet / painted The Sunflowers ? (Van Gogh)

7 the Maracanã Stadium / Real Madrid play ? (The
Bernabeu)

8 the Beaufort Sea / separates Alaska from Russia ?
(The Bering Sea)

9 Apollo 10 / first landed on the moon ? (Apollo 11)

10 Fredrick Forsyth / wrote the Da Vinci Code ? (Dan
Brown)

11 Your question + give student A 3 alternative answers.

12 Your question + give student A 3 alternative answers.

UNIT 3
Fame for fame's sake

1 Read the quote and answer the questions.

In the future, everyone will be world-famous for 15 minutes. (Andy Warhol, 1968)

1 What was he saying about the nature of fame? Has it come true?

2 In your country are people desperate to become famous and what do they do to achieve this?

3 In 1996 a national newpaper survey found that 10% of British teenagers would give up their education just for the chance to appear on TV once. What does this say about young people today?

4 What are the dangers of a society becoming too obssessed with fame?

2 Work with a partner. Read one of the texts each and try to remember as much as you can. Tell your partner what you remember.

Celebrity A

Before becoming famous, celebrity A worked in a supermarket as a cashier. She came to public attention when she became a contestant on a TV reality show, and she spent a large part of the money she earned on plastic surgery to improve her figure. Since then she has gone on to make an estimated $12 million fortune in other reality shows and she appears almost constantly in celebrity, trivia and gossip-orientated magazines. Celebrity A is famous for coming out with strikingly daft answers to interview questions. She thought that Buenos Aires was a basketball player; that Prince Hussein was a rock star and that India was near Florida. She now owns a night club and has launched her own brand of clothes.

Celebrity B

Celebrity B began his career playing guitar in a 1980s pop group. The group had several minor hit records, but never quite made it to the top. Celebrity B was spotted by a TV company when giving an interview on a children's TV show, and he was asked to become a presenter of a weekend children's TV programme. The blend of music, comedy and an ability to communicate with children was hugely successful. But celebrity B did not want to restrict his talents to children's TV. He went on to co-write and star in several award-winning adult comedy series, and more recently he has branched out into playing serious roles in the theatre. He regularly co-hosts a number of high profile TV shows, and his huge comedy and acting talent makes him one of the most sought after TV personalities.

3 Discuss these questions.

1 What are the main similarities and differences between the two celebrities?

2 How can you explain the success of Celebrity A? Why are we as interested in someone like Celebrity A as Celebrity B?

3 Are there celebrities like Celebrity A in your country? What TV programmes can you see them on?

4 Work in groups. Which would you choose? Justify your choices to the group.

1 To be famous but not wealthy, or extremely wealthy but unknown.

2 To be incredibly talented but unsuccessful, or of little talent and successful.

3 To be moderately successful during your life, or massively successful after it.

4 To be extremely intelligent and ugly, or unintelligent and beautiful.

5 To have a long ordinary life, or a short extraordinary one.

6 To have a very short extremely successful career, or a longer moderately successful one.

Van Gogh was unknown and penniless during his lifetime. James Dean starred in only three films and has become a cultural icon. Both men died young.

5 What other famous people do you know who only achieved celebrity status and fame after their death?

What's the idiom?

Let your hair down.	By the skin of your teeth!
Use your head!	You can't fill his shoes.
Get off my back.	Keep it under your hat.
Grit your teeth and get on with it.	Pay through the nose.
He's always licking his boss' boots!	Keep your eyes open.
Pull your socks up.	You scratch my back and I'll scratch yours.
By the seat of your pants!	Get out of hand.
Put the boot in.	Follow your nose.
She has egg all over her face.	Go weak at the knees.
Thumbs up!	A pain in the neck.

Securing freedom?

1 Look at these examples of freedom. Rank them from most important to least important. (1 = most important, 5 = least important)

- freedom to say and write anything you want ☐
- freedom of information (access to government documents) ☐
- freedom to educate your own children ☐
- freedom to travel anywhere ☐
- freedom to park your car wherever you like ☐

2 Discuss these questions in groups.

1 What other kinds of freedom can you think of? Examples: *religious freedom, linguistic freedom*

2 Do you think that the world in general is becoming more or less free? Give examples.

3 Are restrictions on freedom necessary in the fight against crime and terrorism? If so, what kinds of restrictions?

3 Read the text on the government's plans for new security measures. Is it essentially factual or written from one viewpoint?

Row over latest freedom bill

The government yesterday announced its long-awaited plans for new security measures designed to aid the fight against terrorism. Donald Smith, the Home Secretary, unveiled a package of measures which he said would 'help the honest citizen sleep easy at night.' Opposition parties and libertarian-oriented pressure groups reacted with anger, saying that the measures amounted to a strong attack on ancient personal freedoms. Airport authorities denounced the plans as 'unworkable.'

Among the measures were proposals for the government to be given new powers to collect and store information from both public and private agencies including banks, doctors' surgeries and employers. Mr Smith argued that such powers were necessary in order to 'prevent the kind of terrorist atrocities and serious crimes which this country has experienced over the past few years.' He defended the government's position, saying that 'those with nothing to fear' would not be inconvenienced by the measures.

Further measures include powers to limit personal travel, by monitoring departures and arrivals at airports and sea ports. More details of the measures, including a timescale of when they are likely to be introduced, are expected over the coming few days.

4 Discuss with a partner your personal reaction to the measures detailed in the text.

5 Read the examples of different restrictions on personal freedom. Decide for each one whether you would be prepared to allow it in support of the government's strategy for greater national security and the fight against terrorism. Use this scale:

4: I would never allow this.
3: I would be unwilling to allow this.
2: I might allow this.
1: I would happily allow this.

Which freedoms would you sacrifice?

(a) Limits on practising certain religions without persecution. _____

(b) Police monitoring of personal movements based on CCTV footage. _____

(c) Having to check in to a government department to give any reasonable information they ask for. _____

(d) Government collection of lesson attendance information from schools and universities. _____

(e) Sharing of information on citizens between all government departments, including health, education, police and employment. _____

(f) Restrictions on the wearing of traditional and religious clothing in public buildings including schools and universities. _____

(g) Government monitoring of internet use and emails sent from home and work. _____

(h) Restrictions on what you can say about religion, race and politics in a public place, and on what you can write in a public or published document. _____

6 Compare your ideas with other students. Choose at least three of the restrictions from Ex 5; the items with the most support will become law. Which three would you choose? Why?

Crimes of the century

Student A

1 Work with a partner. Read and listen to complete the two crime stories. Start by telling your partner the first line of Millennium Dome.

Millennium Dome

	then attempted to steal the diamonds but didn't get very
	going to be an attempt to steal the diamonds and on the
1	In November 2000, the most audacious crime ever
	getaway by speedboat. However, first the robbers had to
	ready to catch the gang red-handed. Had they succeeded it
	a glittering diamond collection worth £200m from the
	with worthless fakes, just in case the robbers succeeded.
	armed not with guns but with smoke bombs,

Mona Lisa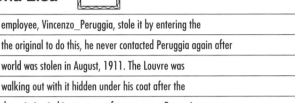

	employee, Vincenzo_Peruggia, stole it by entering the
	the original to do this, he never contacted Peruggia again after
	world was stolen in August, 1911. The Louvre was
	walking out with it hidden under his coat after the
	the painting in his apartment for two years, Peruggia grew
	that enigmatic smile could once again be enjoyed by everyone.
	Eduardo de Valfierno who had commissioned a French art forger to make
	without success: the painting couldn't be found and the

2 Using both handouts to help you, retell the Millennium Dome story. Then listen to your partner retell Mona Lisa.

3 Discuss these questions.

　1　Could either of these crimes have succeeded? Do you have any sympathy with either group of criminals?

　2　What's the most famous or daring crime anyone has committed in your country?

　3　What should the punishment be for these criminals?

- -

Student B

1 Work with a partner. Read and listen to complete the two crime stories. Listen to the first line of Millennium Dome and then tell your partner the second line.

Millennium Dome

	infamous Millennium Dome in London. The gang of six criminals
	would have been the crime of the millennium.
	stink bombs and a JCB had planned to make their
	far. Senior police officers had suspected that there was
	smash their way into the dome using the JCB and they
	attempted in Britain took place: the broad-daylight theft of
	night before the raid they had been removed and replaced
	Undercover police officers and sophisticated CCTV were

Mona Lisa

	museum had closed. The theft was masterminded by
	impatient and was caught attempting to sell it. Returned to the Lourve,
1	The Mona Lisa, arguably the most famous painting in the
	building during regular hours, hiding in a cupboard and
	investigation ceased. However, it turned out that a Louvre
	copies of the painting so he could sell them as the missing original. Not needing
	the crime. The Mona Lisa might have been lost forever but having kept
	closed for an entire week to aid the investigation but

2 Listen to your partner retell Millennium Dome. Then, using both handouts to help you, retell the Mona Lisa story.

3 Discuss these questions.

　1　Could either of these crimes have succeeded? Do you have any sympathy with either group of criminals?

　2　What's the most famous or daring crime anyone has committed in your country?

　3　What should the punishment be for these criminals?

Alternative lifestyles

1 What do you know about the lifestyles of the following?

   diplomats   members of communes   travellers

2 Work in groups of three. Each of you reads <u>one</u> of the texts. Remember the details and report them to the other members of your group. Make notes if you need to.

> My dad is a diplomat and he works in the Canadian Embassy in Seoul, South Korea. We've lived here for just over three months and I really like it. The last place we lived was Ljubljana in Slovenia and Seoul is completely different. My dad moves a lot with his job and I've now lived in five countries; Germany, Mexico, Romania, Slovenia and now here. The hardest thing is making new friends and saying goodbye to old ones, but then you get used to it. At the moment I go to the American School here, and I've made a couple of friends already.
>
> **Chloe, aged 12**

> I live with my parents in a commune in France. We live in a really big house with five other families. There are 13 adults and 11 children in total. It's absolutely great fun as all the children play together. I'm the oldest and the youngest is six, apart from Sylvia my baby sister, she's only 8 months old. We moved here when I was 7 years old, so I've lived here almost half my life. The only bad thing about it is that I am sometimes teased when I go to school. They tease me because I don't live in a 'normal' family.
>
> **Sam, aged 13**

> My mum and dad are travellers. We live in a big van and drive around looking for cool places to live. Some things are good, like not going to the same school all the time, although I do miss having friends. I spend most of my time with my younger brother, Tom, and my sister, Bea. My mum's family have always been travellers and she says we have to keep our traditions. My grandmother is famous because she is a fortune teller and she often works at fairgrounds around the country. When I'm older I want to race motorbikes. I'll also buy myself a van so I can carry on being a traveller.
>
> **Tim, aged 15**

4 Read this extract from a newspaper article and answer the questions.

> A recent report into diplomatic life has revealed that children of diplomats are more likely to be unhappy than their peers. It also shows that later in life they can find it difficult to settle down and have steady relationships. The report goes on to …

   1 What's the article about?

   2 Why do you think children of diplomats might be unhappy?

   3 What do you think the rest of the article might say?

   4 Do you think there are any advantages for diplomat's children?

3 Work in your groups and discuss these questions.

   1 Is there anything you find interesting about each lifestyle?

   2 Do you find any of these lifestyles appealing? Why / Why not?

   3 What do you think is the hardest thing in each child's life?

5 Hold a debate on the topic 'Is it right for parents to choose unusual lifestyles?' Use your answers from Ex 3–4 to help you, and add your own ideas. At the end of the debate have a class vote.

Ellipsis and substitution

Complete the tasks to win the game. There are two task types.

1   Complete the sentences using ellipsis or substitution.

My wife loves shopping, but I _____. → *My wife loves shopping, but I don't.*

2   Rephrase the sentences using ellipsis or substitution.

I've tried to get a job, but I haven't been able to get a job yet. → *I've tried to get a job, but I haven't been able to do so yet.*

START

1 I wanted to buy some trainers, but I couldn't find _____ I liked.

2 'Do you want a large family?' 'No I _____.'

3 I didn't see him, but everyone else _____.

4 This new machine washes better than the old machine washes.

5 I wanted to leave home, but my parents said I wasn't ready _____.

6 She says she hasn't got it but I think she has got it.

7 'How do you know it's cancelled?' 'He said _____.'

8 If you want to learn how to swim, this book shows you how to swim.

9 She gave him a kiss, but she didn't want _____.

10 We want to move to a bigger house but we _____.

11 'Will your children grow up to be like you?' 'I hope _____.'

12 'Have a good time!' 'Yes, we _____.'

13 'How do you know they're Polish?' 'They told me they were Polish.'

14 I'd rather be buying clothes instead of buying food.

15 I went skiing once, but I'll never _____ again.

16 She said she would phone me, but _____.

17 'It wasn't Max that called.' 'OK. I thought it wasn't Max.'

18 Someone sent me a Valentine's card but I don't know _____.

19 I told her as soon as I was able to tell her.

20 'Do you want to have kids?' 'I think _____.'

21 'Are you going to get married?' 'Yes, _____.'

22 I thought she'd be cross but she _____.

23 'Will he come to the wedding?' 'Unfortunately he might _____.'

24 We'd love to go on holiday but we can't go on holiday at the moment.

25 He loves to work out, but since the accident he can no longer _____.

26 'Do you regret buying a car together?' 'Yes, _____.'

27 'Do you think there's enough food?' 'I hope there is enough food.'

28 He's got plenty of time, but not enough time to see me, apparently.

FINISH

UNIT 2

What's in a word?

1 Work in pairs. Can you guess which languages these English words came from? Try to match them.

1	sofa	Arabic
2	tattoo	Carib
3	penguin	Czech
4	shampoo	Dutch
5	mammoth	Hindi
6	barbecue	Malay
7	robot	Polynesian
8	yacht	Russian
9	ketchup	Turkish
10	kiosk	Welsh

Can you guess what the words originally meant?

2 Discuss these questions in groups.

1 Does your language 'loan' words to English? Which words?

2 Are there many English 'loan' words in your language?

3 Is this increasing?

3 Quickly read these two newspaper articles. Which country has a more protective attitude towards its language, Japan or France?

4 Discuss these questions in groups.

1 What are the advantages and disadvantages of loan words entering languages? Why do think both the French and Japanese people ignore their governments' suggestions?

2 In your country, is there an organisation like the *Academie Française* to protect your language? Should there be?

5 Work in groups and discuss which language …

- is the best for a world language?
- is the best for song lyrics / poetry?
- is the most romantic / sounds the nicest?
- is the best for swearing?
- is the easiest / most difficult to learn?

- is the richest / has the most words?
- has the most speakers?
- is geographically the most widely spoken?
- has the most characters / longest alphabet?
- would you like to learn?

6 English is itself made up of words that are derived from Germanic languages, Greek, Latin, French and other languages. Try to guess which of these languages these percentages represent.

28%   28%   25%   5%   8%

The new Japanese

The adoption and 'Japanisation' of English words by the Japanese continues at a rapid pace and Japanese is looking and sounding more and more like an English dialect, or a new language, depending on your perspective. In a new edition of a popular Japanese dictionary, 43,000 entries, along with an additional 7,000 acronyms were of English origin, and that's already behind the times. There have been calls from the top levels of society, including former Prime Minister Junichiro Koizumi, for a reduction in the number of loan words used in official documents. In 2002, a panel of experts convened to come up with 'native' Japanese words to replace loan words, mostly from English, but their endeavours appear to be futile.

How do you say that in *Franglais*?

France's cultural watchdog, the *Academie Française*, has been battling to repel the invasion of English words and phrases by producing new batches of official alternatives. These include *la bonne heure* (happy hour), *bloc-notes* (blog) and *dialogue en ligne* (chat line), all of which are widely ignored. Even the *Academie* has conceded that *Franglais* such as 'le weekend', 'le fast-food' or 'le marketing' are lost causes. However, this doesn't stop experts in government ministries constantly proposing French versions of these loan words. But it's a time-consuming process and even when the *Academie* gives a phrase fast-track approval, for example, *telechargement pour baladeur* for podcasting, it's usually too late to stop the French sticking with the English version.

Adjective endings

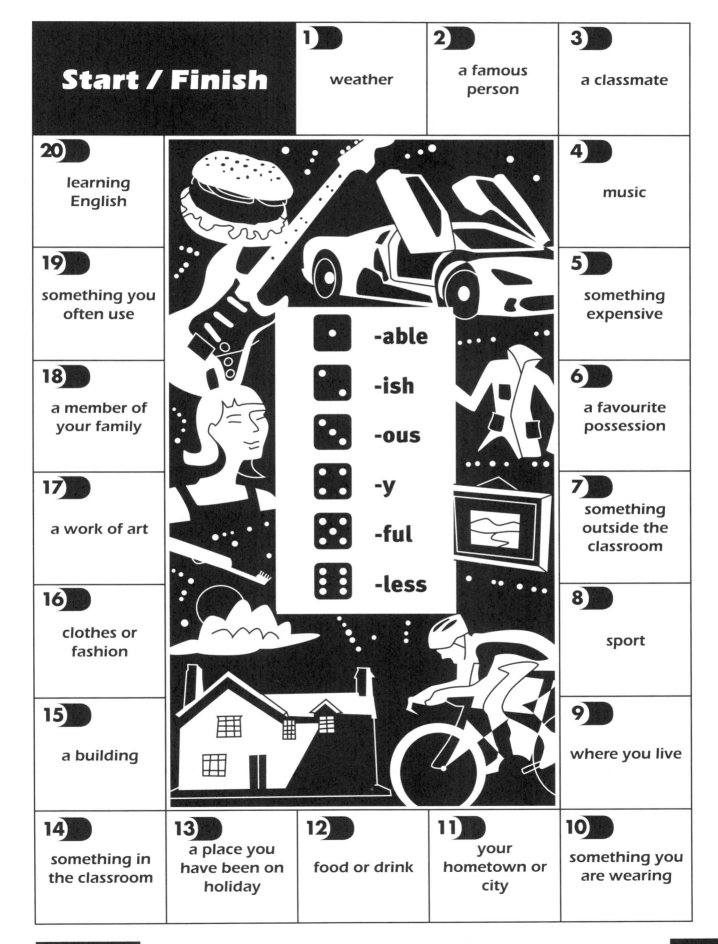

| Start / Finish | 1) weather | 2) a famous person | 3) a classmate |

Start / Finish

1) weather
2) a famous person
3) a classmate
4) music
5) something expensive
6) a favourite possession
7) something outside the classroom
8) sport
9) where you live
10) something you are wearing
11) your hometown or city
12) food or drink
13) a place you have been on holiday
14) something in the classroom
15) a building
16) clothes or fashion
17) a work of art
18) a member of your family
19) something you often use
20) learning English

-able
-ish
-ous
-y
-ful
-less

Caught on the Net

In touch or out of touch?

Internet sites such as Friends Reunited in the UK and Classmates.com in the USA have become extremely popular over the last few years. At one point in 2005, for instance, up to 20,000 people were joining Friends Reunited every day, and for a site that was only launched in July 2000 this is amazing.

The website was the idea of Julie Pankhurst and her husband Steve. At the time Julie was about to have their first child and she started wondering whether her school friends were also married and had families. The main idea was simply to provide a way in which old school friends, who had lost touch with each other, could be reunited. However, as with most things some of the uses that it is put to are not the same as the original intentions. One problem is that the information that is entered is written by the person themselves, and therefore it's impossible to say how accurate it is. There's nothing to stop people posting information that is totally untrue and even malicious. In some cases this has led to serious problems including visits from the police when someone has been accused of a crime. Friends Reunited has also been blamed for a number of marriage break ups. The cause, supposedly, is old school couples getting back together!

Of course, there are also some happy stories where people who had lost touch with each other are suddenly reunited. The fact that it's all done by the touch of a button means that people who have moved away from the area where they went to school are easily able to communicate with people who are still in the same place.

1 Read the article about Friends Reunited and note down the key points.

2 Discuss these questions.

1 What are the advantages and disadvantages of websites like Friends Reunited?

2 In what situations might you use a site like Friends Reunited?

3 What's your opinion of these kinds of sites?

✂ ···

LOOKING for Mr Right!

Over the past ten years or so the growth of internet dating sites has been incredible. There are now so many sites to choose from that it is often difficult to know where to look. Many sites now offer lots of extra services such as chat rooms, webcasts and message boards. Of course, the basic idea of most of these sites is to put people in touch with each other with the idea of having a date or finding a partner. Most sites allow people to put up photos of themselves as well as writing a profile. People then search through all the entries trying to find someone they are interested in meeting. The whole idea sounds very simple and relatively easy. However, as with every idea there are a number of problems and issues. The first is the reliability of the information posted. There's nothing to stop someone writing completely inaccurate information or even posting a fake picture. For example, a man who is only 1m 60cm tall could claim to be 1m 85cm and the only way the lie would be discovered is if an actual meeting took place. Although this may sound fairly harmless, imagine what other incorrect information could be included. And there are also dangers of safety once a meeting has been arranged. There is no way of telling whether the person you are going to meet is beautiful and friendly or possibly an axe-murderer! Of course, there are also lots of happy stories. Some people who have met through internet dating sites have ended up getting married, and it's certainly an advantage that distance is no longer an issue. It's now quite easy to meet someone who lives a long way from you, possibly even in a different country, whereas without such sites this simply would not be possible.

1 Read the article about internet dating websites and note down the key points.

2 Discuss these questions.

1 What are the advantages and disadvantages of internet dating websites?

2 In what situations might you use an internet dating site?

3 What's your opinion of these kinds of sites?

Strike a deal

Student A: supplier

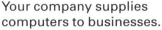

Background

Your company supplies computers to businesses.
You have a meeting with a customer who you supplied with a computer system three years ago.

Points for negotiation

- You need to tell the customer about the improvements you've made to the product. Think about memory size, processor speed and new functions.

- The software has been updated slightly but you believe it was fine before.

- You don't really want to sell fewer than 20 units as this reduces your profit margins.

- You certainly don't want to offer a discount for selling fewer than 20.

- You are offering a one-year warranty.

- Your technical support is extra.

- Installation usually takes place 14 days after the order is placed.

Prices

- One computer costs £700.

- Technical support costs £1,000 per year.

- Warranty extension: one year costs £1,000 per order.

Student B: customer

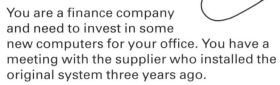

Background

You are a finance company and need to invest in some new computers for your office. You have a meeting with the supplier who installed the original system three years ago.

Points for negotiation

- You need clarification on how their product is now better – the system is a bit slow.

- You want updated software as this is the main problem.

- Your company wants a maximum of 15 computers and expects a discount for this bulk order.

- You want a two-year warranty.

- You expect to get free technical support for a year.

- You want the system to be installed next week.

Prices

- You expect to pay about £500 a computer.

- Your budget is £10,000 but you want to spend as little as possible

Student A

Use these phrases to try and reach a deal.

- What I'm getting at is … ☐
- I suppose I'm really saying … ☐
- Do you know what I mean? ☐
- Do you follow? ☐
- What do you mean by …? ☐
- So what you're trying to say is …? ☐

Student B

Use these phrases to try and reach a deal.

- What I mean is … ☐
- To put it a different way … ☐
- Are you with me? ☐
- Do you get me? ☐
- In other words … ☐
- If I've understood you properly …? ☐

Move Advanced Teacher's Book © Macmillan Publishers Limited 2007

1 Work with a partner. Discuss how you think the following activities are best achieved: individually or in a team? Write *I* or *T* next to each activity.

1 writing a soap-opera script ___

2 writing a poem ___

3 setting up music equipment ___

4 decorating a room in your house ___

5 planning a holiday ___

6 managing a shop ___

7 planning a party for a friend ___

2 For the team-based activities describe the make-up of the team: its size, roles and lines of communication.

3 Have you ever been part of a team that has been unsuccessful in achieving its aims? If so, what were the problems? If not, what might be the main difficulties?

4 Grade the following characteristics of working in teams on a scale of:

3 = necessary 2 = useful 1 = unimportant
0 = to be avoided

1 having a common objective _____

2 having a team-leader or director _____

3 working to a non-negotiable deadline _____

4 having individuals who are willing to compromise _____

5 having team members who know each other well, such as good friends or family _____

6 run democratically (the majority decision is carried) _____

5 Work with a partner. Discuss your choices in Ex 4. Are there any more characteristics of successful team-work?

6 Read each of these scenarios about team-working. As you read, think about what went wrong and why.

1 A group of colleagues has been asked to come up with a new strategy to promote their company's latest service: motivation and leadership training for people who lack confidence. The team is comprised of three people: Jaku, who feels that the new company training package has not been well-designed and is too expensive; Rada, who tends to talk a lot and deliver less; and Mikoy, who is keen to be promoted soon. They have a deadline of three weeks, but it soon becomes apparent that they are not all pulling in the same direction. The other two accuse Mikoy of stealing their ideas and seeking credit for them, while Mikoy responds by saying Rada is an ignorant woman who comes up with endless irrelevant comments. Jaku says little, but gives the impression that his heart is not in it. The deadline approaches and Mikoy cobbles together an incoherent strategy document which is quickly rejected by their line managers. All three participants are blamed equally for the failure and lose out on that season's bonus.

2 Twelve teenage members of a youth group have been asked by their leaders to put up a shelter by nightfall in a wood, for themselves and a group of six visitors to sleep in. They aren't allowed to use tools or rope, just the materials that they can find in the woods. They begin enthusiastically by going off in different directions in search of useful materials. With many of the young people venturing far and wide, this takes quite a long time. When they finally all return they start putting together what they have found, but after some time they realise that the structure is not going to hold up and needs redesigning. Arguments break out over which type of design is best. They cannot agree, and a dominant member of the group forces the others to accept his idea of a wigwam-type structure with leaves to protect them from rain. At this point it starts raining, and it becomes apparent that leaves will not keep out the rain. A quieter member repeats his idea for a design, which was for a large hole with a roof made from sticks and earth. Half the teenagers back him, but the other half refuse to, and start building a third type of structure nearby. Time quickly runs out. The visitors arrive, shocked to see that there are no proper sleeping arrangements, and darkness falls as they face a night without protection.

7 Discuss these questions for each scenario.

1 Think about everyone who was involved. Who is most to blame for the failure?

2 Why do you think each person acted in the way they did?

3 What would you have done differently?

4 What would you say to each person involved?

5 What useful lessons, if any, do you think the people involved will learn?

Teamwork

1 Work in groups to complete the following text. Use the words on your cards. Write two words in each space.

What's *in a* team?

Teams are not just for those who (1) _____ traditional team sports like football and basketball. Individual sports like tennis and swimming also have teams. This is because teams can in fact be (2) _____ two types: sports like football and basketball have 'interdependent' teams but there are also 'independent' teams for sports like tennis or swimming. 'Interdependent' teams need a (3) _____ complementary components, that is different players (4) _____ different things and if there is the right balance of skills, you have the (5) _____ a good team. Therefore, strong individual performance is directly (6) _____ strong overall team performance. In contrast, an 'independent' team is (7)_____ this in that every person performs basically the same actions, and winning or losing has little direct (8) _____ the other team members. It is therefore easier for overall failure to be (9) _____ individuals and a player can make fewer (10) _____ poor team performance if they lose their match or race.

The (11) _____ managing the two types of team differ greatly too. An 'interdependent' team coach would be (12) _____ building team spirit and would use activities that (13) _____ members getting to know each other socially in order to build trust. With 'independent' teams, where this is less important, coach and players have (14) _____ what everyone *individually* needs to do to improve their performance. However, regardless of team type and individual performances, the (15) _____ being part of a team is sharing the glory of victory with your team mates and this is something that all players (16) _____.

2 Discuss how you worked together as a team.

1 What kind of team were you: interdependent or independent?

2 Did everyone participate equally? Who was more dominant and who was less dominant?

3 Was there a clear leader or did different people assume this role at various stages?

4 Apart from being a leader, did different people take on different roles?

5 Did your team work well together? Were there any problems? What caused them?

6 Rate your team's performance from 1 (the lowest) to 5 (the highest).

7 Rate your individual performance from 1 (the lowest) to 5 (the highest).

specialising, impact, participate, focus, into, from, of, of

responsible, split, agreement, blamed, in, of, from, about

excuses, makings, translated, benefit, on, in, on, on

aspects, best thing, mixture, different, into, on, for, for

Teacher's resource notes

Module 1

Unit 1 Everyone's different

Lead-in
Ask students if they have ever shared a house or flat. If they have, ask them to tell you some good and bad points about sharing.

Procedure
1 Students discuss the question in pairs.
2 Students work individually to read about the people and give them a mark on each of the scales. Students then compare their answers with a partner. Discuss some of the results with the class.
3 Students work individually to write a similar text about an imaginary housemate and give him / her marks on the scales.
4 Students discuss the questions in groups and decide which person they would most / least like to share a house with.

Unit 1 The office

Lead-in
Ask: *Do / Would you prefer to work in an office of your own or in an 'open plan' office? Why?*

Procedure
1 Students work in pairs. Give each pair a copy of the office plan and the sentences for each student.
2 Explain that students read information to each other and complete the office plan with the names and character adjectives. Explain that they will need to listen carefully to each other for synonyms of the character adjectives.
Example:
Student A: *Mrs Ingles is a bit stupid.*
Student B: *The dim person sits next to the drinks machine.*
Students work out that 'stupid' and 'dim' have similar meanings and that Mrs Ingles (desk I) is 'dim'.
3 At the end of the activity, students should be able to answer the question 'Where does Ms. Francis sit?'

Vocabulary
dim, bright, inquisitive, pig-headed

> **Answers**
> Desk A = Mr Atkins,   Desk F = Miss Carter, bright
>   opinionated   Desk G = Mr Gerard, cheerful
> Desk B = Ms Francis, curious   Desk H = Ms Bishop,
> Desk C = Mr Evans, gloomy   rebellious
> Desk D = Mr Dawson,   Desk I = Mrs Ingles, dim
>   mischievous
> Desk E = Miss Harris,
>   conventional

Unit 2 Energy-efficient house

Lead-in
Ask: *What do we mean by energy-efficient?* Elicit examples of energy-efficient equipment.

Procedure
1 Students work in pairs and discuss the questions. Elicit feedback from the pairs in a brief whole class discussion.
2 Check students understand what 'carbon saving' means. Ask them to read the texts and decide which they think is the best idea and why.
3 Students read the texts again and make notes under the headings.
4 Students work in pairs to come to an agreement. Pairs then compare their answers. Discuss the choices with the whole class.

> **Answers**
> 1 Possible renewable energy sources include wind, wave and solar power. All those mentioned in the text are suitable for domestic use. People use them to save money, protect the environment or to be fashionable.

Vocabulary
renewable energy, CO_2 (carbon dioxide), solar panel, carbon-neutral, boiler, turbine, generate

Unit 2 Adjective dominoes

Lead-in
Write the following on the board and ask the students to match the halves to make compound adjectives:
old-   strange-   well-   -looking   -known   -fashioned
(Answers: old-fashioned, strange-looking, well-known)

Procedure
1 Explain that the students are going to play a game of dominoes where the first and second halves of compound adjectives have to be matched.
2 Divide the students into groups of three or four and give each group a set of cut-up and shuffled dominoes. Ask the students to divide the dominoes so that each student has the same number.
3 The first student places any one of his / her dominoes on the table. The next player plays a domino to make a natural compound adjective and must make a sentence using it.
4 Students check with you if they are not sure whether a natural compound adjective has been made. If a student cannot play a domino that makes a compound adjective, he / she misses a turn.
5 The first person to play all their dominoes is the winner. If none of the players can play, the winner is the person with the fewest dominoes left.

Unit 3 Two sides to everything!

Lead-in

Ask: *What do you think the title 'Two sides to everything!' means?* (Two sides to every argument). Ask: *Do you agree that there are always two sides?*

Procedure

1 Students look at the newspaper headlines and discuss what they think the 3 stories might be about. Students read the three articles and match the headlines. They check their ideas in pairs.

2 Students read the statements in Ex 2, match them to the articles and decide which viewpoint each statement supports / opposes.

3 Students work in pairs and write one more statement in support and one opposed to each of the actions. Collect these and collate them on the board.

4 Choose one of the topics. Divide the class into two groups, A and B. Group A thinks of arguments in support of the music companies / the government / the protesters, and Group B thinks of arguments against. Give each group about 10 minutes to prepare their ideas and hold a debate.

5 Alternatively, assign roles to the students. For example, two students could be the two men from text 1 – Paul Hunter and Hamid Kahn – and two students could be representatives from a music company. Students then work in groups and role play the debate.

Answers

1 1 B   2 C   3 A
2 1 a, e;   2 c, f;   3 b, d

Unit 3 Just a minute

Procedure

1 Students work in groups of three or four. The cards are placed face down in the centre. The first student picks up a card and must speak for one minute on the subject on the card. He / she must also include the two emphatic words or phrases as naturally as possible.

2 Students award points depending on the amount of repetition and pausing: three for virtually none, two for a little and one if they paused a lot or didn't speak for a minute. Students also get one point for using each of the phrases on the cards naturally.

3 One student needs to keep the time and another student needs to keep the score. The winner is the student with the most points when all the cards have been used. Students are not allowed to change the words on the cards, for example 'absolute' to 'absolutely'.

Unit 4 How motivated are you?

Lead-in

Write *motivation* on the board and ask: *What is motivation? In what areas of life do we need motivation? How motivated are you?* Students discuss this briefly with a partner and report back to the class.

Procedure

1 Tell the students they are going to do a questionnaire to find out how motivated they are.

2 Students complete the questionnaire individually and then exchange their completed questionnaires with a partner. They calculate each other's scores and read the analysis for their partner. They should tell each other in their own words.

3 Students work in pairs and discuss the questions in Ex 3.

4 Students give themselves a score of 1 (lowest) to 5 (highest) for each of the 'Seven Rules of Success'. They then discuss their scores and any rules they think should be added. Students report anything interesting from their discussions back to the class.

Vocabulary

snooze, rack your brains, grumble, set aside (time), yawn, whizz through

Unit 4 Phrasal verb game

Lead-in

Review the meaning and use of several three-part phrasal verbs. Pre-teach any that are likely to be new to the students.

Procedure

1 Students work in groups of three or four and need a board, counters and a dice. The players take it in turns to roll the dice and move round the board answering the questions or doing the tasks in the boxes as they go. If a student is unable to complete a task satisfactorily, then he / she has to return to the previous square.

2 The winner is the first player to reach the finish.

Vocabulary

come down with, come out with, cut down on, get away with, get up to, look down on

Module 2

Unit 1 Important books in history

Lead-in
Ask: *What's the most memorable book you've read? Why?* and generate some whole class discussion.

Procedure
1 Students work in groups. They look at the list of books and discuss what they know about them and why they might be important. Allow time for whole class feedback. Still in groups students add their own suggestions and work together to make a list of the three most important books.
2 Students read the texts and decide which books are being described (answers: A: Marx's *Das Kapital*, and B: Darwin's *On the Origin of Species*).
3 Students discuss the questions in Ex 4 and Ex 5 in groups.

Unit 1 Can you hide your feelings?

Procedure
1 Make one copy of the worksheet for each 16 students and cut up as indicated.
2 Students work in pairs. Give each student one expression which shows a particular feeling or emotion such as alarm, desperation, hope, annoyance etc. Working with their partner they must make up a short dialogue or role play and include the sentences in their dialogue.
3 Suggest the dialogue is between ten and sixteen exchanges long and that they write down what they will say. This enables them to repeat the dialogue if necessary.
4 Students 'act out' their dialogues and the other students try and guess which two expressions are the ones they needed to use.
5 Alternatively, to make it slightly easier, each pair only gets one expression between them.

Unit 2 Future forecasts

Lead-in
1 Write *2050* on the board and ask: *What technological advances might have been made by the year 2050?* Brainstorm a few ideas.
2 Tell the students they are going to read a text about forecasts and predictions for the future.

Procedure
1 Students work in pairs. Student A reads Text A (web forum posting) and student B reads Text B (newspaper article). They make notes in answer to the questions.
2 Students then explain the main messages of their texts to each other, using the notes they made in Ex 1 to help them. They compare and discuss their opinions about which future scenarios are likely and unlikely.
3 Students work individually or in pairs and decide the meanings of the words and phrases.

4 Students work in groups and discuss the advantages and disadvantages of some of the scenarios in the box. Encourage them to use the sentence beginnings given. Students report back to the class anything interesting from their discussions.

Answers
3 1 causing the growth of a new body part or organ
2 something that is usual or expected
3 agreement among all the people involved
4 events that cause serious damage
5 do or make something again in the same way as before
6 independence, having the power and ability to make your own decisions
7 not needed or wanted
8 using machines or done by machines, instead of people
9 weaknesses
10 not behaving in the same way

Unit 2 Quiz time!

Procedure
1 Students work in pairs. Give one part of the quiz to each student.
2 Students spend some time thinking about what questions they need to ask, using the *Is /Was it* + relative clause form and the word cues provided. If necessary go through the example questions with the students. They write two more questions of their own with three alternative answers.
3 Student A asks student B his / her questions. Student B reads the choices and chooses the answer he / she thinks is correct from the list. Then student B asks student A his / her questions.
4 Students tell their partner their score. Find out who the student with the best general knowledge in the class is.

Unit 3 Fame for fame's sake

Lead-in
Ask: *What does the phrase 'Fame for fame's sake' mean?* Ask students to give examples of who this applies to ('instant' celebrities).

Procedure
1 Read Andy Warhol's quote and discuss the questions as a whole class or in groups.
2 Students work in pairs. They read one of the texts each and then explain the details of their text to their partner.
3 In their pairs, students discuss the questions in Ex 3.
4 Students read the alternatives in Ex 4 and make their own choices. In groups students discuss their individual choices and justify their ideas.
5 Use the illustrations to lead into a discussion about celebrities who died young.

Unit 3 What's the idiom?

Procedure

There are two alternative ways of doing this activity:

1 Make one copy of the worksheet for each four students and cut out as indicated.
    Each student gets five cards and they must explain the meaning of each idiom without using any of the words on the card. The other students have to try and guess the idiom. The student who guesses correctly gets the card and the winner is the student with the most cards. Remind the students that all the idioms contain a part of the body or an item of clothing. Give the students a few minutes to check the meaning of any idioms they don't know. If the students need extra support, give each group one complete idioms sheet to refer to.

2 This is a simpler option. Give teams of three or four students a set of the idioms, cut up as indicated. Read out a definition (from the answers below) and teams compete to find the idiom they think matches the definition. The first correct team wins a point and the team with the most points at the end wins the game.

Answers

Let your hair down = Relax

By the skin of your teeth = Achieve something, but with only a small margin of error / time left

Use your head = Don't be stupid / think something through

You can't fill his shoes = You can't replace him

Get off my back = Stop making my life difficult / leave me alone

Keep it under your hat = Keep it secret

Grit your teeth and get on with it = Be strong and do the (unpleasant) task you need to

Pay through the nose = Pay the top price for something, or get the strictest penalty for something bad you've done

He's always licking his boss' boots = He's doing too much to impress his boss

Keep your eyes open = Be careful and watch what's going on

Pull your socks up = Work harder

You scratch my back and I'll scratch yours = You do me a favour and I'll help you in return

By the seat of your pants = Achieve something but only by taking dangerous risks

Get out of hand = A situation that gets out of control

Put the boot in = Attack someone (either verbally in an argument or physically)

Follow your nose = Follow your instincts / make decisions that you think are right

She has egg all over her face = She's done something that has not worked out and has left her looking foolish and embarrassed

Go weak at the knees = Become really nervous / when someone is so much in love with a person that they can't speak or do anything in their company

Thumbs up = A positive decision

A pain in the neck = Something or someone who is really annoying

Unit 4 Securing freedom?

Lead-in

Write the word *freedom* on the board. Ask for connected words and phrases and write these on the board too. Examples: *freedom of information*; *freedom fighter*; *individual freedoms*.

Procedure

1 Students individually rank each of the examples in Ex 1 from most important to least important. They then compare their ideas with a partner.

2 Students work in groups and discuss the questions. Allow time for whole class feedback.

3 Students read the text individually. Ask: *Is it essentially factual or written from one viewpoint?* (The article is typical of quality press news articles, and is mainly reporting facts).

4 Allow students to give their personal reactions to the text in pairs or as a whole class.

5 Students complete the exercise either individually or as a group discussion.

6 In Ex 6 students are asked to make what may be difficult choices; such choices are similar to those made by governments in the context of freedom versus preventing crime and terrorism. Ask students to explain their viewpoints as appropriate.

Vocabulary

unveil, biased, measure (noun), atrocity, sleep easy, persecution, CCTV footage (closed circuit television recordings), restrictions

Unit 4 Crimes of the century

Procedure

1 Students work in pairs and are given a handout each. The handouts contain two different true stories about famous thefts. The students have to put the stories in the correct order by reading each other lines on their handout. The first line of each story is provided. It's important that students don't look at each other's handout. Tell the students to start with Millennium Dome and to number the lines as they do the activity.

2 After students have completed the stories, student A focuses on the Millennium Dome story and student B focuses on the Mona Lisa one. Students retell their story by using both handouts.

3 Students discuss the questions in Ex 3.

Answers

Millennium Dome		Mona Lisa	
A	B	A	B
9	4	6	9
11	16	12	15
1	6	2	1
7	10	8	7
15	8	14	5
3	2	16	11
13	12	10	13
5	14	4	3

Vocabulary

JCB, catch red-handed, forger, audacious

Module 3

Unit 1 Alternative lifestyles

Lead-in
Ask students to say what is alternative about the lifestyles of bikers, punks and hippies (clothes, what they do, what they like etc).

Procedure
1 Students work in small groups and discuss what they know about the three groups of people. Ask a few groups to report back to the whole class.
2 Students work in groups of three. Each student reads one of the texts and tells the other two students about what they have read.
3 In their groups the students discuss the questions in Ex 3. Allow time for whole class feedback.
4 Students read the extract in Ex 4 and discuss the questions. Check ideas with the whole class.
5 Set up the debate. Divide the class into two groups; one group should support the right of parents and think of supporting reasons. The other group should think about why it might not be a good idea for parents to choose alternative lifestyles in terms of the impact on their children. Give the groups 5–6 minutes to come up with some ideas and then hold the debate either as a whole class or in small groups.

Unit 1 Ellipsis and substitution

Procedure
1 Students play this game in groups of three or four. Before they start go through the instructions carefully with the students, explaining the different task types and the examples.
2 Students need a counter each as well as a board and a dice. Players take it turns to move around the board by either doing an ellipsis or substitution task. If the other students are satisfied by the player's answer then the player stays on that square. If not, they return to their previous square. In some cases you may need to help students as more than one answer is possible.
3 The first player to reach the end is the winner.

Unit 2 What's in a word?

Lead-in
Ask students to make lists of words that are the same in their language and English. Allow time for students to give the class some examples.

Procedure
1 Students work in pairs and try to match the words in Ex 1 to the languages they came from. Students then try to guess the original meanings (see answer key).
2 Students work in groups and discuss the questions in Ex 2. Allow time for whole class feedback.

3 Introduce the two articles. Explain that *Franglais* is a term used to describe a mixture of English and French. Students read the two articles individually. Ask: *Which country has a more protective attitude towards its language?* Encourage students to justify their answers.
4 Students work in groups to discuss the questions in Ex 4 and Ex 5. You may like to change the groups around for Ex 5.
5 Students guess the answers to Ex 6.

Answers
1 1 sofa, Arabic, bench; 2 tattoo, Polynesian, puncture / mark made on skin; 3 penguin, Welsh, white head; 4 shampoo, Hindi, massage; 5 mammoth, Russian, earth animal; 6 barbecue, Carib, wooden frame on posts; 7 robot, Czech, forced labour; 8 yacht, Dutch, hunt; 9 ketchup, Malay, fish brine; 10 kiosk, Turkish, palace / pavilion
5 The easiest is possibly Indonesian as there are no tenses and no tones. Basque (Northern Spain) is widely considered to be one of the most difficult.
There are more than one million English words, about one third are technical terms. Taki, spoken in parts of French Guinea, consists of only 340 words.
Mandarin Chinese has about 1.4 billion speakers. English has about 380 million.
English is spoken on every continent including South America (Guyana) and 58 countries in the world and the United Nations includes English as an official language.
Japanese and Chinese have about 2000 common characters but Japanese uses three different writing systems. The Cambodian alphabet is the world's largest alphabet, with 74 letters. The world's shortest alphabet, used in the Solomon Islands, has only 11.
6 28%French, 28% Latin, 25% Germanic (including Old English, Old Norse and Dutch), 5% Greek, 8% other (6% unknown)

Unit 2 Adjective endings

Lead-in
1 Review with the students the use and meanings of the following adjective suffixes: *-able   -ish   -ous   -y   -ful   -less*
2 Brainstorm adjectives with these endings.

Procedure
1 Explain how to play to the students. Students play in small groups and need one dice and a counter each. The first student rolls the dice, moves that number of spaces and must use the suffix that corresponds to that number to describe something within the category on the square. If a student can't do the task he / she misses a turn. The winner is the first person to reach FINISH.
2 At the end, ask the students to report back some of the things they described.

Unit 3 Caught on the Net

Lead-in
Ask students about the different places that people can meet up or get to know each other. Elicit the idea of people meeting after making contact on the Internet.

Procedure
1 On the board write *internet dating* and *Friends Reunited* and make 3 columns under each heading. At the top of the columns write; *know, want to know, new*. Ask students to work in pairs and write the things they know about these two things in the column 'know', then ask them to write two or three things they would like to know in the second column.
2 Divide each pair into A and B. Give all the A students the 'In touch or out of touch?' text about Friends Reunited and all the B students the 'Looking for Mr Right' text about internet dating. Explain that you want them to read their text, check the things they 'knew' are correct, see if they could find answers to the 'want to know' and add information they think is important to the 'new' column.
3 Give students enough time to read the text and complete their chart. Then, ask them to share what they found out with their partner, but to try and do this without referring to the text.
4 Students discuss the questions in Ex 2 in pairs or small groups. Allow time for whole class feedback.

Unit 3 Strike a deal

Lead-in
Brainstorm collocations with *deal* (*reach, make, strike, close, negotiate*).

Procedure
1 Explain that students are going to negotiate (strike) a deal. Students work in pairs and are given a role card and a phrase card each. Give them a few minutes to absorb all the information and think about what they want from the negotiation.
2 The students obviously have to try to get a satisfactory deal and there is enough room for manoeuvre within the roles for this to be possible.
3 Explain that as well as negotiating a deal, they have to use the phrases on the cards as naturally as possible and tick the phrases as they say them. The phrases can be reused but the object is to make sure all six are used appropriately before the end of the discussion.
4 When the activity has finished, allow time for whole class feedback. Find out who got good deals, bad deals and possibly no deals. Both during the activity and after, students must not look at their partner's cards.

Vocabulary
margins, warranty, installation, bulk

Unit 4 Team breakdown

Lead-in
Write the word *team* on the board and brainstorm collocations. Examples: *team work, team spirit, sports team,*

team decision. Ask: *Do you enjoy working in teams?* Ask for possible disadvantages of working in teams, eg *inefficiency, internal divisions, unequal levels of contribution, bullying* etc.

Procedure
1 Students work in pairs for Ex 1 and 2. Encourage students to discuss their reasons and welcome differences of opinion. There are no right answers.
2 Encourage students to think about their own experiences of working in teams, at school, in hobby groups etc. There should be potential for amusing and embarrassing stories.
3 Students rate the items in Ex 4 individually and then discuss their ideas with a partner. Allow time for whole class feedback.
4 Ask students to read both scenarios, and initially ask for a global reason why they went wrong.
5 Students discuss the possible reasons for failure. Again there are no 'correct' answers and students' perspectives are to be encouraged.

Vocabulary
objective, non-negotiable, cobble together, incoherent, venture far and wide

Unit 4 Teamwork

Procedure
1 Students work in groups of four and are given a copy of the text and a strip of words each. If there are more than four students in a group then two can share the same strip. It's better not to have students working in groups of less than four.
2 Explain that they are going to do an activity to help consolidate some of the dependent prepositions they studied in the coursebook. But what they are actually doing is an activity to evaluate how well they perform in a team. DO NOT tell the students this until after they complete the task.
3 The dependent preposition activity works by students reading through the text together and using the words from the strips to complete the gaps. Each student has a quarter of the missing words. In order to do this successfully, the members of the group have to listen to each other's suggestions for each gap and collectively make decisions about which words are right. The activity can only be done by everyone paying attention and working together. It is possible to make the activity competitive if you have more than one group by making the first team to complete the activity successfully the winner.
4 Give each student a copy of the discussion questions and students discuss how well they worked as a team.

Answers
1 participate in,   2 split into,   3 mixture of,
4 specialising in,   5 makings of,   6 translated into,
7 different from,   8 impact on,   9 blamed on,
10 excuses for,   11 aspects of,   12 responsible for,
13 focus on,   14 agreement on,   15 best thing about,
16 benefit from

Move placement test

Name: _____

Section 1 Language: Total _____ / 50

Section 2 Vocabulary: Total _____ / 25

Section 3 Writing: Total _____ / 25

Section 4 Speaking: Total _____ / 25

Section 1 Language

Circle the correct alternative *a, b* or *c*.

1 _____ a bank near here?
  a Is   b Is it   c Is there

2 Sam speaks English very _____.
  a good   b well   c bad

3 My mother is _____ teacher.
  a –   b a   c one

4 What _____?
  a Sam does want   b does Sam wants
  c does Sam want

5 We had _____ rain last night.
  a a lot   b a little   c a few

6 Sam is _____ than Dave.
  a more old   b more older   c older

7 _____ last night?
  a Did you go   b Have you been   c Have you gone

8 She's in the same class _____ me.
  a to   b like   c as

9 Who _____ this book?
  a gave you   b did give you   c did you give

10 _____ the newspaper.
  a I always read   b I read always   c Always I read

11 Where _____?
  a is Harry going   b Harry is going
  c is going Harry

12 This picture _____ by my friend.
  a painted   b was painting   c was painted

13 A: I love Indian food.   B: _____.
  a I do so   b So do I   c So I do

14 There's a no-smoking sign. You _____ smoke here.
  a don't have to   b don't must   c mustn't

15 If you're hot, I _____ the window.
  a 'll open   b am going to open   c open

16 I'm going out _____ some milk.
  a for get   b for to get   c to get

17 Try _____ late.
  a to not be   b to be not   c not to be

18 _____ here before.
  a I think I haven't been   b I don't think I've been
  c I don't think I haven't been

19 Someone _____ the meeting was cancelled.
  a said me   b told me   c told to me

20 If you _____ me your email address, I'll write to you.
  a will give   b give   c gave

21 Life would be easier if I _____ a bit more money.
  a would have   b have   c had

22 I'm late for school _____.
  a sometimes   b never   c always

23 I look forward _____ you next week.
  a seeing   b to see   c to seeing

24 He speaks with _____ strong accent.
  a –   b the   c a

25 I'm going to the hairdresser's _____.
  a to get my hair cut   b to get cut my hair
  c to cut my hair

26 I _____ in Rome since 2003.
  a 'm living   b 've lived   c live

27 Is it alright _____ I open the window?
  a –   b that   c if

28 We complained to the waiter _____ the food.
  a for   b of   c about

29 _____ it was raining we went for a walk.
  a However   b But   c Although

30 Sam was only pretending _____ upset.
  a be   b to be   c being

31 My parents never let me _____ computer games.
  a play   b to play   c playing

32 I _____ call you yesterday, but I didn't have time.
  a would   b would be going to   c was going to

33 Peter came out with us last night _____ feeling ill.
a yet   b although   c despite

34 I was surprised _____ Tom at the party last night
a to see   b seeing   c for seeing

35 If you're tired, _____ to bed.
a go   b you go   c you will go

36 Have you any idea where _____?
a does she live   b she does live   c she lives

37 I wish I _____ to David yesterday.
a had spoken   b would have spoken   c spoke

38 A: What does this word mean?
B: Look _____ in the dictionary.
a up   b it up   c up it

39 This time next week, I _____ on a beach in Greece.
a 'm lying   b 'll lie   c 'll be lying

40 I could see a small road _____ into the distance.
a disappearing   b was disappearing
c disappeared

41 It _____ Pete who broke the window – he wasn't here at the time.
a mustn't have been   b couldn't be
c can't have been

42 This is the first time _____ Vietnamese food.
a I've eaten   b I'm eating   c I eat

43 I can't give you a lift because my car is _____.
a still repairing   b still being repaired
c still repaired

44 _____, that everyone stayed indoors.
a The weather such was   b Such was the weather
c Such the weather was

45 Phone me when you _____.
a have arrived   b will arrive   c will have arrived

46 I'd rather you _____ in the house.
a didn't smoke   b not smoke   c don't smoke

47 Nobody rang me, _____?
a did anybody   b did he or she   c did they

48 _____ realised, I would've told you.
a Had I   b Would I have   c If I would have

49 Sam doesn't work, _____ he always seems to have a lot of money.
a whereas   b yet   c however

50 _____ all the questions, James felt quite pleased with himself.
a Has finally answered   b Finally answering
c Having finally answered

Total mark _____ / 50

Section 2 Vocabulary

Add the missing word.

1 I _____ born in Paris.
2 I _____ 21 years old.
3 My birthday is _____ July.
4 Last month, I went _____ the USA.
5 I stayed in New York _____ two weeks.
6 Did you _____ many photos on holiday?
7 What does Katy's new boyfriend look _____?
8 Did you _____ your homework last night?
9 It's a good idea to try _____ clothes before you buy them.
10 As _____ as I'm concerned, internet shopping is a great idea.
11 Oxford is famous _____ its university.
12 Have you any _____ what time it is?
13 I get on really _____ with my brothers and sisters.
14 We went to lots of places last night, but we ended _____ in Bar Soleil.
15 Sue's new dress is very eye-_____.
16 We used to be friends, but we lost _____ a few years ago.
17 I don't know how old he is, but he looks to be in _____ late-twenties.
18 The sea was very cold – in fact it was absolutely _____.
19 Can you _____ a secret?
20 Lizzy has got a great _____ of humour.
21 After being off school for a week, he found it difficult to _____ up with the work he'd missed.
22 You're the only person I've told. No-one knows about it _____ from you and me.
23 The advantages far _____ the disadvantages.
24 Central Park in New York is a great place to while _____ a few hours.
25 She'll be very successful – she's a real go-_____.

Total mark _____ / 25

This page contains guidance for teachers for Section 3 Writing and Section 4 Speaking.

Section 3 Writing

Write about *one* of the following topics. Write a maximum of 150 words.

a   My family
b   My home town or city
c   My job / studies
d   My hobbies and interests

> **Give a score out of 25**
> out of 5 points for accuracy
> out of 5 points for vocabulary use
> out of 5 points for cohesion
> out of 5 points for complexity of language used
> out of 5 points for general impression

Section 4 Speaking

Choose from the following questions / instructions. Within each section the questions become progressively more challenging.

Home town / city

Where are you from?
How long have you lived there?
Can you tell me something about (student's home town / city)?
How do you feel about living in (student's home town / city)?

Family and friends

Do you have a large or small family?
Can you tell me something about your family?
What kinds of things do you do together as a family?
Can you tell me something about your friends?
What kinds of things do you do with your friends?
What do you think are the important qualities of a good friend?

Work / study

Do you work or are you a student?
What do you do / study?
How long have you had this job / been a student?
Can you tell me something about your work / studies?
What do you enjoy most about you work / studies?
Is there anything you don't like?

Leisure

Have you got any hobbies or interests?
Are you interested in sports / music / cinema / reading etc?
What's your favourite sport / kind of music / film / book etc?
What else do you like to do in your free time?
How did you become interested in (student's hobby or interest)?
What do you generally do in the evenings and at weekends in (student's home town / city)?

Future plans

What do you hope to do in the next few years?
Do you have any long-term plans?
Where do you see yourself in ten years' time?

Learning English

How long have you been studying English?
Why are you learning English?
How do you feel about learning English?
How important is English for you?

What do you want to gain from this English course?

Which areas of English are the most important for you to work on during this course?
– speaking
– writing
– reading
– listening
– grammar
– vocabulary
– pronunciation

> **Give a score out of 25**
> out of 5 points for accuracy
> out of 5 points for vocabulary use
> out of 5 points for cohesion
> out of 5 points for complexity of language used
> out of 5 points for general impression

See page 154 for answers to Section 1 Language and Section 2 Vocabulary.

Most students should be able to complete Sections 1 and 2 in approximately 30 minutes.

Test

Name: _____

1   Choose the correct alternative.

What is regarded as unconventional behaviour often depends on who you are talking to and how old they are. For example, teenagers will often wear clothes that their parents will disapprove of (1) _____ they are aware that it will cause problems. In fact, teenagers generally do this to provoke their parents, (2) _____ then complain when their parents get upset. (3) _____, parents should know what to expect as they were once the same, (4) _____ for some reason they seem to forget this. (5) _____ most teenagers grow out of this kind of behaviour there are a few whose rebellious nature is part of their personality. (6) _____, even these people often try to find other ways of being accepted in society by becoming actors, artists or pop stars, roles in which eccentricity is regarded as par for the course. One of the strangest things about such people is that they often insist that they are individuals and (7) _____ still try to fit in with what is regarded as normal. (8) _____, the same patterns can be observed almost everywhere in the world.

1   a whereas   b even though   c but
2   a yet   b despite   c however
3   a While   b Nevertheless   c On the other hand
4   a while   b even though   c but
5   a While   b However   c Yet
6   a Whereas   b However   c Despite
7   a yet   b but   c nevertheless
8   a While   b On the other hand   c Nevertheless

2   Complete these sentences by adding the word in brackets in the correct place.

a   I'm not very happy about the idea, I know I can't change your mind. (but)

_____

_____

b   It hasn't been decided, I think the choice is rather obvious. (while)

_____

_____

c   He's very mischievous, everyone likes him. (yet)

_____

_____

d   She's rather unconventional, her sister is quite ordinary. (whereas)

_____

_____

e   Her clothes are a bit strange, she's quite a conventional person really. (although)

_____

_____

f   Everything seemed to be going wrong, he still had a positive outlook. (nevertheless)

_____

_____

g   I will lend you the money to buy a new pair of shoes, this is the last time. (however)

_____

_____

h   I studied hard, I still failed the exam. (even though)

_____

_____

3   Complete the dialogue with the expressions in the box.

Can I finish what I was saying?   Where was I?
That reminds me of   Hang on!   Talking of

Tom: So tell me about your childhood …

Pam: When we were young everyone mixed us up; we are identical twins. Although we looked the same, we were very different when it came to behaviour. I was the good one …

Amy: (a) _____ That's just not true …

Pam: (b) _____

Amy: Well, only if it's the truth.

Pam: OK, OK. (c) _____

Amy: You were saying how you were the good one …

Pam: Oh, yes. Mum and Dad thought I was really well behaved. When something happened, they always blamed Amy …

Amy: It was so unfair and you always got what you wanted.

Pam: Mum and Dad would believe anything I said.

Amy: (d) _____ the time you drank Dad's whiskey and then told him it was me!

Pam: (e) _____ whiskey, do you want a drink?

Amy: Pam, don't try to change the topic.

Tom: Why don't I get us all a drink?

4   <u>Underline</u> the word that doesn't collocate.

a   He's got such a / an *fertile / overactive / sympathetic* imagination.

b   Joan is a / an *keen / feminine / avid* collector of film memorabilia.

c   It's important to try and have a *vivid / sunny / positive* outlook on life.

d   Frida Kahlo had a *fertile / dark / creative* side.

e   Jack's a bit eccentric. He's got some *unconventional / avid / unusual* traits.

5   Replace the <u>underlined</u> words with an adjective in the box. There is one extra word.

> conventional   curious   gloomy   intelligent
> mischievous   opinionated   rebellious

a   Max is so <u>dogmatic</u>. If you're talking about something he'll always tell you what he thinks, even when you don't ask him! _____

b   I'm always very <u>inquisitive</u>. I love to know everything that's going on. _____

c   As a teenager I was really <u>disobedient</u>, but as I grew older I became quite <u>ordinary</u>. _____ _____

d   Come on! Try and cheer up. You always look so <u>miserable</u>. _____

e   Mary is such a <u>playful</u> child and she's always smiling in that cheeky way. _____

6   <u>Underline</u> the stressed syllable in these words.

a   conventional   e   mischievous
b   curious   f   opinionated
c   gloomy   g   rebellious
d   intelligent   h   unorthodox

7   Read the first part of the article and complete it with the phrases in the box. Write the numbers.

> 1   by the time she formed the band
> 2   for her weird clothes and quirky music
> 3   before she was even in her teens
> 4   after six years playing with
> 5   as a girl she dreamt of being a pop star

Björk

In 2006, Björk was voted the world's most eccentric star (a) _____. Björk Gudmundsdóttir, was born in Iceland in 1965 and like many of her contemporaries (b) _____. However, unlike many teenagers who simply dream of stardom Björk actually did something about it. In fact, (c) _____ she had become something of a legend in her native Iceland. She was just eleven when she recorded her first album and (d) _____ The Sugarcubes in 1986 she was well on the way to international recognition. Björk left to start a solo career (e) _____ The Sugarcubes.

8   Read the second part of the text about Björk and answer the questions.

Her first solo album was called *Debut* and included four hit singles. In 1993, she appeared at the Brit Awards and then the following year co-wrote the title track to Madonna's album *Bedtime Stories*. In 1998, she recorded her third solo album *Homogenic* and began her acting career and in 2000 she won the Best Actress award for her role in the film *Dancer in the Dark*.

Björk has made it part of her persona to be regarded as unorthodox and in 2004 she hit new heights with the release of *Medúlla*. The album featured hundreds of vocals instead of instruments.

a   In which year did Björk co-write the title track to *Bedtime Stories*?
_____

b   How many solo albums did she record between 1992 and 1997?
_____

c   Was Björk successful as an actor?
_____

d   Is Björk a conventional artist?
_____

e   What was unusual about the album *Medúlla*?
_____

Exercise	Score
1 Language	_____ / 8
2 Language	_____ / 8
3 Vocabulary	_____ / 5
4 Vocabulary	_____ / 5
5 Vocabulary	_____ / 6
6 Pronunciation	_____ / 8
7 Reading	_____ / 5
8 Reading	_____ / 5
Total:	_____ / 50
	_____ %

UNIT 2
Test

Module 1

Name: _____

1 Put these words in the correct order to make sentences.

a modern-looking / over there / I / building / in / that / live

_____

b owned / company / a building / which is / a Swiss-based / by / to / live / close / I

_____

c Microsoft / is / over there / the building / of / new headquarters / the

_____

d landmarks / best-known / one / it's / in / of the / the city

_____

e featured / travel magazine / the / that's / on the / of that / front cover / building

_____

f in one / apartments / recently built / near / of those / he / the sea / lives

_____

2 Complete these sentences by putting the word in brackets into the correct place.

a Abbotabad is a tourist-friendly situated in the foothills of northern Pakistan. (town)

_____

b Uluru is a strange-looking rising 348 metres out of the desert. (rock)

_____

c It's a ruined overlooking the Aegean sea. (temple)

_____

d The Medrassa in Samarkand has thousands of hand-made covering the outside walls. (tiles)

_____

e It's an old-fashioned perched on the edge of a mountain. (castle)

_____

f Stonehenge is an ancient stone built as a temple in the south of England. (circle)

_____

3 Read these sentences and match the grammar points in the box to the underlined words in each sentence. One grammar point applies to two sentences.

1 adjective
2 relative clause
3 clause beginning with a present participle
4 noun used as an adjective
5 phrase beginning with a preposition

a I recently bought a <u>sea-facing</u> flat near the beach. It's fantastic! _____

b The man <u>living in the house over there</u> is my brother. _____

c <u>Outside the building</u> is a beautiful park with a small lake. _____

d <u>Standing close to the front</u> of the building is an eight-hundred year old tree. _____

e The building, <u>which was bought by his father,</u> is now worth millions. _____

f It's really quite a <u>tourist</u> trap. _____

4 Complete these dialogues with the expressions in the box.

a shame   awful   dear. I'm sorry
it can't be that bad   stop moaning   the record
you're not the only one with problems

a A: What's wrong?
   B: I've just lost my job.
   A: Oh _____.

b A: Work, work, work.
   B: _____!
      All you do is complain.
   A: Yeah, I know, but it's just that I've got so much to do.

c A: Sorry, but I won't be able to go out tonight. My car was stolen earlier today.
   B: How_____!

d A: You look terrible. What's wrong?
   B: Everything!
   A: Come on, _____.
   B: It is.
   A: Well, _____.

e A: Matt phoned. He won't be able to come.
   B: Oh, what _____!

f A: You're always late.
   B: It wasn't my fault.
   A: It never is and you never apologise.
   B: Oh, change _____!

Photocopiable   *Move* Advanced Teacher's Book © Macmillan Publishers Limited 2007   **123**

5 Complete these sentences with the words in the box. There are two extra words.

based	catching	coloured	facing
friendly	known	looking	loved
made	room	saving	smoking

a The Eiffel Tower is the best- _____ building in Paris.

b Raul works for an American- _____ media company.

c We're looking at various time- _____ options to try and increase efficiency.

d He designs such eye- _____ buildings, but I wonder how practical they are.

e I'm sorry, but this is a non- _____ restaurant.

f You can't miss it! It's the funny- _____ building on the right.

g I've just bought a new two- _____ apartment in the city centre.

h Come on! It's so badly _____ that I'm not paying that price!

i You can't miss her. She always wears such brightly _____ clothes.

6 Cross out the word which does not form a correct compound adjective.

1 He's always very _____ dressed.
a brightly   b multi   c casually

2 He comes from a _____ -known town.
a good   b little   c well

3 It's important to be _____ -minded and tolerant.
a broad   b badly   c open

4 He's always wearing such _____ -looking clothes.
a expensive   b strange   c casually

5 His apartment is _____ -facing.
a open   b sea   c south

6 We're always looking for _____ -saving ideas.
a energy   b much   c money

7 Read the article and complete the sentences with the correct number.

1 The Parthenon

The Parthenon is one of the most famous landmarks of ancient Greece. Part of a complex of temples on the Acropolis, it was dedicated to the goddess Athena, patron of the city of Athens.

2 Easter Island

This island has interested the world ever since it was discovered in 1722. Its 25-metre-high stone sculptures still puzzle historians and archaeologists. It is believed that they were erected between the 10th and 16th centuries by the ancestors of the original Polynesian settlers. The mystery surrounding them is part of what makes Easter Island so famous.

3 The Taj Mahal

Built by Shah Jahan in memory of his wife Mumtaz Mahal this awe-inspiring palace took 17 years to build. The Taj Mahal stands in magnificent walled gardens and is regarded as the most perfect jewel of Mughal art in India.

4 The Neuschwanstein Castle

The Neuschwanstein Castle was built by King Ludwig II of Bavaria in the 19th century at a time when castles were no longer of military value. The castle, with its beautiful architecture and tall towers looks like something out of a fairy tale.

5 The Great Wall of China

Stretching almost 2,400 km from the sea of Shanhaikuan in the east to the northern frontier of Kansu province in the west, the Great Wall of China is the only man-made monument to be visible from space. The construction was started in around 214 B.C. to protect China from a Mongolian invasion.

a _____ was purpose-built to provide protection.

b _____ is part of a group of buildings.

c _____ is surrounded by mystery.

d _____ is a perfect representation of Mughal art.

e _____ could be from a children's story.

f _____ is so massive it can be seen from a great distance.

g _____ is dedicated to the patron of the city.

h _____ did not have a military purpose.

i _____ was built as a memorial.

j _____ contains objects whose purpose is unknown.

Exercise	Score
1 Language	_____ / 6
2 Language	_____ / 6
3 Language	_____ / 6
4 Vocabulary	_____ / 7
5 Vocabulary	_____ / 9
6 Vocabulary	_____ / 6
7 Reading	_____ / 10
Total:	_____ / 50
	_____ %

Name: _____

1 Complete the text with the words in the box.

> absolutely   at all   complete   even
> simply   so   without doubt

Last year I went on a demonstration march in central London. When we arrived the scene was amazing, we'd been told there would be a hundred thousand people but there were (a) _____ more than that. The march started peacefully and we had (b) _____ no idea (c) _____ what would happen later that day. We'd been marching for about ten minutes when I suddenly started to feel nervous. It was (d) _____ strange. I kind of knew something bad was going to happen before it did. Even so, it was a (e) _____ shock. One minute we were singing songs and having a good time and the next minute we were being attacked by the police. I (f) _____ couldn't understand what had gone wrong. It was (g) _____ the worst day of my life.

2 Choose the correct alternative.

a It's a *complete / completely* waste of time.

b I don't know anything *all / at all* about it.

c That's the *single / simply* most important event this year.

d You'll be pleased to know that the *huge / vast* majority of people agree with you.

e The *all / whole* thing was amazing.

3 Cross out the alternative which is not possible.

1 It was _____ incredible.
   a just   b absolute   c totally

2 It was _____ amazing to see you there.
   a really   b so   c even

3 I was _____ worried you'd forget to come.
   a terrible   b so   c terribly

4 There was nothing we could do about it _____.
   a at all   b even   c you know

5 I _____ don't know what you expect.
   a just   b really   c so

6 U2 are _____ the best-known group from Dublin.
   a absolutely   b by far   c without doubt

7 If you were being _____ honest with me, you'd just tell me what happened after I left.
   a completely   b all   c totally

4 Complete these sentences with the words in the box. There is one extra word.

> do   eradicate   express   give
> raise   show   spread   support

a One of the most important things is to _____ awareness of the issues.

b It's incredibly important to try and _____ poverty in the world.

c We really need to _____ something and not just talk.

d I wear a plastic wristband to show I _____ a particular cause.

e I wish I could do more, but at least I regularly _____ money to charity. I know it's not enough, but …

f There's a demonstration on Saturday. Will you _____ the word?

g You are coming on Saturday, aren't you? It's really important we all _____ commitment, otherwise nothing will get done.

5 Replace the underlined phrases with the phrases in the box. There is one extra phrase.

> very calm   broke the spell   going mad
> took on a special significance   it was physical
> mental snap   moment of stillness

It was amazing, the crowd started (a) getting excited and people were jumping up and down and screaming. The noise was so loud (b) you could almost feel it. Then, as we started playing the song there was a (c) sudden calm. I just have this (d) picture in my mind of that exact moment, it was (e) so peaceful and then all hell broke loose again. For me it (f) was one of the most important days in my life as I suddenly realised that I could make a difference.

a _____
b _____
c _____
d _____
e _____
f _____

6   Match the words in column A to the definitions in column B.

A

a   commitment (n)

b   crowd (n)

c   eradicate (v)

d   guilty conscience (n)

e   issue (n)

f   smug (adj)

g   stand for (v)

h   weirdo (n)

B

1   a subject or topic that people discuss or argue about

2   what a set of letters means or represents, ie UNICEF, UNESCO

3   a large group of people

4   to be self-satisfied, arrogant

5   a feeling that you have done something wrong

6   to get rid of something completely, especially something bad

7   someone who behaves in a way that seems very strange

8   a strong belief that something is good and that you should support it

7   Read the newspaper article and answer the questions.

a   Who were arrested?

_____

b   What was the protest about?

_____

c   Was this the first meeting of the G8?

_____

d   Who talk but don't do anything?

_____

e   What was one of the purposes of the summit?

_____

G8 summit hit by protest

Lars Svenson, Stockholm

Two protesters were injured and more than fifty arrested as fights broke out during a protest outside the G8 summit in Stockholm. Organisers of the protest claim that police started spraying a crowd of people with water. 'One minute we were walking along shouting "Make war on poverty, not people." and the next minute we were being attacked by the police,' said Klaus, from Germany. He, like many others, had made their way to Stockholm to demonstrate outside the latest round of G8 talks. 'They talk and they talk, but when are they going to do something?' said one young woman who didn't want to be named. During the summit, leaders of the G8 countries discussed ways of eradicating poverty including reducing world debt. The next round of talks are due to be held in November in Tokyo.

8   Read the letter. Write T (true), F (false) or NG (not given) in the boxes.

Dear Editor

I'm writing with regard to the protests that took place last week in Stockholm, Sweden. I really don't know what these people expect to achieve. They say they are peaceful and yet every time there is violence. Personally, I think many of them are there just to cause trouble and are not actually interested in the issues. After all, there are better ways of helping people in developing countries. I myself always buy fair-trade products as I think this is one way I can make a real difference. If these young people really want to do something about the situation, they should try and be constructive and do something themselves rather than simply blaming other people for all the problems in the world.

Yours truly,

Mrs W. J. Stubbs

a   The writer holds the protesters responsible for the violence. ☐

b   The writer believes the protesters are indifferent to the problems in developing countries. ☐

c   The writer believes that buying fair trade products may help to eradicate poverty. ☐

d   The writer believes that taking part in protests is a constructive way of drawing attention to problems. ☐

e   The writer believes that the protesters blame other people for all the problems in the world. ☐

Exercise	Score
1 Language	_____ / 7
2 Language	_____ / 5
3 Language	_____ / 7
4 Vocabulary	_____ / 7
5 Vocabulary	_____ / 6
6 Vocabulary	_____ / 8
7 Reading	_____ / 5
8 Reading	_____ / 5
Total:	_____ / 50
	_____ %

Test

Name: _____

1   Choose the correct alternative.

1   We really need to come up _____ a solution to this problem.
a against   b for   c with

2   I'm going to stand up _____ what I think is right.
a against   b for   c with

3   People often look up _____ sports stars, so they have to set a good example.
a to   b for   c with

4   Remember, if you can't cope you can always fall back _____ me. I'll always try and help you if I can.
a to   b against   c on

5   It's very important you face up _____ the situation and do something about it.
a to   b against   c on

6   I'm not going to worry about it. I'm just going to get on _____ what has to be done.
a for   b with   c to

7   Every time I try to do something I come up _____ another problem! It's so frustrating.
a against   b with   c for

8   You really don't need to put up _____ his behaviour any more.
a against   b with   c for

9   I promise I'll make up _____ all the problems I have caused.
a to   b with   c for

2   Match the phrasal verbs in Ex 1 to the definitions below. Write the question numbers.

a   to accept a bad situation exists and to try and do something about it _____

b   to accept an annoying or unpleasant situation _____

c   to admire or respect someone _____

d   to defend someone or something that is being criticised or attacked _____

e   to devote time to sorting out something and making progress _____

f   to do something in order to improve a bad situation _____

g   to have to deal with something difficult or unpleasant _____

h   to rely on someone when you can't manage something on your own _____

i   to think of something such as an idea or a plan _____

3   Complete these sentences with the correct form of the words in the box.

come	cut	face	get	keep	look	run

a   I'm really _____ forward to seeing you on Saturday.

b   I think we've almost _____ out of milk. Can you stop at the supermarket and buy some?

c   I think I'm _____ down with a cold. I keep on sneezing!

d   You really should _____ down on the amount of coffee you drink. It can't be good for you.

e   There's no way you're going to _____ away with it! He's sure to find out.

f   Come on! Try and _____ up with me. I don't want you to get left behind.

g   The sooner you _____ up to the problem, the sooner you'll find a solution.

4   Replace the underlined phrases with the phrases in the box.

are fighting a losing battle   by hook or by crook
make it big   get off to a flying start
sink or swim   steal the show   throw in the towel
pass with flying colours

a   Don't worry about the exam! I'm sure you'll get through very easily. _____

b   What ever you do, don't give up. There's no point giving up after all the effort you've put in.
_____

c   Sometimes it's important to know when you can't win. _____

d   I'm sure you'll be very successful.
_____

e   You need to be careful with Mary as she's bound to attract most of the attention.
_____

f   Watch him! He'll win whatever it takes.
_____

g   They are so similar, I'm sure they will get on together from the moment they meet.
_____

h   I'm sorry but you're going to have to succeed on your own. _____

5 Complete these sentences with the phrases in the box.

| after seeing | down to | due to | owe |
| rooted in | role model | spurs me on |

a   If it was _____ me, you wouldn't get a second chance.

b   You really don't know how much I _____ her, do you?

c   It's the knowledge that I can succeed if I try hard enough that _____.

d   My mother was always my _____.

e   I'm really not sure what advice I can give _____ the situation you face.

f   You do realise you're only here _____ some exceptional circumstances.

g   Her fear is _____ her childhood experiences.

6 Read the article about Beyond Boundaries and complete it with the phrases in the box. There are two extra phrases.

1	working together
2	in just 28 days
3	by attempting a journey
4	nothing can stand in the way
5	by doing the impossible
6	escorted by armed soldiers
7	climbed a live volcano

Beyond Boundaries

In 2005, eleven people made history (a) ____ that had never been made before. They walked across Nicaragua from the Atlantic coast to the Pacific Ocean. Starting on the treacherous Mosquito Coast, and (b) ____ to protect them from bandits and drug traffickers, they hacked their way through impenetrable jungle, crossed crocodile-infested rivers and (c) ____. Travelling 220 miles (d) ____, the most remarkable thing about this journey was that all eleven were physically disabled. Eight men and three women working as a team tried to overcome their disabilities and prove that (e) ____ if you are determined enough. The entire journey was both physically and emotionally challenging for all the participants and has been made into the TV series 'Beyond Boundaries'.

7 Read the article and answer the questions.

At 45 years old, Karl Sacks was one of the participants in the Beyond Boundaries expedition across Nicaragua. He decided to take part because it sounded like the adventure of a lifetime and would be both tough and challenging. Back in 1995, Karl lost his leg when it got caught in the propeller of a boat when he was diving and since then he has worn a prosthetic leg. However, this disability doesn't stop him from doing what he wants and he leads quite a full on life at home where he normally gets up at 4:20 a.m. every day, takes his dogs for a walk and then goes swimming. Taking part in the trip has made Karl even more restless and he is planning to trek to the North Pole sometime in 2007.

a   What expedition did Karl Sacks participate in?
_____

b   Why does Karl wear a prosthetic leg?
_____

c   What effect does the disability have on his life?
_____

d   How is his life described?
_____

e   What has happened to Karl since finishing the trip?
_____

Exercise	Score
1 Language	_____ / 9
2 Language	_____ / 9
3 Language	_____ / 7
4 Vocabulary	_____ / 8
5 Vocabulary	_____ / 7
6 Reading	_____ / 5
7 Reading	_____ / 5
Total:	_____ / 50
	_____ %

 Move Advanced Teacher's Book © Macmillan Publishers Limited 2007 **Photocopiable**

Module test

Name: _____

1 Complete the text with the words in the box. There are two extra words.

a bit	absolutely	all	but	complete
highly	however	tiny	whereas	

We stayed in a (a) _____ beach hotel that your sister told us about and it was (b) _____ wonderful. I'd chosen it because it was (c) _____ recommended and because I wanted somewhere out of the way, and it was certainly that. (d) _____ in the past I would have wanted to go somewhere with plenty to do, (e) _____ I wanted this time was somewhere secluded and tranquil. I was prepared to be (f) _____ disappointed (g) _____ in the end it turned out to be perfect.

2 Choose the correct alternative.

a I *absolutely* / *just* couldn't believe it when he told me! Incredible!

b I was sure. *Nevertheless* / *Whereas* I still wanted confirmation.

c It was one of the *most* / *single* terrifying moments in my life.

d *Despite* / *Even though* I knew what had happened, it was still difficult to accept it.

e I didn't regret what had happened *at all* / *without doubt*.

f *Although* / *However* I knew it would be difficult, I was still determined to have a go.

3 Replace the underlined words with a phrasal verb in the box. There are three extra phrasal verbs.

come back from	come up against
come up with	fall back on	get on with
look up to	make up for	put up with
run out of	stand up for	

a As you aren't very tall you'll need to find ways to <u>compensate for</u> it. _____

b Can you <u>think of</u> any other ideas for what we can do for his birthday? _____

c Which athlete do you <u>admire</u>? _____

d I don't know how you <u>tolerate</u> him. If my boyfriend was so unkind, I'd have left him by now! _____

e If you have a problem is there anyone you can <u>rely on</u>? _____

f Come on! Just <u>do</u> it! The longer you delay it, the worse it'll get. _____

g Sometimes it's very difficult to <u>return from</u> a serious injury. _____

4 Put the letters in order in each gap and complete the text about Bob Geldof. The first letter has been given.

Over the course of his life Bob Geldof has had many roles from punk singer to political activist. He is certainly one of the most (a) o_____ (dtnaeipion) and outspoken people around. His music career started in 1975 with the Boomtown Rats. Their (b) e_____ (gticeern) music combined with Geldof's (c) r_____ (ioueblels) nature catapulted them to the top of the UK charts. Then in 1984 Geldof saw a BBC news report on the Ethiopian famine and he decided that he needed to do something to help raise (d) a_____ (swnraees) and encourage people to donate money. His unique idea – a music single to raise money for (e) c_____ (ityarh) was followed a year later by the historic Live Aid concert. His (f) u_____ (cnvntalioneno) look and his (g) g_____ (ooyml) outlook are (h) t_____ (aitrs) that mean people often love him or loathe him. But, whatever you feel about him as a person, no-one can deny his (i) c_____ (ttnmeiomm) to the cause of African (j) p_____ (yterov).

5 Match the words in column A to the words in column B to make compound adjectives.

A		B	
a	child-	1	storey
b	energy-	2	saving
c	sea-	3	run
d	three-	4	friendly
e	family-	5	facing

6   Complete the text with the compound adjectives in Ex 5.

Stay in this luxury 4 star hotel in the wonderful resort of Costa del Rios in Costa Rica. This 'green' hotel has many (a) _____ features including solar powered water systems ensuring round-the-clock hot water. The hotel is suitable for families as it is extremely (b) _____. In fact, as a (c) _____ business your kids might end up making friends with the three children from the hotel as well as the numerous pets. Ask for a (d) _____ balcony and, if you can afford it, stay on the top floor of this (e) _____ building as this gives you the best views of the Pacific Ocean.

7   ● **03** Listen to three students talking about non-conformity. Who says each statement? Put a ✔ in the boxes.

	Alex	Mette	Natsuko	
a	◯	◯	◯	… thinks she / he is rather conventional.
b	◯	◯	◯	… is too lazy to be different.
c	◯	◯	◯	… thinks Berlin is a great place.
d	◯	◯	◯	… says it isn't difficult to be a non-conformist where she / he lives.
e	◯	◯	◯	… everyone dresses the same where she / he lives.
f	◯	◯	◯	… people always do things together where she / he comes from.
g	◯	◯	◯	… thinks Japanese TV is wild.
h	◯	◯	◯	… wears the same clothes as her / his friends.
i	◯	◯	◯	… thinks being a non-conformist is about how you behave not how you dress.
j	◯	◯	◯	… is a bit of a loner.

8   ● **10** Listen to four people talking about motivation and complete these sentences.

a   When we played games, they always let me win _____ and told me how clever I was.

b   The downside is, though, that I just can't _____ criticism.

c   I'd passed my exams with _____ and had started college.

d   Maybe it was the anti-climax after studying so hard for exams and the high of _____ them.

e   And suddenly there she was in New York looking so _____.

f   When I as 16, I decided to _____ at school.

g   I don't think I'll ever _____ as an artist, but I love what I'm doing.

h   They've accepted what I do and are even quite proud of the fact that I _____ what I wanted.

i   When I was older, my mum told me she knew it was a _____ moment in her life.

j   I've sort of inherited the same … er, determination and strong belief in myself. I _____ to my mum.

9   <u>Underline</u> the stressed syllable in these words.

a   avid

b   dogmatic

c   eccentric

d   gloomy

e   inquisitive

f   miserable

g   overactive

h   serious

i   sympathetic

j   unconventional

   Move Advanced Teacher's Book © Macmillan Publishers Limited 2007   **Photocopiable**

10 Read the newspaper article and complete it with the words in the box. There are five extra words.

> achievement   challenged   compensate
> determination   disappointment   expected
> imagine   motivate   think   tolerated

Natalie du Toit

Competing against the best athletes in the world is hard enough at the best of times, but (a) _____ trying to do it when you only have one leg. Well, this is what Natalie du Toit has been trying to do for the past few years. Natalie was ranked second in her country (South Africa) and was (b) _____ to pick up a medal or two in the Olympics in Athens. Unfortunately, she was involved in a scooter accident in February 2001 on her way home from training in Cape Town. The accident was so bad that she had to have her leg amputated just above the knee. But her (c) _____ to fulfil her dream of competing at an international level meant that within four months she was back in the pool! At first everything seemed strange and she had to adjust the balance of her body to (d) _____ for the missing limb. However, all her hard work was to pay off when, in August 2002, she became the first swimmer with a disability to compete in the finals of the Commonwealth Games against able-bodied athletes. In the race – the 800 metre freestyle – she finished eighth, but it was an amazing (e) _____ to have made it to the finals.

11 Read the text again and choose the correct alternative.

a   Competing at the top level is *always difficult / impossible* when you're disabled.

b   Before the accident Natalie was *the best swimmer / one of the best swimmers* in her country.

c   Natalie *had finished her training session / was taking part in her training session* when she had her accident.

d   After the accident Natalie retrained for *many years / about one year* before competing in the Commonwealth Games.

e   She took part in the Commonwealth Games against *other disabled athletes / athletes without disabilities*.

12 Think of one of the best days of your life. Where were you and what happened? Write about 200 words.

Exercise	Score
1 Language	_____ / 7
2 Language	_____ / 6
3 Language	_____ / 7
4 Vocabulary	_____ / 10
5 Vocabulary	_____ / 5
6 Vocabulary	_____ / 5
7 Listening	_____ / 10
8 Listening	_____ / 10
9 Pronunciation	_____ / 10
10 Reading	_____ / 5
11 Reading	_____ / 5
12 Writing	_____ / 20
Total:	_____ / 100
	_____ %

UNIT 1
Test

Name: _____

1 Choose the correct alternative.

1 What _____ been doing since we last met?
   a had you   b have you   c will you have

2 I'm sure he _____ before we arrived.
   a had left   b has left   c will have left

3 In a recent survey one hundred couples were asked what annoyed them most about their partner. The results _____ and there are a few surprises.
   a had been released   b have been released
   c will have been released

4 How long _____ been married when you celebrate your next anniversary?
   a had you   b have you   c will you have

5 She _____ by the time we get there, unless we hurry.
   a had left   b has left   c will have left

6 They _____ working together for six months before they went out on their first date.
   a had been   b have been   c will have been

7 I _____ the Simpsons ever since the series started.
   a had been watching   b had watched
   c have been watching

2 Complete these sentences with the correct form of the words in brackets.

a I knew I _____ (see) her somewhere before, but I couldn't work out where.

b I'm sorry, she _____ (just / leave), but she'll be back soon.

c They _____ (live) together for a year when they finally decided to get married.

d They _____ (argue) since we arrived an hour ago.

e We _____ (be) together for exactly two years next Saturday.

3 Match the sentences (a–e) in Ex 2 to the tenses (1–5) below.

1 Present perfect simple   _____

2 Present perfect continuous   _____

3 Past perfect simple   _____

4 Past perfect continuous   _____

5 Future perfect   _____

4 Replace the underlined words with a word from the box.

| alarmed   annoyed   astonishment |
| desperate   hesitant   hopeful   perplexed |

a You really shouldn't be underlined{frightened}, it's not that dangerous. _____

b She can be so timid sometimes. She really needs to learn to be more confident. _____

c You look really puzzled, what's wrong? _____

d How can you be so optimistic? Be careful you don't become disappointed. _____

e It was so funny, the look of surprise on his face when you turned up. He definitely wasn't expecting that. _____

f You seem to get angry so easily. You really need to lighten up and relax. _____

g You're becoming more and more worried. If you're not careful you'll have a heart attack! _____

5 Choose the correct alternative.

a There was a look of *desperate / desperation* in her eyes.

b I can't believe how *annoyed / annoyance* you can get!

c I really *hope / hopeful* you get on alright.

d He just grabbed hold of it without a moment's *hesitant / hesitation*.

e They were *dismay / dismayed* by his behaviour.

f Their *alarm / alarmed* was quite obvious. I don't think they'll try that again.

6 Complete these sentences with the words in the box.

| badly written   controversial   hilarious |
| in-depth   monotonous   poetic   slow- starter |
| tearjerker   trashy   unputdownable |

a It was a real _____. I couldn't stop crying.

b I found it a bit of a _____, but after a while I could hardly put it down.

c I love travel books, especially when they are _____ and full of useful information.

d The book was so _____ and boring that I almost fell asleep reading it!

e Why do you keep reading her books? They're so _____, at least you could choose someone who can write properly.

f I stayed up all night and read the whole book, it was _____, you just had to know what happened next.

g I really hate _____ novels that are really rubbish, but they always seem to be on the bestseller lists and the shelves of all the high street bookshops.

h Bill Bryson has got such a light style and his observations are so _____ that I can hardly stop laughing sometimes.

i Her writing is so _____, it's just beautiful to read.

j His biography was a bit _____, especially the bit about his ex-wife.

7 Read the magazine article and complete these sentences with C (Carla), A (Abigail), F (Frankie), G (Gerald) or S (Sandra).

a _____ buys more than one copy of the same book.

b _____ doesn't have time to read serious books.

c _____ enjoyed the last book he / she read.

d _____ enjoys reading different types of books.

e _____ finds poetry helps him / her relax.

f _____ is into fantasy books.

g _____ likes books that aren't too long.

h _____ reads a couple of books simultaneously.

i _____ reads mostly non-fiction.

j _____ sometimes has to read for his / her job.

In this month's profile of our readers we take a look at literature and reading habits. We have interviewed five readers about the books they read and why. Here is what they said.

Carla
What do I like reading? Oh! That's easy. I'm a real history buff so anything about historical people, biographies, autobiographies, that kind of thing. I'm also a big fan of 18th and 19th century poetry – Wordsworth, Byron and so on. I find it really helps me unwind.

Abigail
I don't really have time. When I do it's normally light-hearted stuff. You know the type of thing you read on a plane journey. The last book I read was one of those Grisham novels – great stuff!

Frankie
Anything at all. I'm an avid reader and I quite like trying out new genre. I often have more than one book on the go. At the moment I'm reading a thriller by Dan Brown and a poetry anthology.

Gerald
Fantasy, not sci-fi, but stuff like *Lord of the Rings*. I even like reading Harry Potter! I know it's meant for kids, but … I bought the first one for my son and got hooked, now I buy two copies, one for him and one – the one with the alternative 'adult' cover – for me.

Sandra
You're going to laugh at this, but as an actress I hate reading plays. If I have to read one then it's work, not pleasure. For pleasure I like short stories. I don't have much time so I like to be able to finish something quite quickly.

Exercise	Score
1 Language	_____ / 7
2 Language	_____ / 5
3 Language	_____ / 5
4 Vocabulary	_____ / 7
5 Vocabulary	_____ / 6
6 Vocabulary	_____ / 10
7 Reading	_____ / 10
Total:	_____ / 50
	_____ %

Name: _____

1 Complete these sentences with the phrases in the box.

> It's how   It was   One thing   The problem
> The worst thing   What   What is   What was

a _____ her reaction that upset me so much.

b _____ most concerning is the sudden increase in attacks.

c _____ that really annoys me is all this talk about perfect babies.

d _____ about eating organic is that it's so expensive.

e _____ really frightening was how little he seemed to care.

f _____ they proceed that concerns me the most.

g _____ worries me most is what he's going to say.

h _____ is what people are going to do to stop it happening.

2 Put these words in the correct order to make sentences.

a about it / problem is / the / what to do

_____

_____.

b Mike / was / who suggested / it / it

_____

_____.

c she didn't / was / what / believe me / that / worrying / was

_____

_____.

d it / I / understand / is / what / don't / how / actually works

_____

_____.

e none of my business / is / what / do / you

_____

_____.

f it's / not / or / the issue / is / whether / dangerous

_____

_____?

3 Complete each sentence using the prompt so that the meaning is the same as in the first sentence.

a I'm amazed at how popular GM food is.

What amazes _____

_____.

b Nobody knows exactly what harm it might cause.

The worst thing is _____

_____.

c What really surprised me is how little we know about it.

It was _____

_____.

d It is surprising how much controversy there is.

What surprises me _____

_____.

e It's strange that we haven't heard anything about cloning for a long time.

What is _____

_____.

f Watching the news every night can be very worrying.

The worst thing about _____

_____.

4 Complete the text with the words in the box.

> concern   controversy   debate
> headlines   precedent   sympathy

In recent years stories about designer babies have been making (a) _____ in many of the newspapers around the world. Although stories of couples having lost a child often inspire (b) _____, people still worry about the issues surrounding genetic engineering. The idea that people might choose the sex of their baby is cause for (c) _____ and even the idea that people can select things such as the colour of their baby's eyes and hair have created an amazing amount of (d) _____. The recent story of baby Adam has rekindled the (e) _____ into the rights and wrongs of genetic selection and many worry that it has set a (f) _____ which will lead to a sudden increase in such cases.

5 Choose the correct alternative.

a I'm sure if you wait a while the whole issue will *play down / die down* and be forgotten.

b In the article it *spells out / touches on* some of the main concerns, but it doesn't go into enough detail for you to make a judgement.

c I'd really like to know how this *came about / died down*. It seems a very unlikely coincidence.

d You really can't *play down / spell out* the importance of GM foods.

e I'm sorry, but we really can't *touch on anything / rule anything out*. We'll do whatever is needed.

f Could you try and *spell out / rule out* exactly what you mean? I'm not sure I completely understand.

g I'm not really sure how things will *pan out / come about*, but I'll let you know.

6 Complete these dialogues with the words in the box. There are two extra words.

| cares | like | matter | me | me on | never |
| way | what | whatever | | | |

1 A: I'm sorry, I don't eat meat.

B: You're kidding (a) _____. I spent hours cooking this! Now what will you eat?

A: It doesn't (b) _____. I'm not very hungry.

2 A: Can I turn the TV off?

B: Yeah, if you (c) _____. I'm not watching it.

3 A: Have you seen the news? They've cloned a dog!

B: So (d) _____? It's not so bad, is it?

A: Are you having (e) _____? Who knows what they'll do next?

4 A: I'm thinking of having plastic surgery.

B: No (f) _____! What would you want to do that for?

A: Well, my boyfriend thinks my nose is too big.

B: What? Well, who (g) _____ what your boyfriend thinks?

A: To be honest, I do. I want him to think I'm perfect.

7 Read the article and complete it with the words in the box.

breakthrough	carbon	creation	embryos
genetically	interfere	opponents	
organs	premature	species	

In 1996, a group of scientists in Scotland made a scientific (a) _____ which made the news across the world; they cloned a sheep named Dolly. Cloning itself had been around for a number of years and scientists had already cloned mice and frogs, but these were from (b) _____. What made Dolly so special was that she was cloned from the DNA of an adult. And, not only did she take after her mother but she was, in fact, a (c) _____ copy.

Scientists hailed the breakthrough and claimed that it would lead to many benefits including the ability to save endangered (d) _____, reproduce (e) _____ modified animals for farming purposes and even provide replacement (f) _____ that could be used for humans.

However, problems soon materialised with Dolly. It was claimed that she suffered from (g) _____ ageing and arthritis. This raised new questions about the validity of cloning.

There are, of course, other issues as well. Many people are frightened by the idea that someone might decide to clone an entire person thus creating a modern Frankenstein monster. Some (h) _____ of cloning say that we do not have the right to 'play God' and that we shouldn't (i) _____ with nature.

Whatever our take on the morality of cloning, it is quite clear that with the (j) _____ of Dolly, science has reached a new level.

Exercise	Score
1 Language	_____ / 8
2 Language	_____ / 6
3 Language	_____ / 6
4 Vocabulary	_____ / 6
5 Vocabulary	_____ / 7
6 Vocabulary	_____ / 7
7 Reading	_____ / 10
Total:	_____ / 50
	_____ %

Test

Name: _____

1 Match the words in column A to the words in column B to make phrases with *say* and *speak*.

A   B
a   as I was   1   they say
b   as   2   speak
c   I have   3   and I'll say it again
d   I've said it before   4   saying
e   personally   5   of
f   so to   6   speaking
g   speaking   7   said
h   that   8   say
i   let's   9   to say

2 Complete these sentences with the phrases in Ex 1.

a   They were on top of the world _____.

b   That was terrible! _____, it could have been worse, but only just.

c   _____ celebrities, what would you do if you were famous?

d   It was OK, but _____, I was expecting it to be better.

e   _____ movie stars get paid far too much. I feel quite strongly about it!

f   _____ I'd rather go and see a thriller as I hate sci-fi movies.

g   I'll meet you outside the cinema at, _____, six o' clock.

h   _____, some people are just lucky.

i   _____ before, we should go and watch the latest film together.

3 Complete the idioms with the words in the box.

bottom   eyebrows   fingers
hair   hand   heads   heart   lips

a   waited on _____ and foot

b   she always turns _____

c   from the _____ of his heart

d   her name is on everyone's _____

e   try and let your _____ down

f   raises a few _____

g   his _____ and soul

h   keep your _____ crossed

4 Replace the underlined phrases with the expressions in Ex 3.

a   <u>She's the topic of all the conversations</u> at the moment.

_____

b   He expects to be <u>looked after all the time</u>, but I'm not his slave!

_____

c   Just <u>relax and enjoy yourself</u>.

_____

d   He often <u>surprises people</u>.

_____

e   She is so beautiful that <u>everyone looks</u> when she walks down the street.

_____

f   He puts <u>all his energy</u> into everything he does.

_____

g   He always thanks people <u>sincerely</u>.

_____

h   Can you <u>wish me good luck</u>? I'm taking my exams tomorrow.

_____

5 Complete these sentences with the words and expressions in the box.

antics   freeloaders   glimpse   red-carpet
seventh heaven   star-struck

a   They're such a bunch of _____. They've never done any work in their lives.

b   Did you read about the _____ he got up to?

c   We were given the _____ treatment. It was fantastic!

d   She stood there with her mouth hanging open. I've never seen anybody so _____ in my life.

e   We hung around for hours trying to get a _____ of her as she left the hotel.

f   When he came over and said hello I was almost in _____.

Move Advanced Teacher's Book © Macmillan Publishers Limited 2007   **Photocopiable**

6 Read the text and answer the questions. Put a ✔ in the boxes.

Roy

A lot of so-called celebrities are not talented in the least, they are purely marketing products or the result of some trashy reality TV show. I find it increasingly annoying to have these people thrust down my throat and it annoys me that they are paid so much for doing very little. I also get fed up with all the stories of these celebrities in the news. I mean, who cares what they get up to in their private lives? I think that our society is getting very shallow when we pay these airheads vast sums of money because they are willing to make fools out of themselves on TV. Whatever happened to the idea that celebrities should be positive role models? Unfortunately, it isn't the case with many of these people today, is it? I don't want to meet any celebrities and, thank God, I haven't so far.

Jill

I love reading about my favourite celebrities in the gossip columns of magazines and newspapers. It's so interesting to find out who's dating who and what people are up to. I know some people think these celebrities are simply a bunch of freeloaders, but for me they are a great source of entertainment. I often gossip about the exploits of the stars with my friends. We love it. If I got a fleeting glimpse of my favourite star, I'd be in seventh heaven, but it's yet to happen. Of course, if they died, I'd be absolutely devastated. And, when it comes to buying something, if one of the celebrities I like has endorsed the product I'm much more likely to buy it.

	Roy	Jill	Neither
a Who cares what happens to certain celebrities?	☐	☐	☐
b Who has met a celebrity?	☐	☐	☐
c Who is a big fan of celebrities?	☐	☐	☐
d Who is upset with the attention celebrities get?	☐	☐	☐
e Who values what celebrities say about certain products?	☐	☐	☐
f Who regularly visits celebrity websites?	☐	☐	☐
g Who thinks many celebrities are paid too much?	☐	☐	☐
h Who thinks most celebrities lack talent?	☐	☐	☐
i Who would like to meet or see a celebrity?	☐	☐	☐
j Who thinks today's celebrities set a bad example for youngsters?	☐	☐	☐

Exercise	Score
1 Language	_____ / 9
2 Language	_____ / 9
3 Vocabulary	_____ / 8
4 Vocabulary	_____ / 8
5 Vocabulary	_____ / 6
6 Reading	_____ / 10
Total:	_____ / 50
	_____ %

Name: _____

1 Look at these sentences. Are they about real (R) or unreal (U) past situations?

a   I had to give my personal details when I opened my bank account. ☐

b   I'm sure he couldn't have taken your money. ☐

c   He promised he wouldn't be late. ☐

d   I'm sorry I couldn't lend you any money, but my account was completely empty. ☐

e   He might have given a false name. ☐

f   They must have left early. ☐

2 Choose the correct alternative.

Last week I went to get some money out of my bank account and I (a) *couldn't believe / couldn't have believed* it, my account had been cleaned out. I'm not sure how it (b) *could / should* have happened as I'm very careful with my cards and all my details. The bank told me that I (c) *must / should* have checked my account on a regular basis and that it was my fault that the money had gone. But I just can't accept that. It (d) *must be / must have been* an inside job and I think the bank (e) *could / should* look closely at the people who work there. I spoke to some friends and they said that the bank (f) *must take / must have taken* responsibility if I can prove I didn't take the money out. I guess it (g) *might be / might have been* worse, as they (h) *could use / could have used* my credit card as well, but they didn't.

3 Complete these sentences using the correct form of the words in brackets.

a   He _____ (might / trick) me if I hadn't already seen him before.

b   I'm sorry I didn't come. I _____ (could / get) the time off work.

c   I was lucky really. It _____ (could / be) a lot worse than it was.

d   He said he _____ (would / pay) me back when he went to the bank.

e   I asked the bank manager whether I _____ (could / take out) a loan.

f   I'm sure you _____ (must / feel) terrible when it happened.

g   Tell me what you _____ (would / do) if it had happened to you.

4 Complete the dialogue with the words in the box. There are three extra words.

| balance   banking   credit   current |
| date   identity   pay off   take out |
| transfer   withdraw |

Man: Excuse me! I'd like to (a) _____ some money from my (b) _____ account.

Bank clerk: Certainly. How much would you like to (c) _____?

Man: Umm, let's see. Could you tell me what my bank (d) _____ is?

Bank clerk: Of course. Do you have any proof of (e) _____?

Man: I've got my (f) _____ card. Will that do?

Bank clerk: Yes, that's fine. Can I ask you one more question?

Man: Of course.

Bank clerk: What's your (g) _____ of birth?

5 ~~Cross out~~ the alternative which is not possible.

1   I'd like to _____ €200, please.
    a clean out   b deposit   c transfer

2   Do you have lots of _____?
    a bills   b debts   c account

3   How much would you like to _____ today?
    a take out   b default   c pay off

4   I'm sorry sir, it looks like your bank account has been _____!
    a closed   b cleaned out   c opened

5   Can I have your credit card _____?
    a details   b interest   c number

6   I've never _____ a loan.
    a withdrawn   b taken out   c defaulted on

6 Complete these sentences with the words and phrases in the box.

| believe | come to the conclusion | convinced |
| no doubt | support | would have thought |

a   I'm _____ that online banking is safe.

b   I firmly _____ that people who commit identity theft should go to prison.

c   I have _____ at all that CCTV cameras reduce crime.

d   I've _____ that criminals will always find a way of getting people's personal details.

e   I _____ it was obvious that giving your bank details over the phone isn't safe.

f   I definitely _____ the introduction of new laws against identity theft. It's become a really big problem.

7 Read the article. Write T (true), F (false) or NG (not given) in the boxes.

a   Cases of identity theft are on the increase. ☐

b   The Internet has made people more aware of identity theft. ☐

c   Criminals use people's credit cards to do illegal things. ☐

d   People are more likely to be victims of identity theft because of the Internet. ☐

e   Sue Bailey had taken out a £50,000 loan. ☐

f   Sue was planning on taking her kids on holiday. ☐

g   Figures show that 20% of Americans have been victims of identity theft. ☐

h   The number of people affected by identity theft in Europe is higher than in the US. ☐

i   A man in Texas was sent to jail for bigamy. ☐

j   The use of biometric cards will stop identity theft. ☐

Identity theft

Identity theft is nothing new, the only difference nowadays is its proliferation and broader awareness of its existence. Much of the increase is due to the Internet, which facilitates the use of identity fraud for immediate gains. It is also much easier to use someone else's details to get credit, buy things and commit criminal activities. Due to these factors, most people have either been affected by identity theft themselves, or know someone who has.

Sue Bailey didn't realise she had a problem until her bank contacted her and told her she'd missed a payment on her £50,000 loan. Alarmed, Sue phoned her bank to try and find out what had happened. 'It turned my life into a complete hell' 37-year-old Sue said. 'One minute I'm thinking about where to go on holiday with my kids and the next I'm simply wondering whether I can afford to feed them, let alone go on holiday.' Unfortunately for Sue someone had used her personal details to borrow £50,000 and she was left with the debt.

This type of situation is increasingly common. In the US, around 1 in 5 people have had some kind of identity theft perpetuated against them and in Europe the figures are not much lower. One man in Texas was prosecuted for bigamy when it was revealed he was married to five different women. In the end, it turned out to be a case of mistaken identity, or rather of someone pretending to be him. But, this type of thing is likely to become far more prevalent and there is little we can do to stop it.

One suggestion has been the use of biometric identity cards but there are questions not only over the practicality of such a system, but also as to whether it will actually solve the problem or simply lead to a more sophisticated form of identity theft.

Exercise	Score
1 Language	_____ / 6
2 Language	_____ / 8
3 Language	_____ / 7
4 Vocabulary	_____ / 7
5 Vocabulary	_____ / 6
6 Vocabulary	_____ / 6
7 Reading	_____ / 10
Total:	_____ / 50
	_____ %

Module test

Name: _____

1 Complete the text with the correct form of the verbs in brackets.

A recent survey into arguing (a) _____ (show) that having a row can actually be good for you. Researchers (b) _____ (ask) more than fifty couples, who (c) _____ (live) together for at least three years, a series of questions from what caused their arguments to how they resolved them. 'One of the most interesting things was how many people bottle things up and don't talk about what is bothering them,' said Kim O'Connor, one of the researchers. ' "I (d) _____ (not / speak) to him yet" and "It (e) _____ (would not / do) any good" are the two most common phrases we (f) _____ (hear).' she said. Learning to talk about disagreements and to compromise is one of the key things about a successful relationship.

Rachel and her partner Josh (g) _____ (be) together for eight years. 'I (h) _____ (not / had) a relationship that was longer than six months until I met Josh,' said Rachel. 'At first it was very difficult, but I (i) _____ (learn) that the worst thing you can do is keep things to yourself. There's no point thinking "I (j) _____ (should / tell) him" when it's already too late, get it out in the open and deal with it together, that's the only way.'

2 Choose the correct alternative.

a *What irritates me / What* is how rude he is.

b It *might be / might have been* better if you hadn't told him.

c *As I was saying / I have to say* before you interrupted me …

d *What was / One thing* so unusual about his idea was that it was so obvious.

e I *can't have believed / can't believe* nobody thought of it before.

f *I have to say I / What amazes me* really don't understand your decision.

g The *worst thing / problem with* being famous is that people always come up and talk to you wherever you are and whatever you're doing.

h *Personally / Let's say* we agree to disagree.

i She *couldn't tell / couldn't have told* him, because if she had he wouldn't be here.

j *It's / The key issue is* what do we do next?

3 Complete the text with the words in the box. There are five extra words.

alarm	attention	controversial	debate
desperate	desperation	dismay	
entertaining	eyebrows	eyes	headlines
heads	outrageous	superficial	sympathy

Recent events surrounding a number of celebrity couples have rekindled the (a) _____ as to whether these kinds of people are the best role models for our children. More often than not these so-called stars make the (b) _____ for all the wrong reasons. It's one thing to turn people's (c) _____ when you walk down the street, but quite something else when what you are doing is either illegal, (d) _____ or both. In many cases it seems that some stars deliberately do things in order to raise a few (e) _____ and hopefully gain more publicity. In some cases what has happened to some of these stars inspires (f) _____, but in many cases it simply makes one wonder if they give any thought to what they are doing or whether they are so (g) _____ that their only thought is their own ego. In fact, so (h) _____ are some of the things that people do to get (i) _____ that it makes you wonder whether they do it from (j) _____ or simply to see just how far they can go before they get into serious trouble.

4 Replace the underlined words and phrases with a phrasal verb in the box. There is one extra phrasal verb. Sometimes you need to change the form.

come about	die down	play down
rule out	spell out	touch on

a Give it some time and I'm sure all the fuss will become less intense. _____

b You really need to explain how this could happen, I'm not sure I understand! _____

c I'd avoid mentioning money, it's really quite a sore point with him at the moment. _____

d You really shouldn't try to minimise the importance of this. I actually think it could be the most important factor. _____

e Can I suggest you don't dismiss anything at this stage? _____

Photocopiable

5 Complete the text with an appropriate word in each gap. The first letter has been given.

> Over the past few months I've been receiving suspicious emails at home and work. One of the most worrying factors is how these people have obtained my home email (a) a_____. I can understand why they have my work one, but the other one is private and only for personal use. These messages claim to be from my bank, but they're asking for some very strange information. Why would my bank need to know my medical (b) d_____ and if I have any political (c) a_____? And surely they already know my (d) s_____ as it's paid directly into my account? It seems very strange. Some of the other questions make sense, for example asking me if I have a criminal (e) r_____ or convictions for driving offences. I've tried ringing the bank, but of course I can't get to speak to anyone as it's one of those annoying automated telephone systems. I hate them!

6 ● **17** Listen to Zoe and Ellie talking and complete the gaps with one to three words.

a What's all that noise? ... Ellie, it's _____ in the morning.

b It's just well, you know _____ and I want everything to look tidy.

c You're _____, aren't you?

d She'll be peering _____ and the oven and checking out the bathroom ...

e Yeah, but so what. I mean _____, she won't be expecting everything to be perfect.

f My mum's a perfectionist ... she's really _____ about everything she does.

g She even _____!

h Perhaps I'm more like my mum than I imagined. What _____!

i All your CDs in alphabetical order and your shoes together _____.

j I think I'll just _____ before I go to bed ...

7 ● **23** Listen to the radio programme about CCTV cameras. Are these sentences true (T) or false (F)?

a Jody thinks CCTV cameras are a good thing. ☐

b She didn't use to feel safe. ☐

c Where she lives has always been OK. ☐

d Naseem's friend broke into a local supermarket and was caught. ☐

e The CCTV images were poor quality. ☐

f His friend wasn't at the supermarket when the break-in happened. ☐

g Lily thinks the main issue is invasion of your private life. ☐

h Lily is worried about who monitors the cameras. ☐

i Alvin was attacked recently. ☐

j Lots of people saw what happened to Alvin. ☐

8 Underline the letter in each word that is pronounced differently in British and American English.

For example: v*a*se

1 tomato

2 stupid

3 hostage

4 nobody

5 simultaneous

6 vitamins

7 glasshouse

8 coffee

9 freelance

10 patriotic

9 Read the texts. Write T (true), F (false) or NG (not given) in the boxes.

Rob

What annoys me about Sandra? Oh! How long have you got? No, I'm only joking! One thing that really gets to me is that she thinks she's always right, but she isn't. The problem is, if I point this out she gets upset and tells me to prove it. If I do, she gets even angrier and goes off in a huff. I really can't win, can I? Then there's the fact that she is a clean freak. She is constantly dusting and vacuuming and she does it at the most inconvenient moments. For example, I'll be watching a football match on TV and suddenly the vacuum will start up. And, finally, she complains that I never pay attention to what she's wearing. This is blatantly untrue. I do notice, it's just that I don't say anything.

Sandra

Oh my! So, do you want a list? Let's start with the most annoying habits and then carry on. I guess the number one thing has got to be the fact that Rob is always laughing at his own jokes. It would be OK if they were funny, but they aren't. And, half the time he'll start telling you a joke and burst out laughing before he's finished it. I mean, how annoying is that? Then there's the fact that he's blind. I can buy a new dress, or have a new haircut and will Rob notice? You've got to be kidding. And, last but definitely not least, is his habit of using pet names for me when we're in public. I don't like being called 'Honey bun' at home, let alone in the middle of the supermarket. One day I'm going to hit him when he calls me that!

a According to Rob, Sandra is always right. ☐

b When Sandra is wrong she admits it. ☐

c Sandra always wants everything to be clean. ☐

d Sandra chooses the most inappropriate moments to do the hoovering. ☐

e Sandra often stands naked in front of Rob to get his attention. ☐

f Rob has lots of annoying habits. ☐

g Rob's jokes are very funny. ☐

h Sandra often buys new clothes or has her hair done. ☐

i Sandra doesn't mind Rob using pet names at home. ☐

j Sometimes Rob calls her 'Honey bun' when they are shopping. ☐

10 You have seen a competition that asks you to write about your favourite book, or a book you have recently read. Write your competition entry in about 200 words.

Exercise	Score
1 Language	_____ / 10
2 Language	_____ / 10
3 Vocabulary	_____ / 10
4 Vocabulary	_____ / 5
5 Vocabulary	_____ / 5
6 Listening	_____ / 10
7 Listening	_____ / 10
8 Pronunciation	_____ / 10
9 Reading	_____ / 10
10 Writing	_____ / 20
Total:	_____ / 100
	_____ %

Name: _____

1 Examples of ellipsis have been lettered a–g in the following sentences. For each example, write the information which has been omitted.

1 Anna has four children and I've got two (a).
_____

2 A recent survey has revealed that people who have large families are happier than those who don't (b). _____

3 My brother has three kids and he doesn't want any more (c). _____

4 I'd like to get married, but I haven't (d) yet.
_____

5 Children who stay close to their parents are often happier than those who don't (e).
_____

6 We spoke about living together, but in the end decided we wouldn't (f). _____

7 My sister is divorced, but I'm not (g).
_____

2 Replace the underlined words with a word in the box.

he	it	these	they	this	those

In recent years the birth rate has been dropping in many countries. In Britain, (a) the birth rate is down to an all time low. One reason for this is that people are getting married later in life. Is (b) getting married later in life a contributing factor?

Certainly (c) people who get married later often have fewer children but Britain also has the highest rate of single-parent families and one of the highest rates of teen pregnancy. Some people assume that (d) the single-parent families and teen pregnancies should balance out the figures, but surprisingly they don't seem to. In fact, government officials are so concerned with this decline that (e) government officials are launching a campaign to encourage people to have more children. One of the concerns is that the low birth rate and longer life expectancy will lead to a demographic problem. As a government spokesperson said, 'The country is getting older.' (f) The government spokesperson went on to say that if the problem wasn't addressed within the next fifteen years the financial and social consequences would be devastating.

a _____   d _____

b _____   e _____

c _____   f _____

3 Choose the correct alternative.

1 Fred: Are you coming to the party tonight?

   Martina: _____.

   a So am I   b I think so   c I hope not

   Fred: _____, can you bring a bottle of red wine?

   a If so   b Said so   c So it is

2 Annie: You won't be late, will you?

   Rachel: _____.

   a So am I   b I told you so   c I don't think so

3 Kamilla: Your brother's really horrible!

   Natasha: _____.

   a I hope so   b I told you so   c So it is

4 Rick: See you later.

   Sandra: Yeah, _____.

   a I hope so   b I told you so   c so am I

5 Chris: I'm really fed up.

   Alete: _____.

   a So it is   b If so   c So am I

6 Joanna: Isn't that Matt over there?

   Elizabeth: Oh yes, _____.

   a so it is   b so it was   c so am I

7 Andrea: I hear you're moving in with Tom. Good luck! They say he's difficult to live with!

   Sally: Well, _____, but I'll soon find out.

   a if so   b so they say   c so am I

4 Complete these sentences with the words and phrases in the box.

close	give and take	muck in	neglected
out of line	patience of a saint	resented	
squabbling	stick up for	suffer in silence	

a I come from a very _____ family.

b I wish you'd stop _____ all the time. It's giving me a headache.

c Why didn't you _____ me? I felt really let down.

d We always _____ whenever anything needs to be done.

e   She really must have the _____. I don't know how she puts up with those kids.

f   I never felt _____ as a child. My parents always gave me plenty of attention.

g   She _____ the time I spent with you.

h   You don't need to _____. You really should talk to someone.

i   You really should apologise. You know you were _____, don't you?

j   Relationships always need a bit of _____ to work.

5   Replace the <u>underlined</u> words and phrases with a word in the box.

| adopt   conduct   devote   establish   ignore |
| preserve   prohibit   register   shun |

a   I always <u>avoid</u> the limelight as I'm quite shy.
_____

b   We're going to <u>carry out</u> a survey on families.
_____

c   I want to <u>set up</u> a complaints procedure.
_____

d   Please don't <u>pretend you haven't seen</u> me. It really upsets me. _____

e   I wish you wouldn't <u>take on</u> that attitude with everyone. _____

f   You need to <u>put your name</u> on this list over here, please. _____

g   Whatever happens I'm going to <u>take care of</u> my dignity. _____

h   They're going to <u>ban</u> smoking in all public places soon. _____

i   Why do you <u>dedicate</u> so much of your time to other people's problems? _____

6   Read the article and complete it with the words in the box. There are three extra words.

| consumer goods   diversity   impoverished |
| increase   live   privatise   relations   society |

Christiania is in great danger of extinction as the Danish government plans to
(a) _____ all houses. Nobody owns their houses at the moment, and it is therefore possible for anyone to move in. This means that Christiania has a human (b) _____ which makes it a very special place. However, with the new laws proposed by the government

However, with the new laws proposed by the government Christiania will slowly die. Why does the government want to introduce these new laws? Perhaps because Christiania has been successful and thereby drawn unwanted attention to problems in Danish society, such as loneliness and declining social (c)
_____. Or maybe the government fears that the simple lifestyle in Christiania, without the stress and long working hours needed to afford
(d) _____, will become popular in the rest of Denmark. Or maybe it is just in order to sell the valuable land, although a few hundred million Danish kroners are nothing in comparison to the value of Christiania to its inhabitants. Whatever the reasons, the end of Christiania will make Denmark a nation that is more culturally (e) _____.

7   Read the article in Ex 6 again and choose the correct alternative.

1   The article is written by someone …
    a   from the government.
    b   who supports Christiania.

2   Ownership of property is …
    a   what makes Christiania unique.
    b   not part of Christiania.

3   Christiania has been …
    a   very successful.
    b   a bit of a failure.

4   Most Danish people …
    a   live a fairly relaxed lifestyle.
    b   work long hours.

5   The inhabitants of Christiania …
    a   are tempted by the money the government will get for the land.
    b   want to carry on living there.

Exercise	Score
1 Language	_____ / 7
2 Language	_____ / 6
3 Language	_____ / 8
4 Vocabulary	_____ / 10
5 Vocabulary	_____ / 9
6 Reading	_____ / 5
7 Reading	_____ / 5
Total:	_____ / 50
	_____ %

Move Advanced Teacher's Book © Macmillan Publishers Limited 2007   **Photocopiable**

Name: _____

1 Choose the correct alternative.

1 English is such a colour _____ language.
a -ish   b -ful   c -ous

2 I'm sure it's completely meaning _____.
a -ful   b -y   c -able

3 She's such a knowledge _____ person.
a -ible   b -ish   c -able

4 He was always very adventur _____.
a -ful   b -able   c -ous

5 I'm sure the problems are avoid _____.
a -ful   b -able   c -ous

6 Why are you so mood _____?
a -y   b -ish   c -able

7 That was such a fool _____ thing to do!
a -y   b -ish   c -ful

2 Complete the text with the correct form of the word in brackets. Sometimes you have to add a prefix as well as a suffix.

For the (a) _____ (foresee) future English will be the most important language in the world. And this is an (b) _____ (avoid) fact. However, the rise of English as the world's dominant language was (c) _____ (think) five hundred years ago.

Two events have led to the (d) _____ (imagine) rise of English from a small almost insignificant language to a dominant world force. The first was the (e) _____ (predict) spread of the language as British sailors travelled around the world from the 16th century onwards. The second is the (f) _____ (escape) rise of the USA as the world's leading economic and military power.

Whether English is (g) _____ (replace) or not is open to question. And, it is (h) _____ (understand) when people point to the population of China and suggest that quite possibly Chinese will replace English in the same way that English replaced Latin.

3 Complete these sentences with the correct form of the words in the box. Sometimes you have to add a prefix as well as a suffix.

cure	do	explain	harm	number	style

a It's difficult, but it is _____.

b There are _____ reasons why learning another language is useful.

c Smoking is bad for you. It's _____.

d I'm sorry, but your illness is _____.

e For some _____ reason he loves learning difficult languages.

f She always looks so good. She's so _____.

4 Complete these sentences with the words and phrases in the box.

a bit of a	at any rate	I suppose you can say
I tend to	in a way	kind of
perhaps	under the circumstances	

a _____ that I was just too lazy to learn any more.

b You can only do your best and, _____, I'm actually amazed at how well you've done.

c _____ I think it's unfortunate that you no longer speak your mother tongue.

d I guess it was _____ inevitable that you'd forget the words.

e _____ Chinese will become a more important language than English. Who knows?

f _____ work harder when I've got a target and I think that was the real problem.

g I think I have _____ problem when it comes to learning a new language. I really struggle with pronunciation.

h He speaks Hungarian, _____ he says he does.

5 Choose the correct alternative.

a Someone who isn't very tall is *horizontally / vertically* challenged.

b If you're *lazy / dishonest,* then you might be referred to as morally different.

c Someone who isn't very clever is *mentally / motivationally* challenged.

d Someone who is bald is hair *advantaged / disadvantaged.*

e If you are motivationally *different / deficient,* then you are lazy.

6 Replace the underlined words and phrases with the phrases in the box.

> a bit of a tipple   careful with her money
> getting on a bit   must have seen better days
> passed away   short of a penny

> My aunt recently (a) *died* and I was really sad. She'd had cancer for a while and I know she was (b) *old* and she liked (c) *a drink* every now and then, but it still came as a bit of a shock. After the funeral, I went to her house and I have to say that it (d) *was in bad condition*, it was almost falling apart. The strange thing is that my aunt wasn't (e) *poor* she was just (f) *mean*.

a _____   d _____

b _____   e _____

c _____   f _____

7 Read the magazine article and complete it with the phrases in the box. There are two extra phrases.

> and it was adopted   other people
> by the inhabitants of La Gomera
> users of the language   by normal means
> for its difficulties   for its development

The Silbo Gomero is a whistled language used (a) _____ in the Canary Islands to communicate with each other. The exact origins of the language are unknown, but the reasons (b) _____ become obvious to anyone who visits the rugged island. The deep valleys and steep slopes create an environment in which communication (c) _____ can be difficult. Whistling across deep ravines makes communication possible. The original inhabitants, the Guanches, used the language extensively (d) _____ by the Spanish settlers in the 16th century. When the language became endangered in the late 20th century, the local government made it a subject in schools and all local children learnt to use it. The language contains only two vowels and four consonants. The vowels can either be high or low, and the consonants are either rises or dips in the melody. While non-speakers of Silbo hear only whistling, (e) _____ are able to process the sounds in the same way as people process any other language such as Spanish or English.

8 Read the newspaper article and answer the questions.

Just like endangered animals, languages are also dying out. Around half of today's languages have fewer than 10,000 speakers. One of these languages is Sámi, the language spoken by the indigenous peoples of northern Norway, Sweden, Finland and Russia. Anna Karstedt lives with her parents in the northern Swedish town of Gallivare. Not only does Anna speak Sámi, but she also sings using 'yoik' a kind of chanting used in songs about people, animals and the snowy landscape. For Anna, the language is an essential part of her identity. Although once close to extinction, Sámi, like other indigenous languages such as Welsh and Basque, is now making a revival. Nowadays Sámi is taught in primary schools in many Nordic countries and the prospects don't look as bleak as they once did.

a   What percentage of today's languages can be classified as endangered?

_____

b   Which group of people speak Sámi?

_____

c   Why is Sámi important for Anna?

_____

d   Apart from speaking Sámi, how else does Anna help to preserve the traditions?

_____

e   What measures have helped the prospects of Sámi surviving as a living language?

_____

Exercise	Score
1 Language	_____ / 7
2 Language	_____ / 8
3 Language	_____ / 6
4 Language	_____ / 8
5 Vocabulary	_____ / 5
6 Vocabulary	_____ / 6
7 Reading	_____ / 5
8 Reading	_____ / 5
Total:	_____ / 50
	_____ %

Name: _____

1 Complete these dialogues using the words or phrases in the box.

> a sort of   about   and so on   whatever
> and that sort of thing   give or take   -ish

a   Ralph: How long have you been studying computer science?

  Sarah: Three years _____.

b   Pam: How many people are coming to the party tonight?

  Sandra: Well, there's Jane, Julie, Harry, Fred _____. Then there is my family – so quite a lot of people.

c   Pete: How old are you?

  Jenny: Oh, 30 _____.

d   Amber: What have you been doing recently?

  Kim: Studying, going to the cinema, going to parties _____.

e   Ben: How long have you known Rachel?

  Lee: Oh, _____ three weeks.

f   Tim: What do you use your computer for?

  Matt: Sending emails, downloading music, shopping online and _____.

g   Alan: What do you use your webpage for?

  Anna: I use it as _____ diary.

2 Rewrite these sentences adding the words in brackets in the correct place.

a   I get 30 emails a day. (or so)

  _____

b   The file takes two hours to download. (around)

  _____

c   I was just checking out a few websites when the computer crashed! (and stuff)

  _____

d   My favourite sites are music and video sites. (and that sort of thing)

  _____

e   I spend an hour online in the evening. (more or less)

  _____

f   I'm worried about viruses on my computer. (and the like)

  _____

g   I've got a new computer. (ish)

  _____

h   It should take two or three hours to play the new game. (give or take)

  _____

3 Choose the correct alternative.

a   Ray: Do you want Italian or Chinese food tonight?

  Max: Oh, *whoever / whichever*.

b   Paula: What time should we arrive there?

  Jess: Oh, *wherever / whenever* you can.

c   Myles: Can I bring someone to the party?

  Andy: Sure, bring *whoever / whatever* you want.

d   Phil: What's the best place to go on honeymoon?

  Sam: Oh, I'm sure *whenever / wherever* you go Jane will be happy.

e   Larry: I was wondering what we should do tonight?

  Cindy: *Whichever / Whatever* you like.

4 Write the phrasal verbs in the box next to the correct definition.

> boils down to   figure out   get across
> getting at   going on about   point out

a   to make people understand something

  _____

b   to understand or solve a problem

  _____

c   to indicate or focus on something

  _____

d   to be the main reason for something

  _____

e   to try to say something without saying it directly

  _____

f   to be talking about something, for a long time

  _____

5 Complete these sentences with the phrasal verbs in Ex 4.

a   I really have to _____ how bad your addiction to computer games has become.

b   I'm really not sure what you're _____. If you have something to tell me, just say it.

c   What it _____ is that you can't manage without the Internet and your emails.

d   We really need to _____ what you can do before the problem becomes worse.

e   Please stop _____ your new computer. It's getting boring.

f   It's essential that you _____ the importance of this.

6 Replace the underlined words with a word from the box.

```
average    conducted    dependency
hooked on    indicates    respondents
retrieve    track
```

a   It's very easy to get addicted to computer games.

_____

b   About 50% of the people answering the survey said they played a computer game every night.

_____

c   Joe Samuels is just an ordinary gamer who plays most nights.

_____

d   The survey was carried out on behalf of a leading computer games company.

_____

e   Computer addiction is becoming a serious problem.

_____

f   It's quite easy to get back files that you've deleted.

_____

g   Simply place your online order and then follow it until it arrives at your front door.

_____

h   The increase in the number of spam messages shows a serious trend that needs to be addressed.

_____

7 Read the email. Write T (true), F (false) or NG (not given) in the boxes.

> Am I hooked? First thing in the morning I write my diary using a macro which automatically underlines the last entry and inserts the date.
>
> First cup of tea as I attend to my email. I am the moderator of ten TEFL electronic discussion lists, and even non-letter-writing German and English nephews and nieces sometimes send private messages. I log into my German and English bank accounts, and increase overdrafts by ordering books through Amazon, or, feeling guilty, from a real bookshop. I watch BBC 1 TV news and consult a couple of online newspapers. I check two items on a concordance in Japan, look up 'blackbirds' in an encyclopaedia in the USA and work on the CD-ROM on English pronunciation that I am due to review for one of my lists, relieved to find that my microphone is working again.
>
> I've registered for a free, online seminar in November, and, in preparation, spend ten minutes with 'Learn the basics of Romanian' that I found using a search engine.
>
> My wife, real, not virtual, calls me for breakfast.

a   The writer first checks his emails. ☐

b   He has a cup of tea after checking his emails. ☐

c   He feels guilty because by ordering books he increases his overdraft. ☐

d   To order books he must check his online bank accounts. ☐

e   He watches TV news on his computer. ☐

f   He is writing a CD-ROM about English pronunciation. ☐

g   He uses a concordance program to check a couple of items. ☐

h   The microphone on his computer wasn't working recently. ☐

i   He can speak a number of different languages fluently. ☐

j   He hasn't had breakfast yet. ☐

Exercise	Score
1 Language	_____ / 7
2 Language	_____ / 8
3 Language	_____ / 5
4 Vocabulary	_____ / 6
5 Vocabulary	_____ / 6
6 Vocabulary	_____ / 8
7 Reading	_____ / 10
Total:	_____ / 50
	_____ %

UNIT 4
Test

Name: _____

1 Complete the text with the prepositions in the box.

| for | from | in | in | of | with | with |

I've just started a new job. I'm working for a consultancy that specialises (a) _____ organising training events for other companies. I'm really interested (b) _____ my job because it's challenging and varied. In my old job I just did the same thing day after day and I got really fed up (c) _____ it. Now I'm responsible (d) _____ a small team and we have to come up with new ideas all the time. For me my job is a mixture (e) _____ work and pleasure. Sometimes I get to go and do things like white-water rafting, paintballing and so on. The only problem (f) _____ my new job is that I can end up working long hours. But then I also benefit (g) _____ working in such a dynamic organisation!

2 Choose the correct alternative.

1 Make sure you're not late _____ the interview.
a about   b for   c in

2 Does it have an impact _____ anything we do?
a about   b to   c on

3 You need to succeed _____ your next job.
a in   b for   c about

4 I'm not aware _____ any problems.
a of   b with   c about

5 You can dream _____ it, but it won't happen.
a in   b for   c about

6 How do you react _____ problems?
a about   b to   c on

7 Have you had any contact _____ them before?
a with   b to   c of

3 Complete these sentences with the words in the box.

| apologise | comply | delegate |
| difference | lacking | seek |

a The _____ between my last job and this one is that I really enjoy this one.

b It's important to know when to _____ work and not do too much yourself.

c You must _____ with the regulations.

d I _____ for the delay. We'll try and sort it out as soon as possible.

e You don't need to _____ approval for everything you do.

f We're _____ in the expertise to complete this task properly.

4 Complete the job advertisement with the words in the box.

| approval | decisions | tackle | delegate |
| expectations | initiative | potential | utilise |

job **advertisement**

Project manager

Are you able to implement (a) _____, even when they're unpopular? Or do you always seek the (b) _____ of your colleagues?

Are you able to (c) _____ work and (d) _____ the strengths of the people working for you?

Can you take the (e) _____? And do you have high (f) _____ of yourself?

Can you (g) _____ problems quickly and effectively?

If you answer 'Yes' to these questions and you want to realise your (h) _____, then call us on 020 699 8741 for an application form.

5 Write the words in the box next to the definitions.

| bond | conflicts | confront | enhance |
| open-minded | participate |

a willing to consider new ideas _____

b to deal with a difficult situation _____

c to take part in _____

d to develop feelings of friendship _____

e to improve something _____

f disagreements between people _____

6   Complete the text with the words in Ex 5.

The purpose of our team-building days is to help people
(a) _____ with each other. The result of
this is to (b) _____ productivity. We believe
that people who (c) _____ in these kinds of
activities together, work better together. Those who are
(d) _____ will get the most out of it. Try and
sort out any (e) _____ you might have and
(f) _____ any problems which might come up
during the day together.

7   Read the article. Put a ✔ next to the
two endings that can complete each statement.

Corporate Bonding:
A fun experience?

Adrian: We went on a Samba course for a weekend,
it was fantastic. When my boss brought up the idea of a
team-building activity, I had images of being huddled on
a mountainside, cold and wet from the driving rain. In
the end, we spent the weekend in a nice hotel learning
how to dance and drinking rum.

Lizzie: Team-building, yeah! Well, I guess it was OK. We
spent the weekend in a hotel on the Yorkshire moors.
The hotel was OK and the activities, basically problem
solving games and a quiz in the evening, were fine and
the people were nice enough. The only problem was
that the location was so isolated. There was nothing
else to do, nowhere to go, but I guess that was the idea.

Lucy: Oh God! It was horrible. We went on one of
those survival weekends in Wales. It rained the whole
weekend and the guy running the event was quite
clearly a masochist. The first morning he woke us up
at half past four in the morning and made us walk ten
miles in the pouring rain. I spent the entire time wet
and miserable and then took two days off work with a
cold when we got back!

Andrei: Wow! Team building they call it, I call it free
food. Every Friday night, the office all go down to
the local restaurant and spend all evening eating and
drinking. It's all free as the company pays for everything.
I guess they think it's a good way for people to get to
know each other. I think it's just a waste of money.

Sam: It was absolutely ridiculous. I felt like I was
being treated like a child or something. One person
was made to dress up as a sheep while all the others
pretended to be dogs or farmers and herded the
person dressed in the costume into a wooden pen by
clapping and whistling. It was the most absurd thing I've
ever done and it certainly didn't make us feel any closer
together. I'm just glad I wasn't the one dressed up.

1   Adrian found the weekend-long Samba course
fantastic because …
  a they were on a cold mountainside. ☐
  b they spent the weekend in a cosy hotel. ☐
  c they learned a new skill. ☐
  d they drank rum to keep warm in the rain. ☐

2   Lizzie found the team-building experience OK …
  a because the people and the activities were
     fairly nice. ☐
  b because of the remote location of the hotel. ☐
  c even though there was nothing else to do. ☐
  d because being in an isolated hotel was the
     purpose of the team-building activity. ☐

3   Lucy felt that …
  a the guy in charge clearly didn't care about
     the comfort of the participants. ☐
  b it was horrible because they were woken up
     before dawn and had to complete ten miles
     in appalling conditions. ☐
  c although she was wet and miserable, at least
     she had two days off sick when she got back. ☐
  d it was horrible because the plan wasn't
     changed according to the weather. ☐

4   Andrei thinks team-building is …
  a not the right word for free food on a
     Friday night. ☐
  b great as the company pays for everything. ☐
  c wasting money on food. ☐
  d is a disguise for a regular free dinner. ☐

5   Sam found the team-building session …
  a ridiculous because it involved dressing up. ☐
  b a childish exercise that didn't help the
     participants get closer to each other. ☐
  c ridiculous because real people pretended
     to be dogs. ☐
  d ridiculous because of all the clapping and
     whistling by the farmers. ☐

Exercise	Score
1 Language	_____ / 7
2 Language	_____ / 7
3 Vocabulary	_____ / 6
4 Vocabulary	_____ / 8
5 Vocabulary	_____ / 6
6 Vocabulary	_____ / 6
7 Reading	_____ / 10
Total:	_____ / 50
	_____ %

Move Advanced Teacher's Book © Macmillan Publishers Limited 2007   **Photocopiable**

Module test

Name: _____

1 Complete these sentences by adding the appropriate suffix and / or prefix to the words in brackets.

a His response was rather _____.
   (predict)

b That was a very _____ (fool) thing to do.

c We have quite a _____ (size) problem.

d Your behaviour is just _____! (explain)

e Our relationship became quite _____ (rock) and we argued all the time.

f Oh come on! That's just so _____! (believe)

g He never wants to try anything new. He's so _____. (adventure)

2 Complete these dialogues with the words in the box.

for	on	or so	so am I	sort of	stuff
told me so	whatever	wherever	with		

1 Michelle: Hi! Where have you been?

   Jemma: Sorry I'm late I (a) _____ got held up.

   Michelle: What do you mean? Either you did or you didn't.

   Jemma: Look, I'm sorry I just had (b) _____ to do.

   Michelle: (c) _____, at least you're here now.

2 Jay: Shall we go and get a bite to eat?

   Mack: Sure.

   Jay: Where do you want to go?

   Mack: Oh, (d) _____, I really don't mind but let's hurry I'm starving.

   Jay: Yeah, (e) _____.

3 Holly: Wow! That's beautiful.

   Rick: I thought you'd like it. I hope you're not angry (f) _____ me anymore.

   Holly: Don't be silly, but I hope you don't want me to apologise (g) _____ something I didn't do.

   Rick: No, as long as you don't tell me you (h) _____.

   Holly: I won't.

4 Penny: So, what time are we meeting?

   Jane: Shall we say eight (i) _____?

   Penny: Sounds good, but it depends (j) _____ the traffic.

   Jane: Sure, just give me a call if you're going to be late.

   Penny: OK.

3 Look at these sentences from the dialogues in Ex 2. What information is missing in the brackets?

a Michelle: What do you mean? Either you did or you didn't (   ). _____

b Holly: I won't (   ). _____

c Penny: (   ) Sounds good, but it depends on the traffic. _____

4 Complete the text with the words in the box.

boiled	close	devoted	faced
lost	mucked	points	suffer

I come from a very large family, four bothers and three sisters, and I guess because there were so many of us we had to learn to get on with each other or (a) _____ in silence. When I was ten my father died in an accident and my mother (b) _____ herself to us even more. She (c) _____ up to the challenge of looking after seven of us and we all (d) _____ in together. She was quite strict always telling us what we could and couldn't do, but she never (e) _____ her temper with any of us! In the end, what it (f) _____ down to was that this was the only way she could manage. Even now I find it really difficult to understand how she coped, but she just (g) _____ out that she loved us all and that being so (h) _____ helped us get through the tough times.

5 Choose the correct alternative.

1 It's really important to have an _____ mind.
a enhance   b open   c high

2 My mother has really _____ expectations of me.
a implement   b open   c high

3 It's important to me to _____ my potential.
a implement   b enhance   c realise

4 Do you find it difficult to _____ decisions?
a implement   b tackle   c realise

5 What do you think you can do to _____ your performance?
a enhance   b tackle   c realise

6 I want to _____ in everything. I hate feeling left out!
a realise   b tackle   c participate

7 I guess I come into my own when I have to _____ problems and sort things out.
a realise   b tackle   c implement

6 Replace the underlined words and phrases with a word in the box. There are three extra words.

> died   fat   hell   lazy   old   short
> stupid   the toilet

a Mary's just gone to powder her nose.
_____

b I'm sorry to hear that Frank passed away last week. _____

c Whatever you say I think he's mentally challenged! _____

d He's getting on a bit now. He'll be 70 next birthday. _____

e She's a little plump, that's for sure.
_____

7 🔘 04 Listen to three people talking about learning English and the role of English in the world. Choose the correct alternative.

a Tatyana lives in *Russia / Oxford*.

b She *is studying / wants to study* international business and administration.

c She thinks *it's / it isn't* easy to learn English when you are a child.

d Lars *is / isn't* paying for his course.

e He usually uses *English / German* when he's doing business.

f He thinks having English as a lingua franca *could be a useful thing / is a bad thing*.

g He thinks English belongs to *everyone / native speakers*.

h Paulo *enjoys / doesn't enjoy* learning English.

i He *doesn't like / likes* talking to different people.

j He thinks everyone should learn *English / other languages*.

8 🔘 06 Listen to Graham and Layla talking about two internet adverts they have seen and complete the sentences.

a Layla: Oh yeah, they're clever, very dramatic. They really _____ the message _____.

b Graham: Yes, they are good, but I couldn't _____ what it was all about at first.

c Layla: I think most people will say the Internet is a good thing – _____.

d Graham: Yeah, there's a lot of information, _____, but how much of that is useable?

e Layla: So _____, you'd rather live in the good old days. Come off it!

f Graham: What about credit card fraud and identity theft and _____?

g Layla: What it _____ is being careful. You can't stop using something because it has a couple of risks.

h Layla: No, what _____ is that, it isn't an open-and-shut case …

i Layla: Not true. It's 50%, _____, anyway.

j Graham: Yeah, that's the _____ view, …

Move Advanced Teacher's Book © Macmillan Publishers Limited 2007   **Photocopiable**

9 Underline the stressed syllable in these words.

a reputable   f justifiable

b appreciable   g sizeable

c doable   h unstoppable

d manageable   i tolerable

e inescapable   j inexplicable

10 Read the article and complete it with the phrases in the box. Write the numbers.

1	but tend to be able to choose
2	but this is done not to increase success
3	we could learn a lot from looking at the natural world
4	scientists now believe that the social organization
5	the success rate of the chase

When it comes to living together and working with each other (a) _____ and, in particular, animals that cooperate. There are many examples, some quite extreme, of animal communities. Bees and ants, for example, are the epitome of cooperation and so are animals such as wolves.

It was thought that the reason wolves formed packs was merely for hunting purposes. However, (b) _____ exhibited by wolves has more to do with survival than with just food.

A pack of wolves will consist of between two and twenty individuals, with the average size being around eight. The pack is led by two individuals – the alpha male and the alpha female. They are not 'leaders' in the human sense of the word, (c) _____ where to go or what to do. The survival instinct of the pack means that the other wolves usually follow.

It is certainly true that packs of wolves hunt cooperatively, (d) _____ but simply because they are then able to attack larger prey. Hunting revolves around the chase and wolves will run for long periods tiring the animals they are hunting before bringing them down and killing them. In fact, (e) _____ is surprisingly low.

What is a more interesting aspect is the way wolves spend the rest of their time together. Often it is spent playing, mock fighting or simply watching out for each other.

11 Read the article in Ex 10 again. Write T (true) or F (false) in the boxes.

a Bees and ants follow the same rules as wolves. ☐

b The belief that wolves tend to form packs for hunting purposes is only partially true. ☐

c The average pack of wolves consists of about twenty individuals. ☐

d Because wolves hunt together they can attack large animals. ☐

e By hunting cooperatively wolves are more successful than they would be if they hunted alone. ☐

12 Computer addiction is a serious problem. Do you agree? What are the advantages and disadvantages of computers? Write about 200 words.

Exercise	Score
1 Language	_____ / 7
2 Language	_____ / 10
3 Language	_____ / 3
4 Vocabulary	_____ / 8
5 Vocabulary	_____ / 7
6 Vocabulary	_____ / 5
7 Listening	_____ / 10
8 Listening	_____ / 10
9 Pronunciation	_____ / 10
10 Reading	_____ / 5
11 Reading	_____ / 5
12 Writing	_____ / 20
Total:	_____ / 100
	_____ %

Placement test answers

Section 1 Language

(One point for each correct answer)

1   c
2   b
3   b
4   c
5   b
6   c
7   a
8   c
9   a
10   a
11   a
12   c
13   b
14   c
15   a
16   c
17   c
18   b
19   b
20   b
21   c
22   a
23   c
24   c
25   a
26   b
27   c
28   c
29   c
30   b
31   a
32   c
33   c
34   a
35   a
36   c
37   a
38   b
39   c
40   a
41   c
42   a
43   b
44   b
45   a
46   a
47   c
48   a
49   b
50   c

Section 2 Vocabulary

(One point for each correct answer)

1   was
2   am
3   in
4   to
5   for
6   take
7   like
8   do
9   on
10   far
11   for
12   idea
13   well
14   up
15   catching
16   touch/contact
17   his
18   freezing
19   keep
20   sense
21   keep/catch
22   apart
23   outweigh
24   away
25   getter

Section 3 Writing

Give a score out of 25
out of 5 points for accuracy
out of 5 points for vocabulary use
out of 5 points for cohesion
out of 5 points for complexity of
       language used
out of 5 points for general
       impression

Section 4 Speaking

Give a score out of 25
out of 5 points for accuracy
out of 5 points for vocabulary use
out of 5 points for cohesion
out of 5 points for complexity of
       language used
out of 5 points for general
       impression

Score banding

Sections 1–2

0–30   Elementary
31–40 Pre-intermediate
41–50 Intermediate
51–60 Upper-intermediate
61–70 Advanced

Sections 3–4 (suggested)

0–16 Elementary
17–24 Pre-intermediate
25–34 Intermediate
35–42 Upper-intermediate
43–50 Advanced

Unit test answers

(One point for each answer
unless stated otherwise)

Module 1 Unit 1

1
1	b	5	a
2	a	6	b
3	c	7	a
4	c	8	c

2
a I'm not very happy about the idea, **but** I know I can't change your mind.
b **While** it hasn't been decided, I think the choice is rather obvious.
c He's very mischievous, **yet** everyone likes him.
d She's rather unconventional, **whereas** her sister is quite ordinary.
e **Although** her clothes are a bit strange, she's quite a conventional person really. OR Her clothes are a bit strange, **although** she's quite a conventional person really.
f Everything seemed to be going wrong, **nevertheless** he still had a positive outlook.
g I will lend you the money to buy a new pair of shoes, **however** this is the last time.
h **Even though** I studied hard, I still failed the exam.

3
a Hang on!
b Can I finish what I was saying?
c Where was I?
d That reminds me of
e Talking of

4
a sympathetic
b feminine
c vivid
d fertile
e avid

5
a opinionated
b curious
c rebellious / conventional
d gloomy
e mischievous

6
a conventional
b curious
c gloomy
d intelligent
e mischievous
f opinionated
g rebellious
h unorthodox

7
a	2	d	1
b	5	e	4
c	3		

8
a 1994
b 2
c Yes
d No
e No instruments / hundreds of vocals

Module 1 Unit 2

1
a I live in that modern-looking building over there.
b I live close to a building which is owned by a Swiss-based company.
c The building over there is the new headquarters of Microsoft.
d It's one of the best-known landmarks in the city.
e That's the building featured on the front cover of that travel magazine.
f He lives in one of those recently built apartments near the sea.

2
a Abbotabad is a tourist-friendly town situated in the foothills of northern Pakistan.
b Uluru is a strange-looking rock rising 348 metres out of the desert.
c It's a ruined temple overlooking the Aegean sea.
d The Medrassa in Samarkand has thousands of hand-made tiles covering the outside walls.
e It's an old-fashioned castle perched on the edge of a mountain.
f Stonehenge is an ancient stone circle built as a temple in the south of England.

3
a	1	d	3
b	2	e	2
c	5	f	4

4
a dear. I'm sorry
b Stop moaning
c awful
d it can't be that bad / you're not the only one with problems
e a shame
f the record

5
a	known	f	looking
b	based	g	room
c	saving	h	made
d	catching	i	coloured
e	smoking		

6
1	b	4	c
2	a	5	a
3	b	6	b

7
a	5	f	5
b	1	g	1
c	2	h	4
d	3	i	3
e	4	j	2

Module 1 Unit 3

1
a even
b absolutely
c at all
d so
e complete
f simply
g without doubt

2
a	complete	d	vast
b	at all	e	whole
c	single		

3
1	b	5	c
2	c	6	a
3	a	7	b
4	b		

4
a	raise	e	give
b	eradicate	f	spread
c	do	g	show
d	support		

5
a going mad
b it was physical
c moment of stillness
d mental snap
e very calm
f took on a special significance

6   a   8   e   1
    b   3   f   4
    c   6   g   2
    d   5   h   7

7   a   50 protesters
    b   the G8 summit
    c   No ('they talk and talk' indicates there have been previous meetings)
    d   the G8 (leaders & countries)
    e   to discuss ways of eradicating poverty / reducing world debt

8   a   T   d   F
    b   T   e   T
    c   T

Module 1 Unit 4

1   1   c   6   b
    2   b   7   a
    3   a   8   b
    4   c   9   c
    5   a

2   a   5   f   9
    b   8   g   7
    c   3   h   4
    d   2   i   1
    e   6

3   a   looking   e   get
    b   run   f   keep
    c   coming   g   face
    d   cut

4   a   pass with flying colours
    b   throw in the towel
    c   are fighting a losing battle
    d   make it big
    e   steal the show
    f   by hook or by crook
    g   get off to a flying start
    h   sink or swim

5   a   down to
    b   owe
    c   spurs me on
    d   role model
    e   after seeing
    f   due to
    g   rooted in

6   a   3   d   2
    b   6   e   4
    c   7

7   a   Beyond Boundaries (across Nicaragua)
    b   Because he lost his leg in the propeller of a boat (when he was diving).
    c   none
    d   quite a full on life
    e   He's even more restless / he's planning to trek to the North Pole.

Module 2 Unit 1

1   1   b   5   c
    2   a   6   a
    3   b   7   c
    4   c

2   a   had seen
    b   has just left
    c   had been living
    d   have been arguing
    e   will have been

3   1   b   4   c
    2   d   5   e
    3   a

4   a   alarmed
    b   hesitant
    c   perplexed
    d   hopeful
    e   astonishment
    f   annoyed
    g   desperate

5   a   desperation
    b   annoyed
    c   hope
    d   hesitation
    e   dismayed
    f   alarm

6   a   tearjerker
    b   slow-starter
    c   in-depth
    d   monotonous
    e   badly written
    f   unputdownable
    g   trashy
    h   hilarious
    i   poetic
    j   controversial

7   a   G   f   G
    b   A   g   S
    c   A   h   F
    d   F   i   C
    e   C   j   S

Module 2 Unit 2

1   a   It was
    b   What is
    c   One thing
    d   The worst thing
    e   What was
    f   It's how
    g   What
    h   The problem

2   a   The problem is what to do about it.
    b   It was Mike who suggested it.
    c   What was worrying was that she didn't believe me.
    d   What I don't understand is how it actually works.
    e   What you do is none of my business.
    f   The issue is whether or not it's dangerous.

3   a   me is how popular GM food is.
    b   (that) nobody knows exactly what harm it might cause.
    c   how little we know about it that (really) surprised me.
    d   is how much controversy there is.
    e   strange is that we haven't heard anything about cloning for a long time.
    f   watching the news every night is that it can be very worrying.

4   a   headlines   d   controversy
    b   sympathy   e   debate
    c   concern   f   precedent

5   a   die down
    b   touches on
    c   came about
    d   play down
    e   rule anything out
    f   spell out
    g   pan out

6   a   me   e   me on
    b   matter   f   way
    c   like   g   cares
    d   what

7   a   breakthrough
    b   embryos
    c   carbon
    d   species
    e   genetically
    f   organs
    g   premature
    h   opponents
    i   interfere
    j   creation

Module 2 Unit 3

1
a	4	f	2
b	1	g	5
c	9	h	7
d	3	i	8
e	6		

2
- a so to speak
- b That said / I have to say
- c Speaking of
- d I have to say / that said
- e I've said it before and I'll say it again
- f Personally speaking
- g let's say
- h As they say
- i As I was saying

3
a	hand	e	hair
b	head	f	eyebrows
c	bottom	g	heart
d	lips	h	fingers

4
- a her name's on everyone's lips
- b waited on hand and foot
- c try and let your hair down
- d raises a few eyebrows
- e she always turns heads
- f his heart and soul
- g from the bottom of his heart
- h keep your fingers crossed

5
- a freeloaders
- b antics
- c red-carpet
- d star-struck
- e glimpse
- f seventh heaven

6
a	Jill	f	Neither
b	Neither	g	Roy
c	Jill	h	Roy
d	Roy	i	Jill
e	Jill	j	Roy

Module 2 Unit 4

1
a	R	d	R
b	U	e	U
c	R	f	U

2
- a couldn't believe
- b could
- c should
- d must have been
- e should
- f must take
- g might have been
- h could have used

3
- a might have tricked
- b couldn't get
- c could have been
- d would pay
- e could take out
- f must have felt
- g would have done

4
- a take out / withdraw
- b current
- c withdraw / take out
- d balance
- e identity
- f credit
- g date

5
1	a		4	c
2	c		5	b
3	b		6	a

6
- a convinced
- b believe
- c no doubt
- d come to the conclusion
- e would have thought
- f support

7
a	T		f	T
b	NG		g	T
c	NG		h	F
d	T		i	NG
e	F		j	F

Module 3 Unit 1

1
- a children
- b have large families
- c kids
- d got married
- e stay close to their parents
- f live together
- g divorced

2
a	it		d	these
b	this		e	they
c	those		f	He

3
1	b / a		5	c
2	c		6	a
3	b		7	b
4	a			

4
- a close
- b squabbling
- c stick up for
- d muck in
- e patience of a saint
- f neglected
- g resented
- h suffer in silence
- i out of line
- j give and take

5
a	shun		f	register
b	conduct		g	preserve
c	establish		h	prohibit
d	ignore		i	devote
e	adopt			

6
- a privatise
- b diversity
- c relations
- d consumer goods
- e impoverished

7
1	b		4	b
2	b		5	b
3	a			

Module 3 Unit 2

1
1	b		5	b
2	a		6	a
3	c		7	b
4	c			

2
- a foreseeable
- b unavoidable
- c unthinkable
- d unimaginable
- e predicable
- f inescapable
- g replaceable
- h understandable

3
- a doable
- b numerous
- c harmful
- d incurable
- e inexplicable
- f stylish

4
- a I suppose you can say
- b under the circumstances
- c In a way
- d kind of
- e Perhaps
- f I tend to
- g a bit of a
- h at any rate

5
- a vertically
- b dishonest
- c mentally
- d disadvantaged
- e deficient

6
- a passed away
- b getting on a bit
- c a bit of a tipple
- d must have seen better days
- e short of a penny
- f careful with her money

7
a by the inhabitants of La Gomera
b for its development
c by normal means
d and it was adopted
e users of the language

8
a (around) 50%
b indigenous peoples of northern Norway, Sweden, Finland and Russia
c It's part of her identity.
d She sings 'Yoik' (a kind of chanting).
e It is taught in primary schools (in many Nordic countries).

Module 3 Unit 3

1
a give or take
b and so on
c -ish
d and that sort of thing
e about
f whatever
g a sort of

2
a I get 30 or so emails a day.
b The file takes around two hours to download.
c I was just checking out a few websites and stuff when the computer crashed!
d My favourite sites are music and video sites and that sort of thing.
e I spend an hour more or less online in the evening.
f I'm worried about viruses and the like on my computer.
g I've got a newish computer.
h It should take two or three hours give or take to play the new game.

3
a whichever   d wherever
b whenever   e Whatever
c whoever

4
a get across
b figure out
c point out
d boils down to
e getting at
f going on about

5
a point out
b getting at
c boils down to
d figure out
e going on about
f get across

6
a hooked on
b respondents
c average
d conducted
e dependency
f retrieve
g track
h indicates

7
a F   f F
b F   g T
c NG   h T
d NG   i NG
e T   j T

Module 3 Unit 4

1
a in   e of
b in   f with
c with   g from
d for

2
1 b   5 c
2 c   6 b
3 a   7 a
4 a

3
a difference
b delegate
c comply
d apologise
e seek
f lacking

4
a decisions   e initiative
b approval   f expectations
c delegate   g tackle
d utilise   h potential

5
a open-minded
b confront
c participate
d bond
e enhance
f conflicts

6
a bond
b enhance
c participate
d open-minded
e conflicts
f confront

7
1 b & c   4 a & d
2 a & c   5 a & b
3 a & b

Module test answers

(One point for each answer
unless stated otherwise)

Module 1

1 a tiny
   b absolutely
   c highly
   d Whereas
   e all
   f a bit
   g but

2 a just
   b Nevertheless
   c most
   d Even though
   e at all
   f Although

3 a make up for
   b come up with
   c look up to
   d put up with
   e fall back on
   f get on with
   g come back from

4 a opinionated
   b energetic
   c rebellious
   d awareness
   e charity
   f unconventional
   g gloomy
   h traits
   i commitment
   j poverty

5 a 4   d 1
   b 2   e 3
   c 5

6 a energy-saving
   b child-friendly
   c family-run
   d sea-facing
   e three-storey

7 a Alex
   b Alex
   c Mette
   d Alex
   e Mette
   f Mette
   g Alex
   h Natsuko
   i Natsuko
   j Mette

8 a hands down
   b put up with
   c flying colours
   d getting through
   e full of life
   f throw in the towel
   g make it big
   h stood up for
   i sink or swim
   j owe everything

9 a avid
   b dogmatic
   c eccentric
   d gloomy
   e inquisitive
   f miserable
   g overactive
   h serious
   i sympathetic
   j unconventional

10 a imagine
    b expected
    c determination
    d compensate
    e achievement

11 a always difficult
    b one of the best swimmers
    c had finished her training
       session
    d about one year
    e athletes without disabilities

12 Give a score out of 20
    5 points for accuracy
    5 points for vocabulary range
    5 points for organisation and
    cohesion
    5 points for content
    (appropriacy)

Module 2

1 a showed
   b asked
   c have been living / have lived
   d haven't spoken
   e wouldn't do
   f heard
   g have been together
   h hadn't had
   i learnt / have learnt
   j should have told

2 a What irritates me
   b might have been
   c As I was saying
   d What was
   e can't believe
   f I have to say I
   g problem with
   h Let's say
   i couldn't have told
   j The key issue is

3 a debate
   b headlines
   c heads
   d controversial / outrageous
   e eyebrows
   f sympathy
   g superficial
   h outrageous / controversial
   i attention
   j desperation

4 a die down
   b come about
   c touching on
   d play down
   e rule out

5 a address
   b details
   c affiliations
   d salary
   e record

6 a   2 o'clock
   b   my mum's coming
   c   kidding me
   d   in the fridge
   e   we're students
   f   fussy
   g   irons socks
   h   a horrible thought
   i   in neat rows
   j   clean the fridge

7 a T   f T
   b T   g T
   c F   h T
   d F   i T
   e T   j F

8 1 tom<u>a</u>to
   2 st<u>u</u>pid
   3 h<u>o</u>stage
   4 nob<u>o</u>dy
   5 s<u>i</u>multaneous
   6 v<u>i</u>tamins
   7 glasshouse
   8 c<u>o</u>ffee
   9 freel<u>a</u>nce
   10 p<u>a</u>triotic

9 a F   f T
   b F   g F
   c T   h NG
   d T   i F
   e NG   j T

10 Give a score out of 20
    5 points for accuracy
    5 points for vocabulary range
    5 points for organisation and
    cohesion
    5 points for content
    (appropriacy)

Module 3

1 a   predictable
   b   foolish
   c   sizable
   d   inexplicable
   e   rocky
   f   unbelievable
   g   unadventurous
2 a   sort of
   b   stuff
   c   Whatever
   d   wherever
   e   so am I
   f   with
   g   for
   h   told me so
   i   or so
   j   on

3 a   get held up
   b   say I told you so
   c   (meeting at) eight

4 a   suffer
   b   devoted
   c   faced
   d   mucked
   e   lost
   f   boiled
   g   points
   h   close

5 1 b   5 a
   2 c   6 c
   3 c   7 b
   4 a

6 a   the toilet
   b   died
   c   stupid
   d   old
   e   fat

7 a   Oxford
   b   wants to study
   c   it's
   d   isn't
   e   English
   f   could be a useful thing
   g   everyone
   h   enjoys
   i   likes
   j   other languages

8 a   get (the message) across
   b   figure out
   c   on balance
   d   as you point out
   e   in other words
   f   that sort of thing
   g   boils down to
   h   I'm getting at
   i   or 50-ish
   j   rose tinted

9 a   <u>re</u>putable
   b   app<u>re</u>ciable
   c   <u>do</u>able
   d   <u>ma</u>nageable
   e   ines<u>ca</u>pable
   f   <u>ju</u>stifiable
   g   <u>si</u>zeable
   h   uns<u>to</u>ppable
   i   <u>to</u>lerable
   j   inexpl<u>i</u>cable

10 a 3   d 2
    b 4   e 5
    c 1

11 a T   d T
    b T   e F
    c F

12 Give a score out of 20
    5 points for accuracy
    5 points for vocabulary range
    5 points for organisation and
    cohesion
    5 points for content
    (appropriacy)